ENGENDERING THE SUBJECT

SUNY Series in Feminist Criticism and Theory
Michelle A. Massé, Editor

ENGENDERING THE SUBJECT

Gender and Self-Representation in
Contemporary Women's Fiction

Sally Robinson

State University of New York Press

Published by
State University of New York Press, Albany

For information, address State University of New York
Press, State University Plaza, Albany, N.Y. 12246

Production by Christine M Lynch
Marketing by Dana E. Yanulavich

Library of Congress Cataloging-in-Publication Data

Robinson, Sally, 1959–   #22308355
    Engendering the subject : gender and self-representation in
contemporary women's fiction / Sally Robinson.
        p.   cm. — (SUNY series in feminist criticism and theory)
    Includes bibliographical references and index.
    ISBN 0–7914–0728–4 (PB : acid-free). — ISBN 0–7914–0727–6 (Ch.
acid-free)
    1. English fiction—Women authors—History and criticism.
2. Feminism and literature—History—20th century. 3. Women and
literature—History—20th century. 4. Lessing, Doris May, 1919–
—Criticism and interpretation. 5. Carter, Angela, 1940–
—Criticism and interpretation. 6. Jones, Gayl—Criticism and
interpretation. 7. Sex role in literature. 8. Self in literature.
I. Title. II. Series.
PR888.F45R6   1991
823' .914099287—dc20
                                                                90–10249
                                                                    CIP

10 9 8 7 6 5 4 3 2 1

For Carolyn Ertel Robinson and William Robinson

Contents

Acknowledgments

I wish to thank the Andrew Mellon Foundation and Case Western Reserve University for the generous funding which enabled me to finish this book.

Thanks are due to Carolyn Allen and Kate Cummings for their thoughtful comments on early drafts, and their enthusiasm throughout. Numerous conversations with feminist teachers and students at the University of Washington and Case Western Reserve University enabled me to formulate and sharpen my arguments, and for this I am grateful. Particular thanks go to my students at Case Western Reserve, whose questioning often pushed me to deal with issues I had neglected. I thank Martha Woodmansee who, with humor and intelligence, has helped me to see fruitful complexities in feminist, literary, and institutional questions.

Carola Sautter at SUNY Press deserves my warmest thanks for standing behind this project and for her intelligent advice.

To Myra Andrews Sobel I owe thanks for the kind of encouragement only an old and dear friend can give. Finally, I thank Stan Raleigh, who listened endlessly. Without his support this book would not have been possible.

Portions of Chapter Two appeared in *Cultural Critique* No. 13 (Fall 1989), and I thank the publishers for permission to reprint. In addition, I gratefully acknowledge permission to reprint material from the following:

From *The Sadeian Woman and the Ideology of Pornography,* Copyright © 1979 by Angela Carter, reprinted by permission of Pantheon Books, a division of Random House, Inc.

From *Corregidora,* Copyright © 1975 by Gayl Jones; and from *Eva's Man,* Copyright © 1976 by Gayl Jones, both reprinted by permission of Ramdom House, Inc.

From *Nights at the Circus,* Copyright © 1984 by Angela Carter, reprinted by permission of Viking Penguin, a division of Penguin Books USA Inc.

Introduction
Engendering the Subject

Feminist Theory and Identity Politics

Most feminist theorists and critics would agree with Simone de Beauvoir's claim that "one is not born, but becomes a woman." There is considerably less agreement, however, about how that "becoming" proceeds, and, indeed, about what constitutes the category "woman." The question of how one becomes a woman has been complicated by recent critiques of the "subject" and "identity" as ideological fictions necessary for the smooth workings of humanist systems of thought and social regulation. At the same time, these critiques, especially as articulated by feminist theorists, have enabled us to think about how any subject, or any identity, is marked by gender, race, class, and other cultural differences. The mechanisms of that marking are the means by which one becomes a woman: bodies sexed female are produced as "women" by their placement in systems of signification and social practices.[1] Gender, thus, can be conceived as a system of meaning, rather than a quality "owned" by individuals. And, as in all systems of meaning, the effects of gender are not always predictable, stable, or unitary. The processes by which one becomes a woman are multiple and sometimes contradictory, and the category of "women" itself is, thus, a category marked by differences and instabilities. With the fracturing of identity and the deconstruction of the "essence" of gender, feminist theorists have questioned some of the founding principles of feminist study: the authority of experience, the unity of sisterhood, the cross-cultural oppression of all women by a monolithic patriarchy. This questioning has lead toward what Linda Alcoff calls the "identity crisis in feminist theory," a crisis both over the identity *of* feminist theory, and the identity *in* feminist theory.[2] For, in the wake of poststructuralist theory, both feminist and

1

nonfeminist, it is no longer self-evident what feminist theory is (or should be), and for whom it does (or should) speak.

The question of the intersections between feminism and poststructuralism (and postmodernism) has elicited vigorous and sometimes hostile debate. Feminists have chided post-structuralists with being apolitical, while (nonfeminist) post-structuralists have accused feminists of being atheoretical and naively humanist. Yet these debates have ultimately yielded productive results, particularly around the issues of identity and politics.[3] As Elizabeth Weed suggests, the contra-dictions between feminisms' liberal humanist aims and post-structuralisms' anti-humanist critiques have resulted, not in a stalemate, but rather, in new directions for feminist theory:

> [T]here is something distinctive about the meeting of U.S. feminism and poststructuralist theory, and that seems to be the intense challenge both pose to the very grounds of liberalism, that is, to the nature and status of the individual. Indeed, what makes that meeting so inter-esting is that while post-structuralism is squarely "against" the liberal individual, feminism is in no simple way for such an abstraction. Feminism's interrogation of the history of Western Man as the economy of the One and the same, forges a connection between feminism and post-structuralism that further twists the knot of con-tradictions. At the same time, while the liberal rights dis-course and the poststructuralist critique of it are imbri-cated within feminism in complex ways, it is not a question of somehow reconciling the two. On the con-trary, it is that imbrication which produces the ideological contradictions that make feminism such a productive site for cultural criticism. (xi)

While the designation "liberal humanist" has become something of a theoretical liability—connoting, as it does, the whole masculinist Western tradition against which feminism has always worked—[4] the fact remains that any political dis-course which attempts to speak for a class of subjects, such as women, must be rooted, at least provisionally, in some notion of rights. Or, to put the problem in different and less loaded terms, feminisms' projects must always be *positive* as well as negative; that is, even the most poststructuralist of feminists recognizes that the displacement of Woman as Man's other must "continue to supplement the collective and substantive work of 'restoring' woman's history and literature" (Spivak, "Displacement," 186). With the poststructuralist injunction to deconstruct all categories—and to scrupulously avoid constructing new categories—feminist theory and politics risks floundering in negativity.[5] It is important to remember that relations of domination and subordination do not simply go away when they are deconstructed. Rather, as R. Radhakrishnan notes, the positions from which one speaks demand different strategies, depending on the relative power that inheres in those positions. Thus, "whereas the dominant position requires acts of self-deconstruction, the subordinate position entails collective self-construction."[6] It is my contention, however, that it is possible to operate in both directions at once, and that this is precisely how recent feminist attempts to theorize identity politics for women are operating. In other words, feminist theory must negotiate between positive politics and negative critique.[7]

For feminist theory, the deconstruction of unitary identity has meant dismantling the humanist fiction of Western Man as universal subject and of Woman as the negative term which guarantees his identity. Much feminist work in the last decade has been concerned with demystifying a metaphysical and essentialist notion of Woman, signified by the capital "W," and replacing it with a plural and differentially marked category of women.[8] Whereas Woman identifies a singular, often metaphorical, conceptualization of feminine difference, women, as a plural and heterogeneous category fractures that singularity. Thinking women as a multiple, and internally contradictory, category has made it possible for feminist theory to extricate itself from a narrowly conceived, and static, notion of sexual difference: that is, Woman's difference from Man. As Teresa de Lauretis suggests, the time has come to turn attention away from *the* sexual difference, and toward differences between and within women.[9] Such an emphasis on plural differences links feminist theory with poststructuralist theory.

Yet problems remain in the effort to theorize "women." While it might seem that use of the plural gets us off the hook of generalization, universalism and essentialism, such is not necessarily the case. For example, when white feminists speak of "women," are we actually speaking of white women, heterosexual women, middle class academic women? Critiques of liberal (mainstream) feminism as susceptible to racism, classism, and heterosexism have made such categorical statements problematic.[10] It is important to avoid a falsely generic sense of "women," but at the same time, some category is necessary if feminism is to do its political work. The problem with which feminist theory is grappling at this particular historical juncture is how to theorize "identity" (of women and of feminism) without falling into exclusionary practices and falsely universal—or "global"—generalizations.[11] In the face of poststructuralist critiques of "totalizing narratives," as initiated by Jean-Francois Lyotard and others, feminists have become wary of theorizing on the grand scale. Thus, concepts such as "patriarchy," "sexual difference," "Woman/women," and even "gender" have been put into question under the rubric of detotalization. Yet, as Nancy Fraser and Linda Nicholson point out, in their influential essay "Social Criticism Without Philosophy: An Encounter Between Feminism and Postmodernism," the impulse to detotalization threatens to de-politicize feminism by failing to leave a place for "the critique of pervasive axes of stratification, for critique of broad-based relations of dominance and subordination along lines like gender, race, and class" (23). Such critiques are necessary to feminism's projects if they are to be politically efficacious.

A new binary seems to have become entrenched in critical and feminist theory: the local and specific is being privileged over the cross-cultural and systematic. This new hierarchy has resulted in what Susan Bordo calls "gender-scepticism," the fear that any theorizing about gender will inevitably lead us to new totalizations and new metanarratives.[12] Within the terms of poststructuralist theory, all attempts to speak for a constituency risk falling into the traps of unity and sameness. Yet, as Christine Di Stefano points out, scepticism about subject-centered inquiry threatens to plunge feminism into an impossible politics: "To the extent that feminist politics is bound up with a specific constituency or subject, namely, women, the postmodernist prohibition against subject-centered inquiry and theory undermines the legitimacy of a broad-based organized movement dedicated to articulating and implementing the goals of such a constituency" (76). The task, then, becomes a rearticulation of that constituency, a rethinking of the category "women" for which feminism desires to speak. How, then, are we to think "identity" as local and contingent, while simultaneously recognizing that identities are structured by larger systems of power and signification, such as patriarchy, racism, heterosexism, and international capitalism?

Denise Riley suggests that we think of "identities" as "temporary" and strategic, for "identities *can* only be held for a time, both individually and collectively, and both the history of feminism and the semantic logic of 'women' bear witness to this founding temporality" (136). The category "women" has meaning in relation to other categories, and these relations change throughout history. Categorization works through processes of inclusion and exclusion, and "membership" in any category is secured through the exclusion of "outsiders." In this sense, any "identity" must necessarily exclude differences: the One is not, nor can it be, the Other. Yet, in another sense, identity is dependent on difference: the One is only the One in opposition to the Other. For example, woman has meaning in relation to man, and the history of Western thought has conditioned us to think of woman as not-man. But as Riley suggests, "woman" has not always carried the same meaning and, further, the identity of "women" as a collectivity is put into question as soon as we divorce the category from its oppositional relation to "men." That is, the differences within the category "women" disrupt *the* singular and essential difference between man and woman. Rather than seek a consolidation of "women" and identity, then, it is important to operate a continual dispersal or displacement of identity, to theorize the identity of "women" in specific and local historical contexts.[13]

The feminist desire to de-essentialize Woman and women is coterminous with the desire to wrench apart the binary opposition between the masculine and the feminine, and to deconstruct the singularity and unity of the categories "men" and "women." This does not necessarily entail giving up these categories, but rather, entails an approach to gender differences that does not rely on the dubious proposition of an unchanging and "natural" masculinity or femininity. Diana Fuss, in *Essentially Speaking: Feminism, Nature and Difference*, productively intervenes into the critical discourse that has polarized the terms "essentialism" and "constructivism," effectively deconstructing this opposition. In the process, she suggests that even if we think of identity as a construct and as positional, feminist theorists must, nevertheless, "risk" some kind of "essentialism" if we are to think of "women" as a political category. She argues for a use of the category of "women" "as a *linguistic* rather than a natural kind." Making use of Locke's theory of "nominal essence," Fuss claims that such a category is "useful for anti-essentialist feminists who want to hold onto the notion of women as a group without submitting to the idea that it is 'nature' which categorizes them as such" (5). And, while Fuss warns that nominal essence can easily slip into "real essence," she believes that the risk is worth taking, as long as we are clear about the strategies we are using. Those (poststructuralists) who wish to deconstruct Woman, or even "women," to get rid of "essence" at all costs, must be reminded, Fuss tells us, that "the political investments of the sign 'essence' are predicated on the subject's complex positioning in a particular social field, and that the appraisal of this investment depends not on any interior values intrinsic to the sign itself but rather on the shifting and determinative discursive relations which produced it" (20). In other words, there is no essence of the sign "essence," for, like the sign "woman," it has meaning only in specific contexts. This argument leads Fuss to speculate, daringly, that historically oppressed cultural groups have a stronger investment in essence than those who have oppressed them (98). Conversely, we could say that those who want to deconstruct any category of "women," and thus de-mobilize collective action and agency, are those whose power is threatened by that collectivity.[14]

Linda Alcoff comes to a similar conclusion in her critique of cultural feminism and poststructuralism as both limiting the way we can think of the category "women." She proposes a *positional* definition of "woman" that seeks to avoid an essentialist—that is, timeless and unchanging—notion of female identity and experience:

> When the concept 'woman' is defined not by a particular set of attributes but by a particular position, the internal characteristics of the person thus identified are not denoted so much as the *external context within which that person is situated....* The essentialist definition of woman makes her identity independent of her external situation.... The positional definition, on the other hand, makes her identity relative to a constantly shifting context, to a situation that includes a network of elements involving others, the objective economic conditions, cultural and political institutions and ideologies, and so on. If it is possible to identify women by their positions within this network of relations, then it becomes possible to *ground* a feminist argument for women, not on a claim that their innate capacities are being stunted, but that their position within the network lacks power and mobility and requires radical change. (433–34, my emphasis)[15]

What is valuable in Alcoff's positional definition of "woman" is that it negotiates between the local and the systemic, between the subjective and the institutional. It enables us to theorize how individual subjects occupy positions of relative power as these positions are constructed within and by institutions and social practices. And, while Alcoff stresses the "external" rather than the "internal," her definition does not exclude one in favor of the other; rather, she makes room for a conceptualization of "woman" that recognizes how women's placement in cultural and political systems is produced both internally and externally. She is quick to point out that her "view should not imply that the concept of 'woman' is determined solely by external elements and the woman herself is merely a passive recipient of an identity created by these forces. Rather, she herself is part of the historicized, fluid movement, and she therefore actively contributes to the context to which she has access" (434). In short, Alcoff reinstalls "women" as agents of historical process, as subject *to* normative representation, as well as subject *of* self-representation.

The fact that women remain subject to normative representations—of Woman, the feminine, the biologically female —reminds us that such representations continue to exert a great deal of pressure on any attempt to represent women as the subjects of feminism, or, indeed, as the subjects of any discourse or social practice. As Naomi Schor points out, "whether or not the 'feminine' is a male construct, a product of a phallocentric culture destined to disappear, in the present order of things we cannot afford not to press its claims even as we dismantle the conceptual systems which support it" (*Reading in Detail,* 97). Historically specific representations of Woman, and the prevailing gender ideologies they inscribe and reproduce, have effects on women's self-representation. It is in this sense that Teresa de Lauretis speaks of the "*real* contradiction" enabling feminist analysis of culture's texts: "women continue to become woman" (*Alice Doesn't,* 186). By real contradiction, she means to say that the slippages between Woman—a discursive figure most often constructed and mobilized according to the logic of male desire—and women —actual female persons engendered by, and engendering, social and discursive practices—cannot be explained away as an illusion or paradox of discourse. Rather, this contradiction is *real* precisely to the extent that it describes the seemingly impossible position women occupy in relation to the history of Western thought and its representations of history. She writes: "only by knowingly enacting and re-presenting [these contradictions], by knowing us to be both woman and women, does a woman today become a subject" (186).

It is my view that the differences between Woman and women get at the heart of the contradictions that feminist theory is grappling with at the present moment: the general and systematic versus the specific and local; the negativity of critique versus the positivity of transformative politics; unified identity versus situational identities; the sexual difference versus multiplicitous gender differences. Rather than resolve these contradictions, it is necessary to keep them in suspension, to negotiate between their terms in order to theorize how it is that women become subjects. We can now rejoin Simone de Beauvoir's claim, having complicated the subject of becoming woman, and make some claims about the nature of that becoming. Judith Butler suggests that "'becoming' a gender is a laborious process of becoming *naturalized*" (70), yet it is more than that. On the one hand, becoming Woman, in de Lauretis's sense, does, indeed, entail becoming naturalized. To become Woman means to place oneself in a position that is sanctioned by, and guarantees, masculinist structures of representation. It also means to accept the prohibition against female subjectivity within these structures, to give up access to the place of enunciation. Woman is *spoken by* discursive and social practices; she does not speak. On the other hand, to become a woman means to de-naturalize gender and its representations. If gender is a "doing," rather than a "being," as Butler elsewhere suggests, then becoming a woman is a process that can resist naturalization, because performances always threaten to exceed representations. To think of gender as "performative" rather than substantive means that "there is no gender identity behind the expressions of gender; that identity is performatively constituted by the very 'expressions' that are said to be its results" (Butler, 25). Neither identity nor gender, then, exist prior to their articulation in historically specific, and situational, discursive contexts.

"Women's Writing" and Self-Representation

Thus far, my remarks have concerned feminist theory in general, without reference to the uses to which this theory can be put. I now wish to turn my attention toward "women's writing," a phrase that I qualify with quotation marks in order to suggest its provisional nature. "Women's writing" is a construct that is both useful and risky, in the same way that the categories of Woman and women are. It is useful in that it specifies a difference that feminist literary study cannot do without, just as feminist theory cannot do without the category of women. Because standards of literary value have always been masculine standards, and theories of narrative have generally been rooted only in readings of texts signed by men, then it is important to intervene into the production of literature and criticism from the points of view of gender. While traditional literary studies have claimed to be "transcending" gender, feminist readings of texts always foreground gender. For this reason, the construct "women's writing" has proven invaluable, and the controversy which marks its history testifies to its power. The construct is risky, however, in that it can imply a monolithic object of study, as if all women's writing could be represented as homogeneous. If the category of women is multiple, then, surely, the category of women's writing must be more so. The danger in adhering to the notion of a specificity of women's writing is that, first, such adherence threatens to erase differences between and within writing produced by women from different cultural locations; and, second, homogenization of such a diverse field of cultural production can lead to recuperation. We have all seen these dangers at work in syllabus and course designs, and in hiring practices within institutions. Yet, as I hope to show, the risk is worth taking because debates over the specificity of women's writing have not yet exhausted themselves, even if they seem to have generated more divisiveness than consensus. I chose to ground my theorizing about the articulation of gendered subjectivity in readings of women's narratives because I believe, along with other feminist theorists, that narrative is one arena in which gender and subjectivity are produced in powerful ways. I also believe that it is through narrative that women most often become Woman; but that process can be fractured through women's self-representation.

By women's self-representation I mean a process by which subjects produce themselves as women within particular discursive contexts. This process is not always linear, stable, or teleological. On the contrary, women's self-representation most often proceeds by a double movement: simultaneously *against* normative constructions of Woman that are continually produced by hegemonic discourses and social practices, and *toward* new forms of representation that disrupt those normative constructions. The desire to separate writing about Woman from women's writing has been the trend in feminist criticism attempting to theorize the specificity of women's writing.[16] Yet such a separation is counter-productive, if not utopian, for, like it or not, women writing do so in the context of patriarchal prohibitions against women's speech. To isolate women's writing from the context in which it is produced means to complacently ignore that "although 'Woman' does not exist, of course, other than as man's support, the very unified nature of the concept has had its own seductive history and effects" (Weed, xx). The woman writing is not immune to this seduction because she is always placed inside ideologies of gender. But, she simultaneously occupies an "outsider" position, placed on the margins of culture. The contradictions produced by this double positioning fracture women's subjectivity as it is articulated in women's writing, and lead toward the specificity I am reading in women's self-representation, a representation marked by multiplicitous differences.

These differences within can best be conceived as contradictions between the different social and discursive positions subjects occupy. Subjectivity, as I am using the term, is an ongoing process of engagement in social and discursive practices, not some immanent kernel of identity that is expressed through that engagement.[17] It is not constructed, once and for all, at some locatable point in the individual's history;[18] rather, it is a continuous process of production and transformation. Subjectivity, like gender, is a "doing," rather than a being. Subjects are constituted, differentially, across complex and mobile discursive practices in historically specific ways that involve relations of subjectivity to sociality, to power and to knowledge. The woman writing within patriarchal culture is subject *to* the discursive and social practices that require her silence and repression, but also, and undeniably, subject *of* her own cultural productions. To speak as a woman across these contradictions means to disrupt the prohibitions against Woman's speech and, thus, to challenge male privilege and masculine hegemony over the place of enunciation. It is in the process of that speaking that one becomes a woman, that one occupies different subject positions marked by gender, race, class, and other cultural differences. While I would not suggest that the writers I will discuss are *not* women prior to their writing, I would like to focus on the processes by which their identities as female subjects are consolidated and, conversely, dispersed through the process of self-representation. In other words, I am less concerned with the authority of (gendered) authorship and with the woman's signature than I am with the production of gender that operates in the texts.[19]

In what follows, I will be claiming for contemporary women's fiction a subversive potential real-ized through its negotiation of irreconcilable contradictions, a negotiation, in my view, that can provide feminist praxis with a model for reading women's texts. Those contradictions are figured by the encounters these texts stage between conflicting subject positions. I believe, along with Diana Fuss, that "the notion of subject-positions reintroduces the author into literary criticism without reactivating the intentional fallacy" (35). The woman writing always writes from some position, but this position is never singularly and authoritatively inscribed in her text. Rather, the positions occupied by the speaking subject (its author and/or narrator) are multiple and contingent, as are the positions occupied by the subjects spoken in the text (its characters), and the positions occupied by the subjects of the text's address (its readers). These positions are not guaranteed and consolidated by the gender of writers and readers, prior to the text's reading; the (gendered) subjectivities of writers, readers, and even texts themselves, should not be reified or essentialized. These subjectivities are not products, but rather, effects that emerge in the process of reading. As Gayatri Spivak suggests, the idea of a sovereign and identifiable consciousness as the cause of a text's effects obscures the processes by which that "cause" is itself produced as an effect:

> A subject-effect can be briefly plotted as follows: that which seems to operate as a subject may be part of an immense discontinuous network ("text" in the general sense) of strands that may be termed politics, ideology, economics, history, sexuality, language, and so on. (Each of these strands, if they are isolated, can also be seen as woven of many strands.) Different knottings and configurations of these strands, determined by heterogeneous determinations which are themselves dependent upon myriad circumstances, produce the effect of an operating subject. (*In Other Worlds*, 204)

The most obvious way in which the effect of an operating subject has functioned in literary study is in the reification of "character" into person or consciousness. But writers and readers are also subject to the "immense discontinuous network" that is the text, as it is situated in a particular ideological context. Thus, it is possible to read the plotting of subject-effects within and by any text as the process by which the text produces meaning, representation and self-representation. Such a reading goes beyond a focus on how texts written by women *represent* "female experience" toward a focus on how texts *produce* experience, identity, and gender.

"Female experience" never exists in isolation from discursive and social constraints, but, rather, unfolds precisely through women's engagement in discourse and social systems—many of which, in patriarchal cultures, seek to devalue and silence women's worlds and women's words. Experience, like gender, is a process, not a product. It can be most fruitfully conceptualized as the processes by which individual subjects are constituted in their situational specificity. In this way, experience forges a link between representation and self-representation; or, as Teresa de Lauretis puts it, experience is the process through which "one places oneself

[and] is placed in social reality, and so perceives and com-
prehends as subjective (referring to, even originating in,
oneself) those relations—material, economic, and interpersonal—which are in fact social and, in a larger perspective,
historical" (*Alice Doesn't,* 159). This definition of experience
suggests that self-representation is contingent upon the
social context in which all representations are constructed;
but it does not, thus, reduce experience to a fictional guarantee of subjective integrity or authenticity.[20] Experience, in
this sense, is the process by which one becomes a woman. It
is (at least) a twofold process through which one places oneself and is placed in discursive and social systems. And,
while Woman has most often been placed as the negative of
Man, women place themselves in multiple, and often contradictory, positions.

It is important to consider how Woman, or the feminine,
is a masculine construct that has real effects on women's
self-representation. However, to valorize the feminine as that
which can disrupt masculine representation, without considering how such a valorization serves to keep women on the
margins of culture, forecloses on questions of women's subjectivity and makes impossible women's self-representation.
If women are marginal to patriarchal culture, Woman is
absolutely central. As Virginia Woolf observed, many years
ago, woman is both inside and outside the patriarchal
library: "Imaginatively she is of the highest importance;
practically she is completely insignificant. She pervades
poetry from cover to cover; she is all but absent from history" (45). But, rather than trap herself within the walls of this
library, Woolf decides that "the outside of these magnificent
buildings is often as beautiful as the inside" (8). Woolf, I
would suggest, has understood what it means to be both
Woman and a woman and, further, that there is a power in
remaining on the margins, locked out of the library that
"sleeps complacently."

The conceptual and discursive trope of the margins or
the marginal is not, however, without problems as it is
inscribed in recent theoretical discourse. As many cultural
critics have argued, the marginal tends to exist—that is, to

be constructed—only in relation to the central and on its terms. I do not wish to take that leap of faith which argues for the independence of the marginal in relation to the central or hegemonic; such a move is not only recklessly utopian, but it also effectively cuts the marginal voice or subject off from the social. More importantly, however, it is necessary to deconstruct the notion of the (powerless) marginal as it appears in recent theoretical and critical discourse, as well as to diffuse/defuse the equally monolithic notion of the (powerful) hegemonic. As Laurie Finke argues, feminist theory must

> ...evolve from a rhetoric of marginality.... It should enable us to create a position from which we can, as a first step, deconstruct—subvert—the hierarchical center/margin dichotomy, unmasking the reified categories that underwrite gender distinctions. We must, of course, recognize that such a critical position will always be provisional, always subject to revision based on the shifting relations between the centers and margins of social and critical discourse. (266)

As Foucault and his commentators have argued, power is a relation among, rather than a property of, differentially constituted subjects and between these subjects and the discursive and social practices that give them shape.[21] What is important in this work on power and knowledge is the idea that power relations are *mobile,* and that they take historically specific paths based on current notions of "truth," "normality," and their opposites. These paths, the trajectories of desire as they constitute knowledge and power, are always to some extent contradictory and unstable. To put it another way, in more concrete terms, the current truths about what constitutes "Woman" are crossed by contradictions that, if put into play, work to deconstruct this essentialized figure and its construction within a binary opposition.

My aim in this study of contemporary women's fiction is to trace how gendered subject-effects are produced and articulated through the contradictory processes of self-representation. Through readings of texts by Doris Lessing, Angela Carter, and Gayl Jones, I will offer a tentative theory of women's writing that locates sexual/textual difference in the woman writer's negotiation of homogeneous representations of Woman and women's heterogeneous self-representations. This argument implies that we can most productively think the difference in women's writing as a difference within, rather than a difference in opposition to men's writing. Specificity does not have to be coterminous with separatism; to argue for a specificity of women's writing does not necessarily entail a reading of women's texts in isolation from men's texts, the canon, or hegemonic representations of Woman, the feminine, and so on. Women's writing is marked by disruptive contradictions which unsettle any simplistic, or essentialist, notion of sexual difference and, consequently, of subjectivity. The theory is tentative in that I am not arguing for the representative nature of the fictions under consideration; in fact, I have chosen these writers for their diversity, rather than their unity. Yet there are some compelling continuities between these otherwise diverse texts. They articulate gendered subjectivity through their narrative engagement with Woman and women. The voices which speak in these texts occupy multiple positions in relation to gender and other cultural differences, and the texts detail how these voices must continually operate against the discourse systems that work to negate any female subjectivity, to contain women within Woman. They are all contemporary texts that concern themselves with the power of narrative to define "experience" and (gendered) subjectivity: Doris Lessing's novels of colonial central Africa, Angela Carter's fictive explorations of postmodernist theory, and Gayl Jones's deconstructive fictions of Afro-American womanhood. Lessing, Carter and Jones all focus on women-subjects who are readers of culture's master narratives and, thus, I extrapolate from their texts a model for a feminist practice of reading that would work toward disrupting the smooth reproduction of hegemonic ideologies of gender and race. They provide what Elizabeth Meese suggestively calls "reading lessons"[22] that can illuminate both theoretical and practical-political questions of vital concern to feminist study.

My reading of Lessing departs significantly from earlier readings that take the author's humanist ideological vision, including her Marxism, as the single, authorizing paradigm for understanding her texts. My readings of Carter and Jones are meant, in part, to bring critical attention to two neglected contemporary novelists who concern themselves with current theoretical problems in literary study. Before going on to introduce those readings, however, I need to redefine "narrative" as I am using it in this study. I am calling narrative *any discourse that is mobilized by a desire to construct a history, an accounting of the limits and boundaries of gender, subjectivity, and knowledge.* If it is true that history is the supreme narrative, it must also be true that there are alternative narratives and alternative histories that exist in a crucial relation to "official" narratives and history. It is this relation that I will focus on as I argue that contemporary women's fiction *strategically* engages with official narratives—of history, sexual difference, subjectivity—in order to deconstruct them and to forge new narratives. These official or "master" narratives range from the traditional male-centered quest story, to discourses of colonialism, to philosophical and psychological discourses which posit Woman either as a metaphor for difference in man, or as an a priori lack. These discourses construct gendered positions, for writers and readers, and are all mobilized by the desire for coherence or closure—a systematic accounting of difference in relation to hegemonic perspectives that very often leads to the recuperation of that difference.

Toward a Contestatory Practice of Narrative

Most feminist accounts of the narrative production of gender have stressed the masculinist orientation of narrative and narrative theory.[23] Teresa de Lauretis, for example, argues that *all* narrative is Oedipal, that it constructs sexual difference as the difference between male subjectivity and female objectification; and, further, that women should be "suspicious" of narrative because it tends toward sadism.[24] Yet, de Lauretis does not mean to suggest that feminists should, thus, abandon narrative; on the contrary, she suggests that it is only through a reworking of narrative, and its gendering processes, that women can change the terms of that gendering. Laura Mulvey is even more pessimistic about narrative in her account of how classic Hollywood cinema constructs essential masculine and feminine positions for spectators, so that the woman spectator has only two choices: one, she can identify, like a transvestite, with the active male subject of the fiction; or, two, she can identify with the objectified woman in the fiction, a figure who, more often than not, flounders in passivity.[25] But narrative possibilities are not exhausted by the assignation of masculine and feminine positions oppositionally conceived. While it might be true that these are the only two positions *offered* by hegemonic discursive systems, it does not necessarily follow that others cannot be *constructed,* or even wrenched from within those very systems.

Narratives, in the broad sense in which I mean that term, address readers in gender-specific ways and very often seduce women readers into complicity with the erasure of female subjectivity, seduce women into becoming Woman. Yet it is possible to resist this seduction in a number of ways, and the fictional texts to which I now turn model both the success and failure of that resistance. They all represent woman as readers, as well as writers, of cultural narratives and model a contestatory practice of reading. This practice can be metaphorically described as a double, doubled, and doubling interpretive methodology—a conceptualization that is certainly not new to feminist theory or criticism, but which can be further elaborated in the specific context of narrative. The argument I will advance in the chapters that follow is that these contemporary women's fictions inscribe that double movement as a movement between the "inside" and the "outside" of gender as ideological representation, a movement between Woman and women. As Frann Michel suggests, in an article on Djuna Barnes, the woman writer's "engagement with the order of discourse that would exclude the woman writer places her both inside that order, to the extent that she confronts its terms and myths, and outside it to the extent that her position as subject in the act of engagement would be impossible within such an order." Such an engagement "subtly undermines the notions of a single sexual difference and of a simple 'inside' and 'outside' of representation" (39). To be "inside" hegemonic representation of gender means to be framed within/by *the* sexual difference—that is, Woman's difference from Man. To be "outside" does not mean to occupy a space that is somehow "objective," free from ideology; rather, it means to occupy, self-consciously and critically, a position of marginality that enables women's self-representation. And, while the terms "inside" and "outside" are open to deconstruction,[26] that does not mean that these terms do not have strategic use for a theory of women's self-representation.

In Chapter One, "Repetition and Resistance: Doris Lessing's *Children of Violence*," I consider recent attempts to theorize subjectivity in such a way as to avoid both a return to a simplistic humanist male-centered notion of the self, and an equally unproductive move toward an abstract posthumanist notion of the subject that leaves gender all but beside the point. I use Doris Lessing's early, African-based, novels to analyze how gender foregrounds the contradictions both between these two epistemologies, and within each of them. I argue that a theory of gendered subjectivity must account for the complex, and contradictory, ways in which women take up positions in relation to official narratives of sexual difference. With the possible exception of Dorothy Richardson's *Pilgrimmage,* the Martha Quest novels present the most detailed and sustained exploration of a female subject's history that I have encountered—and, thus, provide the ground for an analysis of the ongoing production of women's self-representation as it intersects with hegemonic representations of Woman. In other words, these texts inscribe a history of a female subject's negotiation between Woman and women. The teleological movement of Martha's narrative takes the form of a traditional quest story that underwrites various narratives of sexual difference which frame woman as negativity. Because of Martha's gender, the ways she is placed and places herself in systems of meaning, this narrative line causes much disturbance; she consistently finds herself identifying with the masculine and negating her experience of "becoming" a woman. This disturbance causes Martha's quest to derail time and again and, in fact, leaves the end of that quest indefinitely deferred. Thus, against the teleological movement that ostensibly structures these texts, I am reading another kind of movement—or, more accurately, lack of movement—that foregrounds the problems encountered when a woman desires to be the subject of her own narrative, and of history.

Those problems do not necessarily accompany any narrative of female subjectivity, and I would certainly not propose that women cannot be subjects of narrative. However, Martha's insistence that her experiences go against her "real self" militates against recognition that subjectivity is a process put into play by her self-narrative and the narrative that is history, rather than a product that rests at the end of a quest. She insists on reading as fragmentary, inauthentic, and false the many subject positions she occupies throughout her history, particularly those encoded by the texts as feminine. These positions, together, produce contradictions not coherence, and despite Martha's faith in the possibility that, someday, somewhere, somehow, things will come together for her, the texts continue to pull back from that possibility. The process by which Martha becomes a woman entails her placement and self-placement in relation to ideologies of race and class, as well as gender, for her situation as a white, bourgeois, colonial subject makes it impossible for her to occupy just one position in the complex network of differences that comprise the social fabric of colonial Central Africa in the pre- and post-World War II era. Because Lessing represents Martha as, above all else, a *reader,* these texts provide me with an opportunity to theorize how texts offer culturally specific positions for readers, and how it is possible to resist taking up these positions. To this end, I draw on Paul Smith's ambitious critique of theories of subjectivity and appropriate, for feminist purposes, his interesting proposition that ideological interpellation can *fail* to produce a compliant subject. This proposition has promising implications for a feminist theory interested in articulating how it is that texts address readers in gender-specific ways, and how it might be possible to resist that address, by recognizing the contradictions produced between official representations of sexual difference and heterogeneous self-representations.

Chapter Two, "Angela Carter and the Circus of Theory: Writing Woman and Women's Writing," continues the dialogue between theory and fiction that I begin in the first chapter. My approach throughout the book is to read theory alongside fiction, in order to open up the novels to current questions in literary study, and to ground theoretical insights in specific discursive contexts. This approach, then, is more a dialogue than an application, and is meant, in part, to put current theoretical "truths" into crisis. In this second chapter, I consider the dynamics of marginality and centrality as they are inscribed in a particularly "seductive" account of sexual difference as a difference between phallocratic authority on the one hand, and feminine *différance*, on the other— Jacques Derrida's privileging of "woman" in *Spurs*. In this text, Derrida advances a claim for the "feminine" as the deconstructive lever par excellence. That is, for Derrida's project in this text, woman provides the means toward freeing philosophical discourse from its reliance on a masculine authority, precisely because that woman-figure cannot be pinned down, exists in an unstable movement between all binary oppositions. While this project is, indeed, seductive from a feminist point of view, I argue that Derrida's "new" narrative of sexual difference, despite his claims to the contrary, reproduces woman as other to man, and more precisely, as the difference in man necessary for his "post-phallogocentric" self-representation. The economy of desire in this text can be described as what Irigaray calls a "hom(m)osexual" economy, in which woman is put into circulation according to the dynamics of masculine desire conceived as an exchange between two men. Irigaray's "Veiled Lips," an oblique commentary on *Spurs*, brings these issues into sharp focus as she posits Athena as the figure of Derrida's "affirmative deconstruction." My polemic purpose in offering this argument is to caution against the seduction of Derrida's text. My intervention into his text, mediated by Irigaray, is an example of how it is possible to resist that seduction by exposing the stakes involved in Derrida's displacement of woman and his deconstruction of "women."

In the second half of this chapter, I read Angela Carter's *The Infernal Desire Machines of Doctor Hoffman* and *Nights at the Circus* as deconstructive texts which stage performances of gender through subversive narrative strategies. *The Infernal Desire Machines of Doctor Hoffman* is a postmodern parody of fictions of male subjectivity and desire. Carter parodies both liberal humanist and postmodernist epistemologies by constructing a textual world torn by a war between the forces of rationality and philosophical certainty, and the forces of desire and radical indeterminacy. The narrative unfolds in a textual world where all "reality" is mediated, indeed, *produced* by the articulation of desire. Carter's "hero" Desiderio, is sent to by the Minister of Determination to destroy the diabolical Doctor Hoffman whose desire machines are wreaking havoc on "reality." The goal of his quest, however, becomes less important than the adventures he "experiences"—that is, constructs—in its process. Desiderio's desire participates in the fantasy of colonization that, simultaneously, marks the Doctor's and the Minister of Determination's projects for "liberation." Woman, in Desiderio's narrative, occupies a range of traditional object positions: she is a fetish, a foil, the exotic/erotic object awaiting the hero at the end of his quest, but never a subject. She is, like Derrida's "affirmative woman," an object put into circulation according to the logic of male desire. As object of the male gaze, she is *subject to* regulation, exploitation and violence. Yet Carter's overt and exaggerated masculinization of her narrative subverts the successful narrativization of violence against women—including the rhetorical violence that keeps women in the position of silent object. The text engenders its readers as political by de-naturalizing the processes by which narrative constructs differences—sexual, racial, class, national—according to the twin logics of desire and domination. The text addresses a reader who must negotiate between the Oedipal logic the text flaunts with a vengeance, and another logic that emerges from her/our engagement in that narrative.

Like the earlier novel, *Nights at the Circus* can be read as a feminist parody of the tendency in postmodernist theory to privilege what Linda Hutcheon calls the "ex-centric": the Other(s) of Western culture, who have, historically, had limited access to the place(s) of enunciation.[27] With the postmodernist critique of the self-present, knowing subject, has come a desire to explore the "difference" whose exclusion has guaranteed the identity of the liberal humanist self. These explorations, however, too often become appropriations that do not disrupt the politics of enunciation. In this novel, Carter gives us a carnivalesque world where all identities are performances and where subjectivity is articulated in the intersections of gender, race, class, and sexual ideologies. My points of focus on this text have to do with what emerges as a philosophical-fictive exploration of difference as spectacle. I argue that the protagonist, Fevvers, and other "freaks" in the "magic circle of difference" known as the circus, are denied agency by those in power who construct them as objects of a controlling gaze, and other forms of penetration. These are "outsiders" in several senses of the term; but because they are at the mercy of the "inside," that is, the center, they must negotiate between these two poles of cultural identity and placement.

Nights at the Circus is particularly concerned with enacting the contradictions between Woman as object of official narratives and women as subjects of self-narratives. The text enacts a conflict between the female protagonist's story and the story that a male reporter attempts to tell about her. Fevvers, the famed *aeraliste,* whose "reality" status is put into question by the apparent fact that she is half bird and half woman, baffles the empirically-minded (American) reporter, Walser, who is simultaneously attracted and repulsed by her ambiguous womanhood. While Fevvers is placed as the object of various male gazes in the text, she simultaneously places herself as the subject of her own story. Her strategy to this end is to turn the gaze on herself by actively staging her difference and by intervening into the hom(m)osexual economy that requires Woman be made into a fetish-object to safeguard male subjectivity. This is the economy that characterizes Carter's earlier novel, and *Nights at the Circus* disrupts it through what feminist film theorists have called the subversive potential of the feminine masquerade. This strategy is akin to what Irigaray calls mimicry: a self-conscious performance, by women, of the place traditionally assigned to Woman within narrative and other discourse. It is by this and other similar strategies that Fevvers appropriates the gaze to herself as an index of her subjective agency, and simultaneously, gains control over her narrative. In both of these novels, Carter demonstrates how becoming a woman can mean becoming naturalized. But her focus on gender as performance, rather than substance, subverts that naturalization by showing how the notion of a "universality of female experience is a clever confidence trick," and how mythologies of sexual difference are "consolatory nonsense" (Carter, *The Sadeian Woman,* 6).

In my third chapter, "'We're all consequences of something': Cultural Mythologies of Gender and Race in the Novels of Gayl Jones," I turn my attention to a complex network of mythologies that have constrained Afro-American female subjectivity by positioning the black woman between indeterminacy and overdetermination. While I am arguing for the *productive* function of contradiction and indeterminacy—instability and doubleness as a tool of analysis and resistance—I want to avoid the kind of theoretical abstraction evident in, for instance, Derrida, that posits indeterminacy as an a priori value. Drawing on histories of American slavery, I argue here that indeterminacy as the mark of the black woman stems from an overdetermination of what Hortense Spillers calls the "nominative properties" that have defined and constrained black female subjectivity in American culture.[28] In other words, indeterminacy has been forced on the black woman through the dominant culture's misnaming of her as Jezebel, Sapphire, and other equally reductive terms. Yet it is in the very overdetermination of these namings that resistance can be glimpsed; the ponderous weight of cultural mythologies of gender and race makes them collapse and, with them, normative constructions of black womanhood. Jones's two novels, *Corregidora* and *Eva's Man,* "flirt" with the figures of Jezebel and Sapphire, as one critic has put it; but they do so in order to conceptualize a black female subjectivity in the interstices of hegemonic representations.

I argue that Jones complicates the need for a black female identity and that such a complication is necessary in order to escape the recuperation of minority perspectives by the dominant—that is, white male—perspective. What is problematic in these texts is their refusal to posit a singular and determinate "identity" for their textual subjects and the seeming subjective paralysis that results from this refusal. Ursa Corregidora and Eva Medina Canada are textual figures whose subjectivity emerges from their engagement in official narratives of sexual and racial differences—from a movement between the "inside" and the "outside" of ideologically motivated representations of the black woman as Jezebel and Sapphire. In order to ground my readings of these novels in their historical context, I begin the chapter by surveying the ways in which discourses on American slavery conspired to keep the black woman "in her place," not only in relation to white culture, but also in relation to the black community as sub-culture. The black woman, I argue, emerges as the linchpin of a complex representational system where gender and race interlock to insure the hegemony of the white man as subject of culture and power. More than any of the other fictional texts under consideration in this study, Jones's two novels focus attention on what is at stake in essentialist constructions of gender in (at least) two ways: first, by demonstrating that the slippages between Woman and women within representation serve the interests of the dominant group, especially since such slippages obscure multiple differences in favor of *the* difference between the hegemonic self and its cultural others; and, second, by denaturalizing the construction of entire narratives around the figure of that difference. These narratives depend on the black woman's compliance for their coherence.

Jones's novels demonstrate how American culture's master narratives about gender and race, particularly about the intersection between the two, force an objectification on the black woman from all sides. In order to resist this objec-

tification, and the erasure of their subjectivity, Jones's protagonists must write in the margins of official narratives,
constructing a position from which they can speak without
being recontained within those very margins. But, since the
black woman is always already *spoken by* discourses of
gender and race, it is impossible simply to "break free" from
that historical containment. Rather, it is necessary for
Jones's protagonists to actively take on, if you will, that history, and the two adopt different strategies in doing so. Ursa
undertakes an explicit revision of her history—marked by
the literal experience of slavery and the more metaphorical
slavery enforced on her by masculinist ideologies in her
experience of heterosexual relations, both inscribed here as
gendered property relations. In order to accomplish that
revision, it is necessary for her to re-play the place of her
exploitation by discursive and social systems, to position
herself firmly "inside" ideologies of gender and race. It is
also necessary for Ursa to intervene into these official narratives, from the "outside," by telling another story, her story,
expressed through the productively ambivalent medium of
the blues. It is in the contradictions between these two types
of positioning that Ursa's subjectivity speaks.

At the end of *Corregidora,* however, Ursa finds herself re-
captured within a certain narrative of victimization and
power with no hope of escape, a narrative metaphorically
rendered as a master/slave dialectic. The critical discourses
surrounding this text have made much of the question of
Ursa's complicity in relation to this dialectic, and my reading
of the novel is meant, in part, to disrupt the tendency of this
criticism to offer an easy answer to Ursa's dilemma. The
master/slave configuration is itself a seductive narrative, in
that it *appears* to grant a mutual power to subject and
object; yet, as the ending of this novel illustrates, the real
power remains with the (male) subject. Both parties in this
transaction, moreover, are contained within a metaphorical
figure of master/slave, masculine/feminine, that denies them
agency. In *Eva's Man,* Jones steps beyond this figuration by
creating in Eva a force that cannot be contained within any
official narrative or discourse of power. In prison for castrat-

ing her lover, Eva refuses to "explain" her crime to the
authorities whose power and systems her act has brought
into question. In this respect, Eva stubbornly positions herself "outside" culturally regulated narrative possibilities;
indeed, she refuses to take up any position at all—at least as
they are offered by the representatives of officialdom. But
she speaks to the reader, taking up a number of different
positions in relation to mythologies of gender and race.

I argue that Eva's excessive mimicry of mythological figures of black womanhood—her own versions of Jezebel and,
especially, Sapphire—is a subversive response to the hegemony these figures have always had over the black woman's
construction as subject. Like Ursa's almost obsessive repetition of the slavemaster's narratives about black women,
Eva's mimicry of these figures places her firmly "inside" ideologies of gender and race. Yet, this mimicry ultimately
deconstructs those ideologies and enables Eva to speak her
subjectivity from an unstable, yet subversive, space that
allows her to resist recuperation. Her refusal to explain herself to the authorities who question her furthers this resistance. Jones's two novels, then, enact the contradictions
between Woman and women, and also demonstrate that not
all differences can be reduced to *the* difference between man
and woman. The official cultural narratives that subject the
black woman to objectification, exploitation, and blame are
structured differently than those that have kept the white
woman "in her place." Jones's novels, like Lessing's and
Carter's, work to problematize Woman's place, and to create
other positions from which women can speak *as*
women—that is, as subjects engendered by, and engendering, cultural processes. The difference of women's writing is
not singular, existing only in relation to the masculine, the
hegemonic, or the falsely "universal." Rather, it has to do
with the politics of enunciation—who speaks, to whom, from
where, and to what end. Gender difference *is* a difference in
language; but it is also a difference in experience, widely
conceived as a subject's relation to discourse and social systems. It is toward theorizing these differences that I offer the
following chapters.

Repetition and Resistance in Doris Lessing's *Children of Violence*

In a 1957 essay entitled "The Small Personal Voice," Doris Lessing laments what she sees as the sorry state of literary criticism: "At the moment our critics remind me of a lot of Victorian ladies making out their library lists: this is a 'nice' book; or it is not a 'nice' book; the characters are 'nice'; or they are not 'nice.'" This dig at critics is overdetermined by her anger at the reception of the first two volumes of her *Children of Violence* series, about which she writes: "Not one critic has understood what I should have thought would be obvious from the first chapter, where I was at pains to state the theme very clearly: that this is a study of the individual conscience in its relations with the collective" (14). Against the "Victorian ladies," Lessing poses the "serious" critic who would disdain "private sensitivity" and subjective response in favor of the larger questions pressing on "man." This formulation imposes a gendered framework on literary response; that is, Lessing engenders the "serious" reader and writer of literature, as male, and the frivolous reader and writer as female. Behind this gendered opposition are others: rational/emotional, public/private, political/personal, with the first term of each couple enjoying a privileged status over the second. Thus, despite Lessing's avowed focus on the *relations* between the individual and the collective, her commentary here drives a wedge between the two, separating the private from the public, the personal from the political, the subjective from the serious, and, further, places these oppositions in a gender hierarchy. Thus, it comes as no surprise that it is also in this essay that Lessing refers to herself as a humanist by necessity, as it were: "Once a writer has a feeling of responsibility, as a human being, for the other human beings he [sic] influences, it seems to me he must become a humanist, and must feel himself as an instrument of change for good or for bad" (6).[1] Yet, while Lessing might well have intended a certain reading of her texts, in alignment with her humanist vision, this does not mean that this is the only reading available. Indeed, these texts are rife with gaps in that humanist vision and it is by foregrounding those gaps that I propose to read in *Children of Violence* a deconstruction of the subject of humanism, albeit an unwitting one. My reading of these novels will, thus, attempt to displace Lessing's humanism by tracing the textual effects that contradict her avowed intentions.

My reading of the first four novels in Lessing's series as a deconstruction of the humanist subject—of narrative, of culture, of history—begins by foregrounding a conspicuously absent term in Lessing's claim that the texts form a study of the *individual* (conscience) in relation to the collective. For, it seems odd indeed that the gender of that individual remains unspoken—given Lessing's focus in these texts on how a *woman* situates herself in relation to the social, here conceived, rather narrowly, as the "collective"—and, indeed, even in that first chapter. It is precisely Lessing's faith in humanism that makes it impossible for gender to enter this statement, since humanist conceptions of the "individual" have always assumed that individual to be male, white, and of unspecified class. But gender constantly presses against Lessing's texts, and it does so in the form of a disturbance—a disturbance in the humanist ideology of singular and unified identity that supports, and is supported by, the quest plot which ostensibly structures them. These novels—*Martha Quest* (1952), *A Proper Marriage* (1952), *A Ripple from the Storm* (1958), and *Landlocked* (1958)—[2] present a sustained exploration of the production of *female* subjectivity as a struggle against cultural and narrative conventions.

These cultural and narrative conventions conspire to keep woman in a position of passivity in relation to historical process by constructing man, Lessing's "responsible individual" ("The Small Personal Voice," 12), as the sole subject of narrative and history. I will focus on two interrelated conventions here: the classical quest story, through which the individual passes into adulthood and culture; and, the humanist paradigm of the individual self on which this quest story is dependent. Martha's quest for an identity, and a collective in which that identity can reside, takes the form of a quasi-linear, teleological narrative whose goal is the achievement of a unified and authentic self that can participate in the historically specific functions of a collective. Or, to put it in slightly different terms, the quest narrative is mobilized by a desire to install its "hero" as subject of cultural and historical processes. This hero must pass certain tests, in the form of obstacles to his quest, in order to accede both to selfhood and cultural authority. As Peter Brooks puts it in his study of the ambitious hero of nineteenth-century narrative, the questing hero strives to "totalize his experience of human existence in time, to grasp past, present, and future in a significant shape" (39). For Brooks, as for Martha Quest in Lessing's novels, ambition is the "force that drives the protagonist forward.... Ambition is inherently totalizing, figuring the self's tendency to appropriation and aggrandizement, moving forward through the encompassment of more, striving to have, to do, to be more" (Brooks, 39). Yet, as Brooks also notes, this dynamic of plot "most obviously concerns male plots of ambition. The female plot is not unrelated, but it takes a more complex stance toward ambition, the formation of an inner drive toward the assertion of selfhood *in resistance to the overt and violating male plots of ambition*" (39, my emphasis).[3]

Martha's quest, her ambitious plot, participates in both of these narrative forms at the same time. That is, her narrative is marked both by the desire to have more, do more, and be more; and, simultaneously, by the violation of this desire. Yet it is not the male plot of ambition, per se, that violates Martha's assertion of selfhood; rather, it is the fact that narratives of selfhood and personal development are culturally coded as male. What Martha must resist, then, is that cultural coding, insofar as it prohibits a woman from being subject of the quest for self. Her resistance, however, is continuously compromised by the paradigm of identity with which Lessing aligns her quest story. For Lessing in *Children of Violence,* the "self" is a masculine ideal that is endangered by feminine forces that continuously militate against authenticity, wholeness and, even, "humanity." The texts thus inscribe the same gendered oppositions evident in Lessing's division of literary response into "subjective" and "serious," and Martha's struggle becomes a struggle to avoid becoming a woman. The paradigmatic *Bildungsroman* quest narrative into which Martha attempts to insert herself as subject constructs the subject as man, "the responsible individual, voluntarily submitting his will to the collective, but never finally; and insisting on making his private judgements before every act of submission" ("The Small Personal Voice," 12). For woman, that submission entails aspiring to the universal, "man, the responsible individual," and, subsequently, transcending gender. Indeed, to *foreground* gender would mean to debunk the humanist claims that Lessing espouses. Lessing's desire to transcend gender is mediated by an ironic narrative presentation that, through the distancing effect of irony and sarcasm at Martha's expense, functions to disembody the textual subject. Throughout these four texts, Martha's desire to be a human subject capable of significant action is paralleled by Lessing's desire to distance herself, in true humanist spirit, from the female body that threatens to derail that quest.

For, the subject of humanism is, precisely, disembodied, ungendered, unmarked by social and discursive differences. This subject—or, better, "self"—exists *prior to* its insertion in discourse and social practices. If for Martha the goal of her quest is to *find* her "self," that is because she believes, as does Lessing, that that "self" is an entity that constructs, but is not constructed by, the world. The texts ostensibly support a conceptualization of human identity as an internal essence that exists independent of social and discursive determinants. Against this representation of identity, we have Martha's self-representation: a process through which she is inserted, and inserts herself, into multiplicitous positions offered her by discursive and social practices. This process

is fragmented and discontinuous, rather than linear and teleological. And, while Martha is focused on the goal, the self
that lies at the end of her quest, the texts continually pull
against this goal by showing how Martha's identity is a process, not a product. Since Lessing represents Martha as,
above all, a *reader,* it is possible to articulate the history of
her subjectivity as a history of being addressed, or interpellated, by texts. Martha is a literal reader, always hungry for
an authoritative explanation of her experience, which
amounts to a normative *construction* of that experience. She
is also a reader in the larger sense of producing meaning
through her engagement with the world as text. Because the
texts to which Martha appeals for self-definition position her
in gender-specific ways, these novels present a history of the
production of a female subject as a history of taking up differential positions in relation to discourse. The history of
Martha's subjectivity can be described as oscillating between
seduction by normative representations of the self, and particularly the female self, which support masculinist and colonialist ideologies; and resistance to that seduction, withhold-
ing her compliance in the ideological construction of gender
and other cultural differences.

   Thus, *Children of Violence* inscribes a conflict between
two versions of subjectivity that are radically at odds with
each other: a humanist version that relies on the ideal of
authentic and whole selfhood as the goal of personal development; and an "anti-humanist" version in which subject positions are seen to be temporary, ideological, and situational.
As Biddy Martin and Chandra Mohanty note, humanist conceptions of the "self" obscure the "the fundamentally relational nature of identity and the negations on which the assumption of a singular, fixed, and essential self is based." Such a
"self" can only "sustain its appearance of stability by defining
itself in terms of what it is not" (196–97). Because these novels are set in white-settler Central Africa, in "Zambesia"—a
fictional country that Lessing means to be taken as "a com-
posite of various white-dominated parts of Africa" (Author's
Notes on *The Four-Gated City*)—Lessing's exploration of
Martha's personal history takes on a complex negotiation of

the racial ideologies that structure subjectivities, both hegemonic and nonhegemonic. Martha's desire to discover her
"real self" is complicated by the social codes that continue to
construct her as a white British woman in opposition both to
the "natives" and to white men—a construction that Martha
attempts, sometimes successfully, sometimes not, to resist.[4]

These texts delineate the process by which one becomes
a woman, as a process of normalization/naturalization that
comes into conflict with the desire to resist that process. They
are structured by a doubled movement between two contradictory narrative forces, one represented by Martha's quest
and her conscious desire to preserve the integrity of a "self"
that she only vaguely perceives as a kind of unchanging "center," and the other by the gradually building evidence of the
inefficacy of this paradigm of identity to describe her experience.[5] On the one hand, we have Martha's quasi-linear history, a classical *Bildungsroman* story of her growth from adolescence to adulthood:[6] a history that can be described as a
process of disillusionment with first, a conventional social
body and, later, with various contestatory, "alternative" social
bodies. The forward push of the teleological narrative
depends on the humanist model, but the ambiguities and
ambivalences produced within this movement disrupt both its
linearity and teleology. These ambivalences, or disturbances,
give the texts a counter-movement, less like a narrative line
than like a rhythm of repetition and resistance. A reader coming to these texts with an expectation about how quest narratives are structured—particularly in terms of a teleological
movement toward an end—is likely to find herself disappointed, and her expectations unfulfilled. Such a reader is also likely to experience an extreme frustration with Martha, who
seems to be particularly good at botching up the narrative
that is her life. Yet, as I will demonstrate, a different reading of
these texts, a reading attentive to the contradictions that
structure them, foregrounds the gaps in Martha's narrative
that demonstrate the impossibility of transcending gender
when detailing a woman's quest for meaning and for "self."
Like the repressed of discourse, which some feminist theorists
have called "the feminine," gender returns again and again to

structure Martha's self-representation. Gender, thus, not only disturbs Martha's quest, but also disturbs our reading of the quest plot as paradigmatic of "human" experience. These texts enact the contradictions between Woman and women by demonstrating what happens when the subject of narrative is engendered as a woman.

The Female Oedipus:
Gender and the (De)Structuring of Martha's Quest

The *Children of Violence* novels seem to be governed by what Roland Barthes calls the hermeneutic code of narrative, in that the texts set in motion a trajectory of desire described by the following question: Will Martha ever act on her growing knowledge of the falsity of her many different roles, and find a life that will allow her to be "herself," free of the stifling atmosphere of conventionality and "the nightmare repetition" that characterizes the "white settler mentality" in colonial Central Africa? The hermeneutic code of narrative privileges beginnings and ends over middles and inscribes the drive of narrative as the drive toward a truth to be unveiled at the end.[7] What is situated in the middle are desire and expectation, signified as a disturbance or disorder. The Martha Quest novels follow this hermeneutic code on one level, and the desire expressed in the above question represents pretty closely Martha's desire. But Martha's Quest is, in effect, *overtaken* by the obstacles and complications that Barthes argues keep both reader and character going in narrative, so that it gradually becomes clear that she and we will never reach an answer to the question. In short, these texts are structured less like the classical quest narrative than they are like soap opera, a genre in which, as Tania Modleski so eloquently puts it, "the narrative, by placing ever more complex obstacles between desire and fulfillment, makes anticipation of an end, an end in itself" and, she continues, "Soap operas invest exquisite pleasure in the central condition of a *woman's* life: waiting" ("The Search for Tomorrow," 266, my emphasis).

I have moved in this paragraph from the general to the

(gender) specific in order to suggest, as Modleski and many others have, that narrative characterized by the hermeneutic code is culturally encoded as masculine. The linear quest narrative is perhaps most obviously so. Without essentializing that construct[8] I would like to suggest that there are reasons why such a narrative mode simply does not work so well when one sets out to tell a woman's story, and to read one. Although I question Modleski's generalization about the "central condition of a woman's life," her description of the narrative form of the soap opera evokes a certain social reality that does indeed surface in the Martha Quest novels: a woman on a quest—for meaning, subjectivity, the fulfillment of desire—might well find that her culture places "ever more complex obstacles between desire and fulfillment." And, as Annette Kuhn observes, also in relation to soap opera, a woman in such a narrative might well find herself in a "masochistic" position of being forced to renunciate her quest, or "forever anticipating an endlessly held-off resolution" ("Women's Genres," 27). Martha is impatient with beginnings and impatient for ends; as the narrator sardonically tells us at one point, she "tended to think too much of an end before she had mastered a beginning" (*MQ,* 109).[9] Her imagination and desire projected toward the end of her quest, Martha is bogged down in the middle and does in fact see this condition as specifically female.

  Children of Violence, thus, inscribes sexual difference through what Teresa de Lauretis convincingly describes as a gendering of narrative processes. The quest narrative constructs sexual difference as a binary distinction between activity and passivity: "male-hero-human, on the side of the subject; and female-obstacle-boundary-space, on the other" (*Alice Doesn't,* 121). The "mythical subject" of narrative is male, and the pattern of his narrative is one of movement, progress, transformation. This archetypically masculine "hero" is assumed to be a unitary, rational subject who, in the specific case of the *Bildungsroman* moves toward the "possibility of a conscious choice" about his life and who he wants to be.[10] The feminine in this paradigm is most often represented as a static force, an obstacle that must be overcome if the hero is to find his "true self" and his place in the world. We are, of course, back to Oedipus and his story. As de Lauretis remarks:

> It was not an accident of cultural history that Freud, an avid reader of literature, chose the hero of Sophocles' drama as the emblem of Everyman's passage into adult life, his advent to culture and history. All narrative, in its movement forward toward resolution and backward to an initial moment, a paradise lost, is overlaid with what has been called an Oedipal logic—the inner necessity or drive of the drama—its "sense of an ending"...(*Alice Doesn't,* 125)

Everyman, but of course, not Everywoman. *Her* place in this drama is as "what is not susceptible to transformation, to life or death; she (it) is an element of plot-space, a topos, a resistance, matrix and matter" (119).

The Martha Quest novels almost literally enforce this Oedipal logic, but on a thematic rather than structural level. That is, the texts represent Martha's desire on a thematic level as the desire to be subject of this mythical narrative; while, on a structural level, the texts consistently work against the form that narrative must take. Thematically, the masculine represents progressive movement: man makes history. The feminine represents a more cyclical movement, most often described as an inevitable repetition that ultimately reduces to stasis: woman may reproduce, but she does not produce history.[11] The inevitability Martha assigns to this feminine repetition suggests a particularly dangerous passivity; it is the feminine that participates in an uncontrollable reproduction of conventional ideologies. The masculine, on the other hand, is an active force, capable of change. Her mother, against whom she reacts so violently, is the prime representative of this ideological reproduction; May Quest speaks for the status quo, the "official line" in the colony. For Martha, this ideological reproduction is a monstrous force, effectively beyond "rational" control, and is situated in the nuclear family. Thus, Martha's thinking reproduces what

Denise Riley has identified as the nineteenth-century British conflation of the "social" and the "familial" into the feminine, and the separation of the male "individual" from that realm. The formulation of "individual versus society" becomes the masculine versus the feminine, the former being the realm of "politics" and the latter the realm of "personal life."[12] However, when Martha enters actively into the colony's political scene—where individuals fight against "society"—she begins to identify the "pompous, hypocritical and essentially male fabric of society" (ARS, 19) as that which causes the ideological reproduction she so fears. As is characteristic of Martha throughout the series, she swings from one extreme to the other, an absolutist whose world view is dependent on binary oppositions. Here, she reverses the masculine and the feminine, but fails to displace the opposition.

Martha's rebellion against convention throughout the texts pits the masculine against the feminine in a representational paradigm that depends on other gendered binary oppositions, particularly the opposition between rationality and emotionality. As Lynn Sukenick points out, Lessing situates "self" and personality on the side of the rational in opposition to sensibility or emotion: "Rationality is personality; for Lessing it is intelligence that gives one a sense of self and preserves some approximation of integration in the face of invading irrationalities." Within this paradigm, emotions "disrupt the self as if they, the emotions, are outside of the self" (Sukenick, 104–105, my emphasis). Martha consistently appeals to the masculine gods of reason in order to combat feminine irrationality; she feels that, "above all it was essential to account for every contradictory emotion that assailed one": "Books. Words. There must surely be some pattern of words which would neatly and safely cage what she felt—isolate her emotions so that she could look at them from outside" (APM, 60–61). For Martha, the "outside" view provided through the discourses of the "human sciences," amounts to a kind of universally objective knowledge that can protect her from what she perceives as an assault of irrationality in the form of contradiction. Implicit in the opposition between "rational" and "irrational" is that the latter is somehow "false" or inauthentic. The feminine becomes, in Martha's mind, an obstacle to authenticity, here conceived as subjective agency.

Martha's self-representation thus places her firmly in the camp of the mythical hero; like other "great" heroes of *Bildungsromane*—Stephen Dedalus comes immediately to mind—she feels she must work against those claustrophobic "feminine" forces that conspire to hold her down.[13] She does indeed encounter many obstacles in her journey toward this telos, and they are often encoded as feminine. But they are not, as Sukenick suggests, entirely "outside" forces; rather, these obstacles to progressive movement are situated *both* inside *and* outside Martha, and this sets her apart from her male counterparts. These forces are inside to the extent that Martha feels the existence of a "female self" at odds with her "real self"; and outside to the extent that she thinks those feminine forces and that "female self" have "nothing to do with her"—a phrase that echoes through all four novels. The irrationality that Martha links with the feminine is rooted in the female body that comes to signify the greatest obstacle to her quest for "self." Thus the texts essentialize gender as a being, an internal force that can be located *inside* the individual. Yet, at the same time, Martha's resistance to "becoming a woman"—that is, her resistance to taking up the "natural" position of femininity—serves to denaturalize that becoming. Martha, then, situates herself both inside and outside the ideology of gender which gives the equation "rationality: authenticity:: irrationality: falsity" its meaning. She is trapped, or framed, *inside* discourse and social systems that construct Woman as non-man, and, thus, *outside* the realm of cultural possibilities for action and meaning. The phrase, "the female self," in other words, contains a contradiction in terms. Martha is *subject to* the ideological production of femininity as passivity, which makes it difficult, if not impossible, for her to be *subject of* her quest narrative as self-representation.

This becomes clearest in *A Proper Marriage* where Martha finds herself succumbing to the feminine pattern of repetition, "the dragging compulsion" (24) of domesticity

that she never fails to characterize as static and conventional. She is inexorably drawn toward what she sees as a feminine compliance, while at the same time feeling a desperate
need to rebel against it. In keeping with her construction of
the feminine as conservative repetition, Martha tries to fight
a certain kind of nostalgia—within which "nothing mattered
very much" (APM, 207)—with a "dispassionate, cool eye"
(MQ, 165). Martha situates this nostalgia inside herself as a
private   affliction,   seeing   feminine   compliance   as   an
inevitable force that all subjects gendered female must con-
tend with. Her access, however, to an outsider position signified by the "dispassionate, cool eye"—a phrase connoting
the masculine in these texts—makes it possible for her to
rebel against this supposedly "natural" feminine condition.
While both (feminine) compliance and (masculine) rebellion
are culturally sanctioned positions existing in relation to
hegemonic   ideologies,   Martha's   belief   in   an   internal
essence—of gender and of self—blinds her to the fact that
such essences are the effect of ideologies. The masculine
and the feminine take on their differential meanings only
within a representational paradigm that privileges one over
the other, as we can see through the contradictions which
mark Martha's self-representations. In order to safeguard the
unity of "self," Martha must work to banish contradiction.
But, because her ideal of selfhood comes into conflict with
her experience of becoming a woman, she most often
chooses to align herself with subject positions encoded as
masculine. It is this vicious circle which in Martha's view
keeps her from positioning herself as a woman and as a person; and, in my view, demonstrates how gender disturbs the
humanist ideal of unified and authentic selfhood.

The fact that Martha must consistently battle to banish
contradiction testifies to the irreducibility of contradiction in
her experience of female subjectivity, that experience being
her ongoing engagement in social and discursive systems
which offer her only limited self-positioning. Her self-representation, thus, is marked by confrontations between different ideological systems which define the terms "woman" and
"person" as mutually contradictory. Martha's response to

this confrontation is a drive toward a unity that constantly slips away. She seeks a "woman who combined a warm accepting femininity and motherhood with being what Martha described vaguely but to her own satisfaction as 'a person'" (*APM*, 206). Yet, it is unlikely that Martha will *allow* herself to find this woman because, as Sukenick points out, Martha's "mistrust of female irrationality" works "against an admission of female resemblance" (102).[14] Indeed, Martha feels "obliged to repudiate the shackled women of the past" (*MQ*, 8)—not, it is worth pointing out, obliged to *avenge* them. Women are the "enemy" because Martha opposes "personhood" to femininity in an interpretive move that suggests an unquestioning acceptance of the ideological codes that essentialize gender. Despite her "reasonable" conviction that feminine compliance endangers her "personhood," she nevertheless accepts what official wisdom constructs as "normal womanhood," as can be seen in this fairly typical description of Martha being pulled in opposite directions: "The instinct to comply, to please, seemed to her more and more unpleasant and false. Yet she had to reassure Douglas and kiss him before he left if she was not to feel guilty and lacking as a woman" (*APM*, 264). According to conventional wisdom, the voice of the dominant ideology in these texts, to become a woman means to be passive and compliant; yet Martha's sense that this identity is false keeps her from locking herself within this singular position. Her divided response to conventional wisdom suggests that there are gaps in the prevalent ideologies of gender to which Martha owes her view of women being not wholly "persons." Such gaps leave open the possibility that individuals can resist occupying the subject positions ideologically determined within discursive and social systems. Neither compliance nor rebellion are "false"; rather, they are subject positions that Martha occupies at different times and in different contexts. If the feminine is "false," it is only because the ideologies to which Martha subscribes construct it as such, simultaneously constructing the masculine as the "authentic."

The feminine—messy, emotional, irrational, and, above all, false—disturbs Martha's quest toward selfhood, and disrupts the linear movement of the texts. Martha's desire to be subject clashes with her (self)object-ification. The narrative she creates for herself—her self-representation—is constantly derailed by "feminine" forces that leave her floundering in a kind of freeze frame without progressive movement. Since her occupation of feminine positions stalls her quest, time and again, gender becomes the obstacle toward self-realization. This is because the texts work to locate gender *inside* the "self." Gender becomes something added on to that self, not constitutive of it. If gender is an essence, and if the feminine is naturally in opposition to everything Martha believes a "person" to be, Martha's resistance to becoming a woman must take the form of an intense (self) negation. Throughout the novels, she uses negation as a form of self-defense, a protective measure necessary to preserve a clear receptive space for her "self" to be built in. It is most often a strategy of reaction against everything she feels her "self" should not be:[15] the masculine must defeat the feminine. She reacts against her mother and other women in the colony who are made to represent the conservative force of repetition, yet she must pay a price for this kind of negation. It is not so easy to negate one's experience of gender relations because cultural institutions continually produce those relations, and work to situate each individual within the terms of a sexual difference oppositionally, and hierarchically, conceived.

The difficulty Martha experiences in resisting normative constructions of gender relations takes shape as a contradiction in subject positioning. Despite her desire to realize an internal "self" independent of social forces, Martha takes up multiple and often contradictory subject positions in relation to her culture's narratives of gender. We can see this when she represents herself as a prototypically feminine figure who waits for a man to call her "self" into being. The contradiction between her desire to "find" her "self" and her desire to be "created" by a man signifies a gap in Martha's self-representation where we can see how she continues to become Woman. Contrary to her desire to be the subject of her own narrative, and of history, Martha positions herself as the object of someone else's narrative, a man's. She is seduced by romantic discourses into taking up a gendered position in a type of narrative that can be loosely described as "woman needing a man for fulfillment." This ideal is constructed through a complex of hegemonic discourses which take effect in social practices and serve to normalize male domininance by positing woman as some kind of lack. What ought to be particularly problematic for Martha in this narrative, given her desire for self-determination, is that it assigns her a passive position as the female object who waits for the male subject to give her meaning. In an extended description of Martha's state after her lover William leaves the Colony, the narrator foregrounds the inadequacy of this explanation by placing the word "self" in quotation marks, and suggesting that Martha is less an individual than a member of the category "woman":

> There is a type of woman who can never be, as they are likely to put it, "themselves" with anyone but the man to whom they have permanently or not given their hearts. If the man goes away there is left an empty space filled with shadows. She mourns for the temporarily extinct person she can only be with a man she loves; she mourns him who brought her "self" to life. She lives with the empty space at her side, peopled with the images of her own potentialities *until the next man walks into the space, absorbs the shadows into himself, creating her, allowing her to be her "self"—but a new self, since it is his conception which forms her....* Martha knew, with William gone, she was not so much lonely as self-divided. (*ARS,* 38–39, my emphasis)

The language I've highlighted here suggests that Martha has given up her position as questing, active subject—in favor of occupying the "feminine" position as the object at the end of someone else's quest/story, a man's. The only activity attributed to Martha here is "mourning," an activity which gains meaning only in reference to the man for whom she waits. She is reduced here, she reduces herself, to an empty space, and the language of the passage foregrounds the conventional construction of Woman as feminine "matter" in need of masculine "form" to take shape. We can read her "self-division" in two different ways: first, such a division signifies compliance with the ideological "truth" that a woman needs a man to be "whole"; but, second, *self*-division implies recognition that the passively waiting woman is divided against her own desire to occupy an active subject position in her own narrative.

At the beginning of *Landlocked,* Martha is caught up in another period of waiting, and the narrator asks: "what was she waiting for, in waiting for (as she knew she did) a man? Why, someone who would unify her elements, a man would be like a roof, or like a fire burning in the centre of the empty space" (*LL,* 30).[16] The narrator's description here, beginning with the rather off-hand "why," is ironic—at Martha's expense. The "why" places the comment in brackets, as it were, signalling Martha's belief that, of course, it is only "natural" for a man to arrive on the scene and miraculously "unify her elements." The language of this passage foregrounds a particularly phallocentric conception of female subjectivity, an "empty space" that will be filled by a "fire burning in the centre"; and, as is characteristic of hegemonic representations, this conception "naturalizes" socially constituted differences. It is Martha's susceptibility to this kind of normalizing narrative of gender differences that leads her to essentialize Woman as that "veiled personage that waits, imprisoned, *in every woman,* to be released by love" (*MQ,* 157, my emphasis). *Children of Violence* implicitly problematizes this type of generalization through its socio-political context; the minutely determined racial and class divisions in the colony undermine Martha's attempts to subsume heterogeneous women under a monolithic Woman.

These two examples of the narrator's ironic commentary on Martha's compliance with normative constructions of Woman illustrate Lessing's strategy of distancing herself from Martha. They also point to what might be called the "unconscious" of these texts. If these texts form a "study of the individual conscience in its relations to the collective," they also study how that "individual" is constrained by how the "collective" constructs her gender. Representations of Woman, such as those rendered through these two narratives of female sensibility, have power over women's self-representations. Because maternity, more than anything else, signifies the kind of feminine stasis and repetition that Martha fears, she needs to devise strategies for protecting herself from it. She needs, in other words, to distance herself from her female body—just as the narrator's irony distances Lessing from that body. One strategy she employs is projection, and it comes into sharp focus in a scene where Martha and her friends are engaged in a discussion of abortion. When Alice tells her it's illegal, Martha "flares into animated indignation," with "Do you mean to say that a woman's not entitled to decide whether she's going to have a baby or not?" (*APM*, 19). Martha here espouses what she knows to be a radical view, implying that *all* women should be allowed to decide what to do with their own bodies. Lessing juxtaposes this scene with the appearance of a "native woman" with three small children, a woman to whom Martha's "animated indignation" clearly does not extend. Her own fear of falling into the cycle of childbearing that she sees as the beginning of the inexorable pattern of feminine repetition is projected onto this woman who "summed up her uncomfortable thoughts and presented the problem in its crudest form" (19). The presence of this woman does not prompt Martha to reconsider the conversation about abortion that has just taken place; indeed, Martha seems to place this woman outside the realm of choice altogether.

She represents to Martha that part of herself that simultaneously attracts and repulses her, the susceptibility to the "feminine" rhythm of reproduction and compliance:

This easy, comfortable black woman seemed extraordinarily attractive, compared with the hard gay anxiety of Stella and Alice. Martha felt her as something simple, accepting—whole. Then she understood she was in the process of romanticizing poverty; and repeated firmly to herself that the child mortality for the colony was one of the highest in the world. *All the same...*(*APM*, 19; my emphasis, ellipses in the original).

Either view of this woman, romantic or "reasonable," denies her any specificity or even humanity. And, while Martha disapproves of Dr. Stern's implicitly anthropological, "objective" stance on black women—"'It seems even Dr. Stern is only interested in writing papers about them,'" she says "bitterly"—this does not prevent her from seeing this woman as other to her conception of *all* women. Later in the text, we are told that "during those first few weeks of her marriage, Martha was always accompanied by that other, black woman, like an invisible sister simpler and wiser than herself; for no matter how much she reminded herself of statistics and progress, she envied her from the bottom of her heart. Without, of course, having any intention of emulating her; loyalty to progress forbade it" (63–64).

Implicit in this comment is Martha's exclusion of the black woman from any kind of "progress," what Martha considers to be her own birthright. This woman, then, represents the "feminine" against which Martha represents herself. The "whole of womankind" evoked by Martha, clearly excludes this woman, as does the white women's discussion of abortion as an option for all women. Martha projects a negative part of herself onto this woman in the kind of identification Abdul JanMohamed points out as a standard feature of the "colonial encounter."[17] Throughout these novels, progress is productive, "rational," and implicitly masculine; while acceptance, and perhaps even envy, are conservative forces implicitly encoded as feminine. Progress is the prerogative of the "universal" subject, the mythical hero who is unencumbered by gender and race. Thus, Martha doubly excludes the black woman from participation in history. She represents this "invisible" black "sister" as the female principle incarnate, as evidenced in her rather glib recognition of her only insofar as she "summed up" Martha's own "problem in its crudest form." There are a host of racist assumptions at work here, only some of which reach Martha's "progressive" consciousness. Most particularly, Martha constructs this woman as "cruder," less rational, and implicitly more "natural" than herself—in order to safeguard herself from these qualities, and

in order to fight against a contradictory experience of subjectivity. As Wendy Hollway argues, projection safeguards
unitary subjectivity in that it is a psychic mechanism for
avoiding recognition of contradiction in subjective positioning.[18] In this attitude, Martha is not very far from the official
colonial line on the "natives": they are in need of "civilization"—that is, European values—while at the same time
being "essentially" incapable of such an assimilation.[19]
Martha's projection is a defense mechanism that suppresses the contradictions between her conscious desires and the
"irrational" forces that militate against her desire to be
"rational" and "progressive." In projecting acceptance onto
the black woman, and envying her for it, Martha effectively
complies with the racist structures of colonial society,
despite her conscious desire to fight against them.

Because progress, movement, and subjectivity are
encoded as masculine in these texts, Martha's quest for her
"real self" is consistently derailed, deferred, and even,
denegated by what she perceives as feminine threats to her
self. The fact that she experiences her subjectivity as multiple, made up of "the different selves which insisted on
claiming possession of her" (MQ, 156), militates against the
unity she strives for. This multiplicity, in fact, functions to
undermine the humanist ideal of singular and unified identity that underwrites the quest plot to which Martha appeals
in her efforts at self-representation. Such an ideal cannot
begin to explain how these multiple, and often contradictory,
"selves" can exist in one individual, nor how these "selves"
are provisional, contingent on the social relations that the
humanist conceptualization of identity would locate *outside*
the individual. What Martha needs, as she herself senses, is
a "theory" that will explain how it is that these contradictory
selves keep getting called into existence and how gender is
centrally involved in that process. Such a theory, to which I
will now turn, might be able to explain why Martha gets
seduced into culturally sanctioned gender positions against
her conscious desire to avoid them. It might also suggest
how it is possible for Martha to resist this seduction, to
become a woman without becoming naturalized.

A Theory for Martha:
Gender and the Production of Subjectivity

While it is clear that, as many feminist theorists and critics have pointed out, the subject of humanist discourses has always been constituted as male, it is not quite so clear how a "post-humanist" theory of subjectivity can take gender into account except on an abstract and, thus, recuperable level. Luce Irigaray, for example, suggests that "any theory of the subject has always been appropriated by the 'masculine,'" and will continue to be. When a woman "submits to (such a) theory" she is "subjecting herself to objectivization in discourse—by being 'female.' Re-objectivizing her own self whenever she claims to identify herself 'as' a masculine subject" (*Speculum,* 133). Such has been the trajectory of my argument, thus far, in relation to Martha Quest. However, I am not as willing as Irigaray, and other French theorists, to leave the question of the subject forever trapped within masculine parameters. The question of female subjectivity remains an urgent one, despite what might seem to be a critical consensus on the impossibility of asking that question without returning it to the structures of knowledge that the deconstruction of the "universal" self has brought into question. As Rosi Braidotti argues, since the construction, and deconstruction, of the subject has been an historically male project in Western philosophy, it is possible that the history of the female subject might tell a different story:

> Well may the high priests of postmodernism preach the deconstruction and fragmentation of the subject, the flux of all identities based on phallocentric premises.... The truth of the matter is: one cannot a deconstruct a subjectivity one has never been fully granted.... Just because modern philosophy has discovered an area of twilight within human subjectivity and discourse; and just because this is blurring the century-old distinction between self and other, it does not inevitably follow that there is no more certainty about the self. Just because ever since the end of the nineteenth century the ontologi-

cal security of the knowing subject has been shaken up, it does not mean that all the old notions—such as subjectivity, consciousness and truth—are no longer operational. ("Envy," 237)

I take Braidotti's remarks to be motivated by a desire to bring subjectivity, consciousness, and experience—and even, "reality"—back into the realm of possibility, and into the realm of (feminist) theory. This entails remembering the lessons learned from the extremely convincing critiques of the sovereign subject of humanist discourses that have been forwarded by feminist and other theorists; but it also entails taking that critique as only the first step toward theorizing a different subjectivity and, particularly, a gendered one. Such a theory must be able to account for how it is that women continue to become Woman. My immediate goal in considering the possibility of that theory is to be able to explain how it is that Martha Quest becomes a subject, despite what the novels seem to present as her failure to find her "real self." To that end, I will take a brief detour through a recent book that conveniently demonstrates why it has been impossible, within humanist and even post-humanist discourses, to theorize an agential female subject *of* discourse who is not passively and inevitably subject *to* discourse: Paul Smith's *Discerning the Subject.* Then I will take Smith's insights further, engender them, and finally, re-enter Lessing's texts in order to argue that Martha's subjectivity is constituted in gender-specific terms by the process of her engagement in discourses and social systems.

Smith presents an impressive critique of theories of the "subject" in a variety of disciplines that come under the rubric of the "human sciences." His basic critique of theories of the "subject" in the human sciences is that they have tended to *abstract* the "subject," to produce "a purely *theoretical* 'subject,' removed almost entirely from the political and ethical realities in which human agents actually live" (xxix), and thus the human sciences have foreclosed on the possibility of the subject's being installed as the agent of a "contestatory politics," an agent capable of resistance. The result of such an abstraction is that the "subject" is either posited as the traditional humanist subject of history, the coherent or "whole" individual that exists in opposition to the social; or, is theorized as a passive entity wholly *sub-jected* to structures larger than itself—whether those structures be language, ideology, "society," or text. The opposition between active agency and passive subjection seems particularly apropos for any consideration of gendered subjectivity. This is a gendered opposition within patriarchal culture, and we have seen how it is inscribed in Lessing's texts.

Smith argues that the human sciences have "cerned" the subject, and thus introduces a clever terminology that gives a focus to his study as a whole and, more importantly, for my purposes here, brings gender into the picture. He offers definitions of two outmoded verbs: "to cern" and "to cerne":

> The first [to cern] means "to accept an inheritance or a patrimony," and I use it to suggest that contemporary intellectual abstraction of the "subject" from the real conditions of its existence continues—and is perfectly consonant with—a western philosophical heritage in which the "subject" is construed as the unified and coherent bearer of consciousness. Simultaneously, I have used the second verb, which means to "to encircle" or "to enclose," to indicate the way in which theoretical discourse limits the definition of the human agent in order to be able to call him/her the "subject." My project in this book is, then, to be described as an attempt to *dis-cern* the "subject," and to argue that the human agent *exceeds* the "subject" as it is constructed in and by much poststructuralist theory as well as by those discourses against which poststructuralist theory claims to pose itself. (xxx)

One of the "real conditions" of the subject's existence abstracted within the "western philosophical heritage" is, of course, gender. The first sentence of Smith's definitional passage makes that clear enough by pointing to the fact that the "cerned" subject is a patriarchal construction, linked up with "inheritance" and "patrimony." Despite Smith's use of "him/her" to refer to the subject, however, gender remains only implicit in this passage.

Smith goes on to argue that the "human" agent might be seen to "exceed" its construction by/in the human sciences through a "failure of interpellation." Working beyond Althusser's theory of how the subject is interpellated by ideology, and thus finds its "place" in the social, Smith argues that it is possible for the human agent to resist ideological interpellation. In other words, and against Althusser, Smith criticizes the deterministic view that constructs the subject as wholly *subjected*. Althusser theorizes interpellation as the process by which individuals are "hailed" by ideological apparatuses whose purpose is to construct individuals *as* subjects: "the category of the subject is constitutive of all ideology, but at the same time and immediately I add that the category of the subject is only constitutive of all ideology in so far as all ideology has the function (which defines it) of 'constituting' concrete individuals as subjects" (Althusser, 160). As Catherine Belsey points out in her reading of Althusser, "ideological state apparatuses" are those institutions which help "represent and reproduce the myths and beliefs necessary to enable people to work within the existing social formation" (58). They have, thus, a *normative* function; the "destination" of all ideology is the subject, but a subject who is interpellated as a coherent, singular identity who is then capable of functioning to reproduce the existing social formation. Belsey notes that, for Althusser, the "elementary ideological effect" is to construct people as "unique, distinguishable, irreplaceable identities" so that "within the existing ideology it appears 'obvious' that people are autonomous individuals, possessed of subjectivity or consciousness which is the source of their beliefs and actions" (Belsey, 58). The idea that individuals are the effect, rather than the cause, of ideological systems and meanings undermines the humanist credo of consciousness as originary.[20] But, what Althusser's formulation cannot take into account, as Paul Smith points out, is whether interpellation can fail to construct its appropriate subject, and the question of contradiction between different interpellations and their effects in the subject.

Smith argues that ideological effects are not unified or predictable, and that "each interpellation has to encounter, accommodate, and be accommodated by a whole history of remembered and colligated subject positions.... A singular history always *mediates* between the human agent and the interpellations directed at him/her" (37). This claim seems promising for an analysis of how gender is *produced* through ideological interpellation, and how it might be possible to resist normative positionings based on gender. In fact, my reading of Martha's Quest, thus far, would suggest that the "whole history of remembered and colligated subject positions" is a gender-inflected history. Or, more precisely, gender is *produced* through subjective positioning within an individual's history. Gender, like Althusser's "ideology," signifies a relation between subjects and meaning. Indeed, it is possible to rewrite Althusser's formula, substituting "gender" for "ideology," as de Lauretis does: "Gender has the function (which defines it) of constituting concrete individuals as men and women." De Lauretis goes on to point out that Althusser's "subject" is ungendered and, further, that his theory, "to the extent that a theory can be validated by institutional discourses and acquire power or control over the field of social meaning, can itself function as a techno-logy of gender" (*Technologies,* 6). The point here is that any theory that claims to transcend gender, even if only implicitly, does, in fact, construct gender. While Smith would not claim to be transcending gender, he certainly does not foreground it, despite the fact that "Feminism" occupies a privileged position in his study.

This privileged placement is clear from the outset, in the Preface, where Smith indicates that feminism is capable of "dis-cerning" the subject; indeed, the Preface implies that feminism is the telos toward which the book will move, not only because his discussion of it is deferred to the end in a book that gets less negatively critical as it progresses, but also because feminism is named as the arena of "some of the more relentless and rewarding questioning of the status and representation of the 'subject' in recent years" (xxxii). Here, Smith evokes the "*sexed* 'subject,'" as a key concept, and the reader is left with the idea that the book as a whole will take this notion into consideration. This expectation, however, is disappointed. The "subject" of Smith's book—the human agent capable of resistance—is certainly not the coherent individual of humanism, nor the in-different theoretical subject of post-humanism; but neither is it an "agent" rooted in historical specificity and material practices. It is, like the "subject" of the discourses that Smith critiques, non-classed, non-racial, and non-gendered. Indeed, it is not until the chapter on "Feminism" that Smith even suggests that the "subject" of the human sciences has been always constituted as Western, white, male, and of unspecified class—and, even here, I find no recognition that it is precisely this construction of the "subject" that human agents might *resist*.[21]

The problem, I think, lies in the fact that Smith wants to see Feminism as a discourse comparable to, say, anthropology—that is, as an isolated area of the "human sciences," and *not as a way of reading* those human sciences. I find it odd that a writer who concludes by claiming that "part of [his] project has been to suggest merely that some feminist thinking and feminist practice has found ways toward solving problems which seem to [him] urgent ones" (154), has not once mentioned that the "subject" of the human sciences is *male*—that is, has not suggested it until its proper place, in the chapter on "Feminism." The definition Smith offers of "to cern"—"to accept an inheritance or a *patrimony*" (xxx, my emphasis)—calls out for the feminist analysis that Smith avoids. My point here is not that Smith posits feminism as a commodity—although that could be argued—but, rather, that it is through feminism that Smith *could* have avoided a re-abstraction of the "subject," of ideology and of resistance.

This is not to say that feminist discourse is the only place where such abstraction is avoided, or always so. What is missing from Smith's book is *any* sense of the stakes involved in "cerning" the subject: What ideologies are thus served? In the chapter on anthropological discourse, tellingly entitled "Paranoia," Smith approaches an answer to this question in his discussion of the assumed split between the knowing subject and the object of knowledge, between the Western (white male) subject and the cultures constituted as its Others. Here, Smith might have specified how this particular branch of the human sciences works to ensure the dominance of a specific culture and the exploitation/oppression of its Others, and thus, specified what might be at stake in "resistance." Instead, he makes do with a gesture toward the political implications of his own critique in the following perfunctory statement that receives no elaboration: "a proper account, for example, of the epiphenomenal changes in the representational strategies of anthropologists could not be separable from a history of the West's exploration, exploitation, and colonialization of other parts of the world, nor from the postcolonial emergence of new forms of cultural and economic hegemonies and indirect military imperialism" (89). From here, Smith goes on to offer a clever reading of the meta-paranoid structures of knowledge in the human sciences, most specifically in narratology, and leaves the political questions to founder in a comparison of narrative in general and psychoanalytic accounts of paranoia. More importantly, perhaps, the politically minded reader is left to wonder how it is that the interpellation Smith sees operative in anthropological discourse can *fail* to construct "the object of knowledge" as Other. The notion of interpellative failure and the production of contradiction in subject-positions is an important one, I think; but Smith never specifies *how* this might work, nor does he elaborate how contradiction leaves room for resistance.

Unlike Smith, who seems to assume that the unitary rational subject is simply "bad" because it is a reductive fiction—and assumes that the reader already knows why this is so—[22] Couze Venn argues that this construction has served the interests of hegemonic groups throughout history by positing a "norm" against which all differences must necessarily be constituted as "deviations."[23] The "fiction" of the unitary, rational subject is thus seen to be *motivated* and *strategic,* compatible with "strategies of administration" (*Changing the Subject,* 122). Within psychological discourse, the "norm" of the individual is taken as pregiven, but more importantly, it is a norm that is not "innocent" or "neutral": it is, of course, the norm of the white male subject unencumbered by the exigencies of class. Venn writes:

> [I]t is an unexamined norm, shrouded in the mysterious clarity of common sense and translated into "facts" through quantification.... Thus the norms which psychology constructs and fixes are those consistent with the dominant form of sociality, that is to say that reproduce the social, intersubjective relations and relations of power as they are played out in social institutions of all kinds, from the family to the shop floor. (130)

The idea of "normalization" is vital here, as it can begin to explain how humanist notions of the self—in this case, within psychological discourse—are not without ideological motivation. Theories of the "self" or the subject have not been "innocent," nor have they been, as one is tempted to conclude from Smith's study, simply "wrong" because not sophisticated enough.

My critique of Smith is not meant simply as a "complaint" about a text that does not accomplish what I want it to accomplish. Rather, I discuss his study in detail in order to point out that it—perhaps too conveniently—encapsulates "radical" thought on the subject from a male perspective. The questions Smith raises have to do with the same old subject—once again encoded as male—and, thus, can be of little help in theorizing the female subject. Nevertheless, his critique of theories of subjectivity does provide the ground for my reading of Lessing's texts, as I work toward a theory of how the female subject is constituted through her engagement in social and discursive practices that always work in gender-specific terms. The process by which Martha's subjectivity is constituted has everything to do with what Lessing refers to as the relationship between the individual conscience and the collective, or, as I prefer to term it, the mutually productive relation between subjectivity and sociality. The social world through which Martha moves is intricately dependent on normalized constructions of gender, race and class that take effect on the subjective level through processes of interpellation. Smith's point that "a singular history always *mediates* between the human agent and the interpellations directed at him/her" (37), can help to drive a wedge between representations of Woman and women's self-representation. That is, despite the fact that gender remains mostly beside the point in Smith's analysis, he suggests a two-way relation between subjectivity and sociality, between self-representation and the representations of hegemonic ideologies. As de Lauretis suggests, in another (feminist) context, "to assert that the social representation of gender affects its subjective construction and that, vice versa, the subjective representation of gender—or self-representation—affects its social construction, leaves open a possibility of agency" (*Technologies,* 9).

Gendered Address and Martha's Self-Representation

The *Children of Violence* novels are centrally concerned with how the social construction of gender affects the subjective representation of gender, and vice versa, and with how a female subject's self-representation is always affected by cultural representations of Woman. As we have seen, Martha's attempts to insert herself as subject into a paradigmatically masculine quest narrative reinscribes one particularly stubborn social construction of Woman as passive resistance, the inert "feminine" matter against which the "subject" must fight in order to find an end to his quest. Martha's struggle against the culturally constructed limitations on women's subjectivity—and, thus, women's self-representation—positions her both inside and outside hegemonic representations of gender. She is split between active participation in cultural process, and passive acceptance of those processes, a split that the texts conceptualize in gendered terms. The texts represent Martha as being subject to, and subject of, contradictory desires and split between occupying contradictory positions in relation to systems of signification. As Wendy Hollway suggests in a discussion of the production of gendered subjectivity, self-representations "are a product of a person's history, and what is expressed or suppressed in signification is made possible by the availability and hegemony of discourses. Positions available in gender-differentiated discourses confer relative power by enabling the suppression of significations which would be undermining of power" (*Changing the Subject*, 239). Although I see self-representation as a *process*, rather than a product, I would agree with Hollway's analysis in that Martha reaps a certain power from taking up normative feminine positions because the discourses that offer these positions "carry all the weight of social approval. But successful positioning in these discourses is not automatic, else there would be no variations" (*Changing the Subject*, 238).

We can see this success and failure in *A Proper Marriage*, which witnesses a sluggish, heavy, pregnant Martha. She sees her pregnancy as a betrayal, a trick played on her, against her will, by a recalcitrant body against which she must struggle. She must be seduced into complying with femininity, seduced into becoming Woman against her desire to be subject.[24] This text contains a particularly cogent representation of how ideological interpellation works to constitute a gendered subject, and how discursive and social practices can succeed in constructing a normalizing subjectivity only if certain contradictions are suppressed. When Martha and Douglas first marry, for example, they consult the Book—here, a particularly hackneyed volume of conventional wisdom that gen(d)eralizes about what newly married couples should feel, and thus constructs appropriate subject positions for them based on gender. Martha's marriage to Douglas has stalled her quest because it has placed her firmly in an end position: end of search, end of independence, end of action. Indeed, Martha feels herself to be at a standstill, while Douglas goes on about his business as usual. By marrying Douglas, Martha has opted for an easy way out of the dilemma I have been charting here: namely, the dilemma a woman faces when she desires to be subject of a quest narrative. She has, in short, inserted herself into Douglas's story, rather than continuing her own.

This causes her to experience an assault of "irrational" emotion in the form of contradiction between what she feels and what she thinks she ought to feel, and she appeals to the Book for definition:

> [F]or most of the last week she had been struggling with waves of powerful dislike of [Douglas] that she was too well educated in matters psychological not to know *were natural* to a newly married woman. Or, to put this more precisely, she had gone through all the handbooks with which she was now plentifully equipped, seized on phrases and sentences which seemed to fit her case, and promptly *extended them to cover the whole of womankind.* There was nothing more paradoxical about her situation than that, while she insisted on being unique, individual, and altogether apart from any other person, she could be comforted in such matters only by remarks like "Everybody feels like this" or "*It is natural* to feel that." (*APM,* 23, my emphasis)

The generalizations Martha encounters, and takes comfort in, are not "neutral" or objective knowledge; rather, the language I've highlighted here suggests that generalization is a normalizing apparatus which works to preserve a particular social order. In subsuming women under the category of Woman, by interpellating its readers as subjects known as "normal women," the Book obscures the specific in favor of the general. Because the Book provides her with a "rational" explanation for those very "irrational" emotions she feels, she aligns herself with the subject position it offers her. Paradoxically, then, Martha allows herself to be comforted by fitting neatly into the category she has violently resisted since her adolescence. The Book is a technology of gender;[25] it produces a *generalized* "Woman" in order to *naturalize* a certain cultural construction of femininity. The "rational" explanation offered by this apparatus of social regulation promotes the kind of generalization that militates against the recognition of difference. The subject interpellated by the Book is a white, middle class woman who is constructed as the norm; and even her differences from other white, middle class women are obscured in favor of sameness, the mode of regulation.

The Book brings Martha in line with the gender appropriate position and she accepts this position in order to safeguard a unitary subjectivity. This subject position comes into
conflict with others that Martha has occupied, and desires to
occupy, and results in what the narrator points to as a "paradox." Such a paradox, in my view, stems from Martha's
desire to situate herself "outside" ideology when, in fact, she
so clearly occupies positions *in* ideology. What Martha experiences as a "paradox" of desire is an example of Althusser's
"elementary ideological effect." Hegemonic discourses position subjects as concrete, unique individuals in order to
"seduce" them into normative behavior: "the individual is
interpellated as a (free) subject in order that he shall submit
freely to the commandments of the Subject, i.e. in order that
he shall (freely) accept his subjection" (Althusser, 169).
Such interpellation, in effect, "flatters" the individual into
thinking that discourse is speaking specifically to her; "people 'recognize' (misrecognize) themselves in the ways in
which ideology 'interpellates' them, or in other words,
addresses them as subjects, calls them by their names and
in turn 'recognizes' their autonomy" (Belsey, 61). This process feeds into the illusion of unitary subjectivity, the illusion
that individuals are "free" from discursive and social determination. At the same time, subjects are reduced to "the
Subject," are generalized in order that hegemonic discourses
can take effect on a broader level. Martha is simultaneously
interpellated by the Book as part of a collective known as
the "newly married woman" and as an individual who is
"intelligent" enough to recognize that her fears, etc., are simply the result of a change in her life.[26] Martha's desire to fit
into this new collective overshadows her irritation at being
subject to generalization and, thus, she suppresses the contradictions that mark the Book's address of her. It is in the
interests of hegemonic ideologies to obscure such contradictions in order that the subject can take up an unproblematic
position in relation to social practices.

It is in the interests of the colonial social fabric that
Martha remain married to Douglas, be a "good" wife—which
means, in this context, to do charity work, complain about

the servants, and produce babies. Her entrance into the collective of the newly married woman disturbs her quest toward selfhood, and it is in *A Proper Marriage* that Martha is least likely to resist filling the slot offered her by her world. This entire novel, in fact, represents Martha as being sluggish, *because* pregnant, and becoming "a petty-bourgeoise colonial" (*APM,* 131). She has, in short, become the embodiment of her worst nightmare, the nightmare repetition—and, it is unequivocally because she has become Woman. When Martha is pregnant, she suffers from a surge of contradictory emotions that put into play the gap between what it is to be Woman, and her desire to be subject. The language of the following passage foregrounds the separation of activity and passivity as a difference between participating in cultural processes and being outside of those processes:

> The rainy season began. The child would be born towards its end. Again, she felt the discrepancy between the shortness of the rainy season, a handful of brief months in any ordinary scale of time, and the crawling days which she had to live through. She was consumed, several times a day, by a violent upsurge of restlessness. She could not keep still. She could not read. Above all, she felt there must be something wrong with her, to feel like this. For at the back of her mind was the vision of a woman calm, rich, maternal, radiant; that was how she should be. (*APM,* 130).

Martha's restlessness signifies the beginnings of her resistance both to a feminine position, and to the very identification of woman with a "natural" passivity and conservatism. To succumb to maternal calmness and stasis would mean forever being stuck as an observer of culture, instead of a participator in it. And, although at this point Martha remains seduced by a normative conception of what a woman can do and be, as signified by the "should" in the last sentence, she will resist that self-representation by doing something that threatens to disrupt the ideological bases of her world: she will leave her marriage, and her child and, thus, forcibly (and painfully) extricate herself. That act of resistance prevents Martha from being contained in an idea of Woman that forecloses on the possibility of active participation in history.

Yet Martha does manage to short-circuit her seduction into a compliant femininity, and does so, because, as Smith would put it, her personal history "mediates" all interpellations directed at her. The contradictions between Martha's different desires and between the subject positions she occupies undermines the notion of a unified self whose identity inheres in some essential core. Further, such contradictions work to diffuse the unity of gender difference, as woman's difference from man. As Wendy Hollway argues, the smooth reproduction of gender difference depends on the unity of both the subject and of ideological representation; when contradiction enters the equation, we begin to glimpse the possibility of change:

> The reproduction of gender-differentiated practices depends on the circulation between subjectivities and discourses which are available. The possibility of interrupting this circle is contained in a grasp of the contradictions between discourses and thus of contradictory subjectivities. While one set of desires may be suppressed, along with their signification, by the dominant sexist discourse, the contradictions are never successfully eliminated. They are the weak points in the stronghold of gender difference: taking up gender-appropriate positions as women and men does not successfully express our multiple subjectivities. (*Changing the Subject*, 252)

The multiplicity that marks Martha's self-representations disrupts her complicity in the reproduction of normative gender difference. Her resistance against the culturally sanctioned maternal position is produced through a contradiction in desire which, in turn, produces a contradiction in her subjectivity.

That contradiction surfaces in Martha's recognition that biological reproduction and ideological reproduction go hand in hand to preserve the status quo in the Colony. The equation of the two problematizes the "naturalness" of reproduction as the essence of woman. For example, she resists having a second child because she fears being "sucked into the pattern" of "the great bourgeoise monster, the nightmare *repetition*" (*APM,* 77). But her "rational" decision against maternity comes into conflict with her "irrational" desires, located, quite plainly, in her body: "Martha knew her female self was sharply demanding that she should start the cycle of birth again" (*APM,* 251). The narrator, however, suggests that this desire is not exactly "natural," but is a culturally produced desire supported by such normalizing apparatuses as the Book—different volumes of official wisdom that construct subject positions for wives, husbands, mothers, and so on, and work to regulate their behavior to keep it in line with socially sanctioned norms: "The voice of their female selves was a lure whose ambiguous and double-dealing nature they understood very well—they were not supported by the book for nothing" (253). The book reinforces the notion that the maternal instinct is "natural," and thus displaces socially sanctioned norms onto the "female self," the body.

Martha is able to see that the maternal ideal is a cultural construct, but reduces its ideological force to "false consciousness," and thus cannot explain *why* it is that so many women fall for this "lure":

> That phrase 'having a baby,' which was every girl's way of thinking of a first child, was nothing but a mask to conceal the truth. One saw a flattering image of a madonnalike woman with a helpless infant in her arms; nothing could be more attractive. What one did not see, what everyone conspired to prevent one seeing, was the middle-aged woman who had done nothing but produce two or three commonplace and tedious citizens in a world that was already too full of them. (*APM,* 274)

The fact remains that, despite Martha and her friends' recognition of a "conspiracy" between their bodies and normative ideologies, they tend to accept the "naturalness," indeed the inevitability, of succumbing to this "female self." If the drive toward maternity is natural—biological and instinctual—how is it possible to resist this drive and the reduction of women to mothers? Because Martha conceives of gender as singular, essential, and irreducible—a foregone conclusion, rather than a process of meaning production—she locks herself within normative ideologies of gender. But, as Judith Butler suggests, it is possible to resist these normative ideologies by thinking gender as "the very apparatus of production by which the sexes themselves are established. As a result, gender is not to culture as sex is to nature; gender is also the discursive/cultural means by which 'sexed nature' or 'a natural sex' is produced and established as 'prediscursive,' prior to culture, a politically neutral surface *on which* culture acts" (7). In relation to Martha, we can see that what she conceives as "prediscursive"—a "female self"—is actually a discursive production. The fact that she senses a cultural "conspiracy" aimed at reducing women to mothers points to a recognition, not yet conscious, that motherhood is not so "natural" after all. If there exists a natural "female self," then there can be no "conspiracy" of this sort: the two explanations of the production of women as mothers contradict each other. It is in foregrounding this contradiction that resistance begins.

Martha's resistance to occupying a maternal position stems from the fact that authoritative representations which equate woman and mother delimit the range of positions available to subjects engendered female in a multiplicity of different ways. In other words, these representations produce gender normatively and singularly. For example, to be a mother, according to the hegemonic ideology against which Martha fights, means to forego sexuality and political/intellectual activity. The conventional wisdom in the colony requires that once a woman enters into the cycle of reproduction, any other mode of production is forbidden to her. The power of this conventional wisdom can be seen in the fact that, despite Martha's analysis of the ways in which the Book delimits women's desires, she accepts certain gendered subject positions as "natural" or essential to women. The narrator highlights this "biology is destiny" representation of gender and sexuality in Martha's interpretation of her affair with Thomas during her marriage to her second husband, Anton. Once again, we can see Martha positioning herself as lack in relation to a man, and the irony with which the narrator exposes Martha's assumption that this is "natural": "*Of course,* her real nature had been put into cold storage for precisely this, but when what she had been waiting for happened at last, then she discovered that creature in her self whom she had cherished in patience, fighting and reluctant" (*LL,* 100, my emphasis). Here, Martha's "real nature" corresponds to the "creature in herself," the sexual Martha, that Thomas calls into being; but the fact that Thomas *creates* this Martha suggests that her sexuality is not as "natural" as she might think. This contradiction draws Martha back from her belief in the natural complementarity of heterosexuality by suggesting that even something as seemingly "natural" as sexuality is subject to a particularly powerful form of social regulation: the Law. Sex, "the radically unconstructed" (Butler, 7), is thus seen to be subject to construction within ideology.

Despite the fact that she and Anton have consciously decided to have an "open marriage," Martha feels her affair with Thomas to be a transgression of social norms, and more importantly, feels it in her body:

> If she let her connection with Thomas weaken; if she let her—what?—body (but what part of it?) remember Anton and that he was her husband, well her nerves reacted at once and in the most immediately physical way. She vomited. Her bladder became a being in the flesh of her lower stomach, and told her it was there and on guard. It did not like what she was doing—did not like it at all. Her stomach, her intestines, her bladder complained that she was the wife of one man and they did not like her making love with another. (*LL,* 114).

This reaction, attributed to her body, is a projection. What it indicates is that Martha has internalized the social sanctions against adultery and that the rhetoric of "free love" does not automatically carry with it the appropriate subjective response.

Martha is experiencing a contradiction between two subject positions here; the pay-off in positioning herself as subject in what Wendy Hollway calls the "permissive discourse" of sexuality requires that she forego the pay-off in positioning herself as object of the "have and hold" discourse of marriage.[27] While Martha's "rational" self knows that the property relation in marriage is bourgeoise and thus, in her Marxist interpretive frame, "false," her intrication in practices of social regulation effects her on a different level—what she would characterize as an "irrational" level. The contradictions between these two positions are projected onto the body and internalized as a conflict between "nature" and the law, in order that the "rational" Martha can retain a non-contradictory subjectivity.

Disillusioned with her romantic ideal of fulfillment through marriage and motherhood, Martha seeks out another subject position that will "feed her imagination." After leaving her husband and daughter, Martha finds in political activity another mode of self-representation and thinks, "For the first time in her life she had been offered an ideal to live for" (APM, 286). This ideal is romantic; she is attracted to her friend Jasmine's position in political circles because "nothing could have appeared more glamourous than such a role" (286). Ironically, she brings with her to this "role" a variation on the maternal ideal that she identifies with ideological reproduction: a paternalism that marks all of the colonialists' attitudes toward the "natives."[28] When Martha joins the Communist party, she brings with her an idealistic collective vision that originates in her childhood on the veld. This is a vision of an ideal city that has occupied so many of Lessing's critics and which has generally been taken to be coextensive with Lessing's utopianism.[29] In contradistinction to the sterile and politically abhorrent climate of Central Africa, Martha "refashioned that unused country to the scale of her imagination." This vision is prompted by her pity at the sight of a "native driver" whipping a black child; this pity "flooded out and surrounded the black child like a protective blanket" and sets off Martha's "familiar daydream." Like her pity, and the paternalism she feels for the child, this daydream amounts to a reaction that obscures the material conditions of racial inequality; it is a romantic ideal that is not far from the colonial paternalism that Martha deplores in the white settler mentality:

> There arose, glimmering whitely over the harsh scrub and the stunted trees, a noble city, set foursquare and colonaded along its falling, flower-bordered terraces. There were splashing fountains, and the sound of lutes; and its citizens moved, grave and beautiful, black white and brown together; and these groups of elders paused, and smiled with pleasure at the sight of the children—the blue-eyed, fair-skinned children of the North playing hand in hand with the bronze-skinned, dark-eyed children of the South. Yes, they smiled and approved these many-fathered children, running and playing among the flowers and the terraces, through the white pillars and tall trees of this fabulous and ancient city. (*MQ*, 10–11)

First, this city is clearly European and Martha takes for granted that such an architecture is superior to the "native" setting she sees around her. The repetition of the word "white" can be read as an index of this superiority; beauty shines "whitely" among the "white" pillars. Second, this vision enforces a hierarchy of paternal figures smiling and approving of the "many-fathered children." Third, and most importantly, such a utopian vision suggests that racial harmony can be achieved simply by an effort of individual good will, and thus forecloses on any analysis of the material political uses and effects of racism. As Julian Henriques points out in his discussion of the politics of racism, the "common sense" explanation of racism as the result of "false consciousness" or distortion in individual information processing mechanisms, obscures the power relations operative in racial division.[30] To blame racism on false consciousness—just as Martha blamed the lure of the female self on a conspiracy by her world to hide the "truth" of maternity—means to reify both the individual and the social, and to avoid analyzing how the subject is complicit in reproducing ideology, and how ideology, conversely, constructs the subject in sexual and racial terms. In believing that the "colour bar" is simply a result of white ignorance, Martha exonerates herself from racism, and simultaneously, denies the deep structures of racism that shape the dominant ideology of the colony. Indeed, she decides to exclude her parents and their friends from her ideal city "because of their pettiness of vision and small understanding; they stood grieving, longing to enter, but barred by a stern and remorseless Martha" (11). This last comment lends credence to Claire Sprague's interpretation of Martha's vision as "little more than a revenge fantasy" ("Dialectic, 44)—a personal reaction masquerading as political commitment. That the personal is deeply intricated with the political is obscured by the humanist ideology that separates the individual from "society."

The humanist ideals Martha brings to her "Communist phase" seem absurd in the face of the material political situation in the Colony. Martha and her comrades embody the attitude that Antony Beck attributes to Lessing's humanist politics of liberation: "the real crime of colonialists is to dehumanize the colonized; not so much in the areas of economic exploitation and political exclusion but to violate the moral rules governing interpersonal behavior implicit in the metaphysics of liberal individualism" (72–73).[31] The narrator, however, directs a scathing irony at the young, romantic "Reds." Martha and Jasmine are interpellated by Marxist rhetoric as noble human beings fighting the oppressive injustices of the world—with no reference to historical or geographical specificities and differences. They see themselves as "frontline fighters, fighters like Lenin, afraid of nothing, and armed with an all-comprehensive compassion for the whole of humanity" (*ARS*, 38). Thus, Martha's self-representation, at this point, is produced by and produces a variation on the kind of romance plot that described her seduction into compliant femininity earlier in the series.

The "whole of humanity" is a construction that obscures the differences that Martha and her comrades are not prepared to see. The narrator submits the collective desire of these idealistic communists to a particularly caustic irony: "When members of the group talked of the future, it was as if they were interchangeable with each other, one country the same as another, they were part of the great band of international brothers, and as they talked their eyes met, exchanging looks of infinite devotion and trust" (*ARS,* 27). It is clear enough here that the notion of an international brotherhood is absurd in the context of colonial Africa, where the "natives" risk their lives in even being seen with a "Red." And, despite Martha's apparent membership in the *brother-*hood, she ends up, in many ways, on the margins of the organization, performing the kinds of "feminine" tasks she renounced earlier. Martha's romantic vision, in fact, participates in the same "maternalism" that marks the colonial *grandes dames* who set out to "civilize the natives." We can see this tendency when, outside the window of their meeting room, Martha and Jasmine see a "ragged, barefooted black child, pot-bellied with malnutrition":

> Martha and Jasmine smiled at each other, saying in the smile that because of them, because of their vision, he was protected and saved.... Each saw an ideal town, clean, noble and beautiful, soaring up over the actual town they saw, which consisted in this area of sordid little shops and third-rate cafes. The ragged child was already a citizen of this ideal town, co-citizens with them; they watched him out of sight around the corner smiling: it was if they had touched him with their hands in friendship. (*ARS,* 27)

Their refusal to take account of the material conditions of the blacks in the town, and their underestimation of resistance to change on the part of the ruling class, lead Martha and Jasmine to include this black child in a collective vision that is absurdly idealistic. The problem with all of the "collectives" to which Martha gives allegiance is that they actively work to obscure differences in order to secure a coherence to their own self-representation.

As we saw with the example of the Book, normalization, naturalization and generalization work hand in hand to perpetuate hegemonic ideologies by suppressing the differ-

ences which endanger the smooth workings of social apparatuses. All of the collectives to which Martha belongs
enforce this type of generalization. Within each collective, it
is important to guard against "individualities," differences
that threaten the homogeneity and hegemony of the group.
It is this against which Martha rebels; she deplores the
Sports Club scene because it forces her to suppress her
"real self" by calling into being what she sees as a false identity. But I am not so much interested in considering the ways
in which each of these collectives fails to offer Martha the
appropriate space for the realization of her "self"—as some
of Lessing's critics do;[32] rather, I am interested in how these
micro-societies can only exist as coherent groups by suppressing difference on the macro level. In other words, and
in the interest of homogeneity and coherence, these collectives must work by a principle of exclusion. Thus, Martha
can feel herself to be part of a universal "womankind" only
by excluding from this collective the black women for whom
the Book would be an irrelevant commentary; and, she can
represent herself as a hero of oppressed black children only
by objectifying them. There are two different notions of the
collective that can be extrapolated from the *Children of Violence* novels, and they both work to reduce the complexity
both of individual subjectivity as constituted in social practices, and of the social as a historical process rooted in specific practices, and for specific reasons. In one theory of the
collective, Lessing seems to equate the "collective" with a
static notion of "humankind" that suppresses difference in
favor of homogeneity, as in the notion of "collective consciousness."[33] According to Lessing, this collective consciousness is a kind of force field structured by binary oppositions that exist in complementary relations; it is a kind of
universal repository of emotions that all individuals—regardless of class, race, gender, place, and time—have access to.

In order to elaborate this idea, it is necessary to look
briefly at *The Four-Gated City,* where the mature Martha dis-
covers that she can "plug into hate," which is the "underside
of all this lovely liberalism" (*FGC,* 511): "If I didn't know better and I plugged in to hater by accident, I'd stay a hater. Did

Hitler plug in to hater by accident? (For instance.)...A nation can get plugged in through one man, or group of men, in to—whatever it might be. Here is Martha. I'm plugged in to hate Jew, hate black, hate white, hate German, hate American, hate" (*FGC,* 513). What we have here is a reduction of fascism, racism, and nationalism to a kind of aberration that can happen "by accident" and, more importantly, a reduction of social practices—especially politics—to the province of the individual. There is no recognition here of any specificity of historical experience; that is, if Hitler can be explained as an individual, even arbitrary, phenomenon, then there is no room for a consideration of the ideological climate in which a Hitler could be produced. At the same time as this formulation explains sociopolitical phenomena as individual aberrations, it also forecloses on the question of human agency and the correlative question of resistance; if history is produced simply by individuals or collectives "plugging in to" various emotions, we are stuck with a particularly stubborn form of determinism through which all modes of oppression can be explained in similar terms, and in terms that leave no room for the possibility of social transformation—except, that is, on the level of accident.

The other notion of the collective at work in *Children of Violence* is a more local version, less mystical and more easily graspable in terms of social formations. Here, the "collective" reduces the social to intersubjectivity; the various collectives of which Martha is a part are merely groups of individuals who "interact" with society, but who remain, in certain important ways, external to it.[34] "Society" in *Children of Violence* is conceived of as what is *outside* individuals and, in most cases, what oppresses them and threatens the coherence of the collective. A particularly glaring example of this can be seen in the colonialists' reaction to the impending threat of World War II. The "collective," in this case the British members of the elite "Sports Club," works to insulate itself against outside forces in order to remain unitary and coherent. "Politics" to these people is something that happens in Europe; they enclose themselves in a "magic circle, and inside it nothing could happen, nothing threatened, for some tacit law made it impossible to discuss politics here, and Europe was a long way off" (*MQ*, 139). The absurdity of this comfortable belief in the collective's insularity is highlighted by the material reality of the political situation in the Colony; these individuals are only able to see themselves as "apolitical" by suppressing their knowledge of complicity in exploiting the "native population." Like hegemonic groups tend to, this collective regards its ideological biases as the "natural" state of affairs, It is "apolitical" because it enforces the status quo—in this case, the preservation of white supremacy. It is this self-imposed insularity that prevents the colonials from seeing a parallel between their own "politics" and those of Hitler, and prevents them from seeing the contradictions involved in exhorting the "natives" to join their masters in fighting a "monster" "whose crimes consisted of invading other people's countries and forming a society based on the conception of a master race" (*APM*, 120).

The "Reds," for their part, are just as busy refashioning "reality," and desperately trying to mold the "natives" into what they see as the only correct political position—*their* position. This desire, on the part of the radical whites, results in a number of absurdities, the most telling of which is the blacks' calling them "Comrade Baas." The limits in the group's vision become particularly evident when they attempt to become involved with Africans who are, after all, the reason they have become Communists in the first place—or, at least, this is what they tell themselves.[35] The romantic vision that Martha and Jasmine entertain feeds into a collective vision that obscures difference—not individual difference in the sense of Martha's difference from Jasmine, but social difference in the sense of positioning in relation to the hegemonic group. It is this difference which makes the Africans move away from the "liberal whites" in the colony, and decide to work for their own liberation. Like Martha's earlier envy of the "comfortable" black woman with all the children, she and Jasmine absurdly envy the Africans because they can escape the boredom of bourgeoise life. Explaining why she must leave this place, Jasmine says, "I suppose it's all right for the Africans.... They're persecuted day and night, it gives them an interest in life" (*LL*, 183). Typically, when the group breaks up, Martha feels an explicitly personal loss, instead of a sense of regret for what the group could have accomplished politically: "The group was at an end. At this, Martha felt cut off from everything that had fed her imagination" (*ARS*, 259). These comments highlight these women's investments in political activity, and expose their failure to see beyond their own epistemological framework. That epistemological framework is secured by a humanist notion of identity that rests on an essentialist conceptualization of Self and Other. For Martha and Jasmine, the radical Otherness of the Africans is an a priori fact that no amount of coalition building or shared political commitment can change. Unable, or unwilling, to break down the barriers between Self and Other, the women remain secure in the "home" of their own identities, conceived in opposition to the identity of the Africans.[36] If, as Biddy Martin and Chandra Mohanty suggest, "change has to do with the transgression of boundaries, those boundaries so carefully, so tenaciously, so invisibly drawn around white identity" (203), then Martha and Jasmine cannot effect change because they are so invested in keeping those boundaries intact.

Martha's faith in the existence of a "real self" forces her to erect boundaries between that self and its Others. Her investment in positioning herself against the Africans and against the feminine has to do with securing for herself a unity and coherence, a "core" of identity that is not endangered by class, race and gender difference. The "self," thus, becomes a personal entity that is endangered by social forces that impose on that self restrictions and contingencies. There are, however, moments when Martha not only questions the existence of a "real self," but when she effectively moves outside herself to examine her thoughts and actions. In those moments, Martha is able to go beyond her private obsessions to glimpse briefly that her subjectivity is not just an internal force, but is intricated in social practices. This is a part of Martha that maintains an ironic distance on the Martha who tries on different selves and who is remarkably naive when it comes both to asserting a coherent identity and assuming a stasis in the social.[37] When the "watcher" takes over Martha—or when she occupies this subject position—she is able to make connections between the personal and the political that her other subjective postures militate against. For example, at the end of A Proper Marriage, Martha is struck by a sense of unreality in Douglas's behavior, and is able to see that this is the same quality that marks the political climate in the Colony at this particular time. "Watching the situation from the outside," Martha describes it to herself with "absorbed fascination":

> She was considering such questions as, What did the state of the self-displaying hysteria Douglas was in have in common with the shrill, maudlin self-pity of a leader in the Zambesia News when it was complaining that the outside world did not understand the sacrifices the white population made in developing the blacks? For there was a connection, she felt. Not in her own experience, nor in any book, had she found the state Douglas was now in. Yet precisely the same note was struck in every issue of the local newspapers—goodness betrayed, self-righteousness on exhibition, heartless enemies discovered everywhere. (APM, 334)

Internal factors, Douglas's hysteria at Martha's desertion, and external factors, the leaders of the Colony equally hysterical in their fear that the "natives" will use the war as a catalyst for revolt, come together here. What Martha realizes, although cannot yet articulate clearly, is that Douglas's reaction is not simply personal; it is, rather, a function of his membership in the colony's hegemonic group. Douglas casts himself in the same role as the political leaders of the Colony, in a narrative that takes for granted that the status quo is "natural," rather than motivated. In this narrative, desertion by one's wife is as unimaginable as the fact that the "natives" might take some initiative in their own lives; it is "unnatural," and therefore, impossible. Martha's act is as political as it is personal; that is, she must leave Douglas because the life he represents is politically, as well as personally, abhorrent to her. To the reader, it comes as no surprise that there is a connection between Douglas, the conventional "civil servant," and the newspapers, the spokespieces of white supremacy. But Martha takes this insight even further in noting that the press places the political conflict on a personal level in interpellating its readers as subjects who must feel "righteous" and "betrayed" because it is "natural" to do so. Predictably, however, Martha shies away from her insight here, and resorts to the kind of fatalism that precludes her acting on what she sees in this moment of clarity. She almost decides to stay with Douglas, and thus give up "politics," because "what she did and what Douglas did was inevitable, they were involved in a pattern of behavior which they could not alter" (*APM,* 335).

The "official" reading of these texts, and of Martha's quest, and the one I would imagine Lessing endorsing, is that Martha must leave the colony because it militates against her fulfilling her potential and finding her identity. Such a reading enforces an absolute separation between the subject and the social, the private and the public, the "individual" and the collective; it places the subject *outside* ideology and obscures, at once, the subject's complicity in ideological reproduction, and the subject's constitution in ideology. It also, and this is the important point, forecloses on the possibility of subjective agency and resistance. To focus so doggedly on an end and to discount process results in what Joan Didion so eloquently describes as Lessing's "dilemma":

> What we are witnessing here is a writer undergoing a profound and continuing cultural trauma, a woman of determinedly utopian and distinctly teleological bent assaulted at every turn by fresh evidence that the world is not exactly improving as promised. And, because such is the particular quality of her mind, she is compelled in the face of this evidence to look even more frenetically for the final cause, the unambiguous answer. (123)

Lessing's "trauma," as I have suggested, has much to do with gender, in that it is Martha's gender that, in part, "assaults at every turn" the teleological force of the narrative. As a true humanist, Lessing seems compelled to contain that trauma, to construct the individual as "universal," and to set *him*—Lessing insists on using this pronoun—on a quest for the end, the final solution. It should, then, come as no surprise that Lessing, in 1971 as in 1957, can take a leap beyond gender, and claim that "probably by the time we are through, if we do get through at all, the aims of Women's Liberation will look very small and quaint."[38] Some of us, fortunately, are not so convinced that a cultural apocalypse will render gender beside the point. It is to just such an apocalypse that I will now turn my attention by analysing how the so-called "postmodern condition" reproduces gender in all too familiar ways.

Angela Carter and the Circus of Theory: Writing Woman and Women's Writing

Angela Carter's novels, *The Infernal Desire Machines of Doctor Hoffman* and *Nights at the Circus,* present a postmodernist take on de Beauvoir's claim that "one is not born, but becomes a woman." These novels are much more obviously "deconstructive" than Lessing's, in that they operate a displacement of sexual difference as a "natural" distinction between women and men based in biology. For Carter, to become Woman means to become naturalized into a subordinate position, regardless of one's "official gender." That is, she disrupts an essentialist equation between biological sex and social gender. At the same time, however, she *foregrounds* gender as constitutive of subjectivity by tracing the processes by which "official" women—that is, individuals sexed female—are socially and discursively constructed as Woman according to the needs of the dominant, "official" sex, men. For Carter, gender is a relation of power, whereby the weak become "feminine" and the strong become "masculine." And, because relations of power can change, this construction is always open to deconstruction. These two novels inscribe a tension between the normative construction of gender and its subversive deconstruction. And, although the line between construction and deconstruction is unstable and uncertain, the overall effect of Carter's novels is to drive a wedge between Woman and women, between male-centered metaphysical representations of Woman and the feminine, and women's multiplicitous and heterogeneous self-representations. Both of these texts strategically engage with the theoretical concerns of postmodernism and, in my reading of them, I will focus on their engagement with one relatively new, and predominantly male, theoretical preoccupation which has emerged from the "postmodern condition": a preoccupation with the place of "woman" in the deconstruction of culture's master narratives.[1]

The Infernal Desire Machines of Doctor Hoffman presents an epistemological revolution, not unlike that heralded by theorists of the "postmodern condition," in which culture's master narratives are losing the power and authority to order experience and, conversely, in which "experience" is no longer considered the ground of epistemological certainty. One master narrative, however, remains intact in this world: an Oedipal narrative that places man in the position of questing, speaking subject, and woman in the non-position of object who is *subject to* male regulation, exploitation, and violence. This is the same mythical narrative that caused so much disturbance in Lessing's fictions of female subjectivity. But, in The Infernal Desire Machines, the hero's gender fits with the gender of the "mythical hero." Desiderio is a subject gendered male, but not in the falsely universal sense. Carter's revision of the Oedipal quest narrative *foregrounds,* rather than *transcends* gender, de-universalizing the male subject by engendering him. In Nights at the Circus, Carter continues to explore male fictions of woman but, here, creates a counter-narrative that explodes these fictions from the outside, and implodes them from the inside. In this text, Carter engages with the postmodern desire to privilege what Linda Hutcheon calls the "ex-centric": the Other(s) of Western culture, who have, historically, had limited access to the place(s) of enunciation. With the postmodernist critique of the self-present, knowing subject, has come a desire to explore the "difference" whose exclusion has guaranteed the identity of the liberal humanist self. These explorations, however, too often become appropriations that do not disrupt the politics of enunciation. The politics of the postmodern, thus, can approach a postfeminism in which the gender of the speaking and reading subject is all but beside the point. Such a politics makes irrelevant the historically constituted experience of gender difference, including the differences among and within women. I use the term "experience" in Teresa de Lauretis's sense of a "personal, subjective, engagement in the practices, discourses, and institutions that lend significance (value, meaning, and affect) to the events of the world" (*Alice Doesn't,* 159). And, although experience, like gender, is a construct rather than an essence, it does not necessarily follow that it is, thus, without authority in constituting subjectivity.

It is precisely the neglect of "experience" in postmodern/poststructuralist theory that Carter critiques in her novels. In order to contextualize that critique, I will begin by performing a close reading of one exemplary text concerned with theorizing writing (as) woman: Jacques Derrida's *Spurs.* My goal here is not to generalize about the whole of Derrida's thought, nor even to offer a definitive reading of this text—such an enterprise would, in any case, be impossible. Rather, my intent is to read this one text closely, from a particular (feminist) position, in order to analyze what is at stake in Derrida's privileging of woman and the feminine as that which enables the deconstruction of the humanist subject and his discourses. With the aid of Luce Irigaray's oblique intervention into Derrida's text, "Veiled Lips,"[2] I will argue that *Spurs* constructs a particularly seductive narrative that functions to recontain women within a metaphorical figure of Woman, used, in this case, to bolster masculine self-representation. In my reading of Derrida's text, I focus on two woman-figures which emerge in his reading of Nietzsche's speculations on woman: the affirmative woman and the feminist. While the first woman becomes a figure of male desire, a phantasm of the male imaginary, the second threatens that desire and is disqualified from participating in the elaboration of a "feminine" textual operation. Irigaray's reading of Derrida's reading of Nietzsche foregrounds the (unacknowledged) gender ideology operative in *Spurs,* and thus practices an explicitly feminist critique of Derrida's appropriation of the feminine. In turn, my reading of Irigaray, and of Carter, will question what is at stake in *any* appropriation of the "feminine": the desire to recontain women into a metaphorical conception of Woman.

Derrida: The Affirmative Woman and the Feminist

Irigaray's "Veiled Lips" intersects with other feminist work on Derrida, most notably Alice Jardine's 1985 study *Gynesis*. Jardine traces the explosive "putting-into-discourse" of woman and her textual effects in recent theoretical discourse, particularly in the work of Derrida, Jacques Lacan, and Gilles Deleuze. Jardine names this process "gynesis" and implies that the privileging of Woman in these exemplary texts of modernity represents a "logical" reaction to the deconstruction of phallic authority and privilege. Man, once at the center of all systems of truth, has become decentered, and with him, all notions of paternal authority and mastery. According to Jardine, modernity's crisis is erupting in culture's "master narratives." It is a crisis set in motion by the death of the paternal metaphor—a crisis, in other words, in the masculine perspective. My reading of *Spurs* owes much to Jardine, but I am more interested in critiquing Derrida's ideological agenda than in describing how he figures in a larger cultural trend. To put it another way, my reading of *Spurs* foregrounds the question of the text's desire by considering the stakes involved in Derrida's appropriation of the feminine. Gayatri Spivak, another feminist commentator on Derrida, suggests that we ask the question: "What is man that the itinerary of his desire creates such a text?" To ask this question, as I propose to do here, "restores to us the position of questioning *subject*...a position that the sexual differential has never allowed women a propos of men in a licit way" ("Displacement," 186).

As several feminists have suggested, "gynesis" coincides with a recent increase in feminist discourses—especially discourses concerned with theorizing a female subject.[3] Rosi Braidotti takes this suggestion further in pointing out that woman has been historically made to signify crises in male-centered ontologies and epistemologies:

Ever since Nietzsche, passing through every major European philosopher, the question of woman has accompanied the decline of the classical view of human subjectivity. The problematic of the "feminine" thus outlined is nothing more than a very elaborate metaphor, a symptom of the profound illness of Western culture and of its phallogocentric logic. It is a male disease, expressing the critical state of the post-modern condition. ("Envy," 236)

Although I do not want to posit a simple cause/effect relationship here, I do want to suggest that the increase in feminist discourses has helped to provoke a crisis in the hegemony of the masculine perspective. The reaction to this crisis, I would argue, takes the form of what Robyn Wiegman calls a "renegotiation of the masculine," a reconstitution of the masculine perspective in order to *include* the feminine in its self-representations.[4] The proliferation of woman-effects can be considered as an attempt to reconceptualize the "feminine" in the service of masculine self-representation. The affirmative woman who emerges in *Spurs* is a figure of male desire who is appropriated in order to mark the masculine with heterogeneity. This appropriation keeps the masculine intact despite what might appear to be a "feminization" of Nietzsche and philosophy. It is the male desire to force woman into a certain theoretical space in order that she, in Irigaray's words, "reproduce the masculine. That the masculine also desires the feminine perhaps redoubles the stakes. Doesn't change the game" ("Veiled Lips," 117). The stakes in this particular version of the game involve a displacement of gender as ideological representation and a foreclosure of the question of female subjectivity.

The two terms, masculine and feminine, are not parallel or complementary, although the history of Western thought might lead us to believe this. Rather, there exists an asymmetry between the two concepts—and their representations—in that the masculine has always had the power to construct both itself and the feminine. This is a discursive power, to which accrues a privilege of *self*-representation, a privilege the feminine does not share. The discursive construction of masculinity and femininity can shift—as can the effects of these constructions in the social sphere—because of shifting ideological configurations. Such a shift is evident in the texts Jardine describes, most especially in Derrida. To take Jardine's analysis one step further, I will argue that gynesis, in Derrida, is an ideological strategy for recuperating an always threatening feminine into a safer discursive space, a space articulated from the masculine position. In the process of recuperating the feminine into itself, the masculine perspective changes. And, paradoxically, that which originally helped to provoke the crisis in masculine self-representation—that is, feminism—is now *itself* represented as the masculine perspective. For Derrida, feminism is eminently phallogocentric.

The feminine and woman, as Derrida uses the terms, exist only in representation; that is, the feminine is a theoretical-fictive construct which attempts neither to account for the perspective of female subjects nor for our experiences of female sexuality. He warns that the feminine "should not...be hastily mistaken for a woman's femininity, for female sexuality, or for any other of those essentializing fetishes which might still tantalize the dogmatic philosopher, the impotent artist or the inexperienced seducer who has not yet escaped his foolish hopes of capture" (*Spurs*, 55). This disclaimer provides Derrida with a kind of safety valve; the implication here is that his discourse on woman can somehow operate "uncontaminated" by Western cultural constructions of the feminine. In my view, it is impossible to talk about any discursive positioning of woman without taking into account the "traces"—to use a Derridean term—that masculinist representations of sexual difference have left behind. In other words, it is impossible to talk about Woman outside of the ideology of gender. I read Derrida's comment as a warning not to just any reader, but to an implicitly feminist reader; and this amounts to an attempt to forestall feminist commentary on his text.[5] Throughout *Spurs*, the feminist is linked with the "dogmatic" philosopher; both readers of woman attempt to pin her down, to dis-cover her truth. Derrida maps out a feminine textual space in *Spurs*—divorcing it from "woman's femininity," "female sexuality," and indeed, female *subjectivity*—and proceeds to occupy it, taking Nietzsche along with him.[6]

Why this insistence on the nonreference between Woman and women, this attempt to theorize Woman apart from any consideration of female subjectivity? Or, as Nancy Hartsock asks: "Why is it, exactly at the moment when so many of us who have been silenced begin to demand the right to name ourselves, to act as subjects rather than objects of history, that just then the concept of subjecthood becomes 'problematic'?" (196). The very idea of subjective agency has become suspect in post-humanist discourses, perhaps because the subject has always been theorized as universal—that is, white and male. While feminists might applaud the deconstruction of the (male) "subject-who-knows," are we ready to throw out the idea of subjectivity and all that means in terms of the production of sexual differences? Theories of subjectivity have, after all, enabled feminists to theorize the nexus of gender, representation, and power within patriarchal culture, precisely by showing that ideological apparatuses interpellate subjects in concrete, gender-specific terms.[7] While much feminist work has been concerned with demonstrating that the subject, in hegemonic discourses, is always produced as male—that is, "universal"—this work has also made it possible to theorize a different subject, a subject gendered female.[8] As Teresa de Lauretis points out, "displacing the question of gender onto an ahistorical, purely textual figure of femininity," as in Derrida, amounts to discarding gender as "ideological misrepresentation" (Technologies, 24; 3). She argues that,

> ...only by denying sexual difference (and gender) as components of subjectivity in real women, and hence by denying the history of women's political oppression and resistance, as well as the epistemological contribution of feminism to the redefinition of subjectivity and sociality, can the philosophers see in "women" the privileged repository of "the future of mankind." (Technologies, 24)

I want to insist on two points in response to de Lauretis's comment. First, that this "diffuse, decentered, or deconstructed" subject who inhabits the texts of postmodernism is a subject de-sexualized, "neuter"; and as Luce Irigaray points out, a sexually indifferent subject always returns to the same, that is, the masculine.[9] The tactic, then, of positing a textual femininity, that has no reference to *women,* displaces gender, and we are back to square one—that is, the production of man as subject. And, while feminists certainly have a stake in displacing gender as essence or metaphysical opposition, we must be careful not to *transcend* gender through its displacement. Secondly, what de Lauretis invokes as the feminist "redefinition of subjectivity and sociality" cannot be subsumed under the conception of subjectivity as singular, unified, and male. For the post-humanist (male) philosopher, "Man's non-coincidence-with-himself [has become] positivized"; for Derrida, "wherever there exists the traditional subject present to *himself* in relationship to an object, there exists metaphysics and its attendant phallo-logocentric representations" (Jardine, 106; 109, my emphasis). While it may well be true that "Man" cannot conceive of a different subjectivity, except perhaps a de-sexualized one, his problem is not necessarily "ours," to paraphrase Gayatri Spivak ("Displacement," 184). The "absolutely convincing deconstructive critiques of the sovereign subject" (Spivak, 186) should not prevent feminists from theorizing another, gendered, subject.

Spurs, in its representations of woman, constructs gender, and as with all constructions of gender, Derrida's text participates in a certain ideological agenda. Despite his disclaimer to the contrary, Derrida's text does, in fact, inscribe some rather traditional representations both of woman's femininity and female sexuality. The text also reproduces the masculine discursive gesture *par excellence:* the male subject defines the female object and puts her into circulation according to his desire to maintain control—or mastery—over the discursive space. Woman becomes an object of textual desire in *Spurs,* not exactly as an enigma to be "solved," but rather as the pretext for Derrida's reading of heterogeneity in Nietzsche. He writes: "one can no longer seek her, no more than one could search for woman's femininity or female sexuality. And she is certainly not to be found in any of the familiar modes of concept or knowledge. Yet it is impossible to resist looking for her" (71). This cryptic statement, simultaneously disavowing and affirming the search for woman, is symptomatic of Derrida's discourse on woman; never allowing himself to be pinned down on the question of woman, he plays both sides of the fence, as does Nietzsche. For Derrida, this is the mark of a text's heterogeneity, and he follows Nietzsche in inscribing the contradictions he calls "rigorously necessary" in order to give a text its "style" (57). This textual search for woman, then, puts woman into circulation as the mediator in a philosophical exchange between men, an exchange motivated by the (disavowed) desire to "know" woman and thus, to contain her in a certain space.[10]

Mimicking Derrida's language, Irigaray situates his "spurring operation" within the parameters of a male desire to "penetrate" the enigma that woman represents. She claims that the feminine

> ...remains so foreign to him that, believing he must break this thing open, that he cannot appropriate it except by breaking in, forcing his way beyond present appearances, "man" arms himself with a pointed object—stylet, dagger, sometimes pen—to penetrate it. Bearing down with the weight of his entire being, to force her to fold. In order that she always remain open. ("Veiled Lips," 105)

Irigaray's comment mimics Derrida's emphasis in *Spurs* on feminine "folding-into-self" as the mark of undecidability and doubleness; woman joins the hymen, the pli, and the umbrella as a figure which disrupts the opposition of inside and outside. Following this logic, he posits dissimulation as the woman's operation, and privileges it because it disrupts the priority of truth; like dissemination, and other Derridean textual operations, dissimulation problematizes any notion of authenticity, propriety, and authority. What is interesting in *Spurs,* however, is that Derrida seems pressed to differentiate between a dissimulation that is affirmative—that is, deconstructive—and one that is not. These two types or modes of dissimulation correspond to two types or figures of woman: the affirmative woman and the feminist.[11] The former is a figure who closely approximates traditional cultural constructions of the feminine. It is this woman Derrida has in view when he writes: "There is no such thing as the essence of woman because woman averts, she is averted of herself. Out of the depths, endless and unfathomable, she engulfs and distorts all vestige of essentiality, of identity, of property" (51). I will return to her in a moment. The latter, as she circulates in Derrida's textual economy, resembles the ghost of the "castrating woman," the feminist who threatens male subjectivity. She reacts against man, within his system of truths, and thus "remains within the economy of truth's system, in the phallogocentric space" (97). This woman dissimulates, Derrida suggests, in her own interests; "she takes aim and amuses herself with [truth] as she would with a new concept or structure of belief, but even as she plays she is gleefully anticipating her laughter, her mockery of man. With a knowledge that would out-measure the most self-respecting dogmatic or credulous philosopher, woman knows that castration *does not take place*" (61).

The idea that this woman "mocks" man comes back a few pages later, with added force: "She feigns her castration—which is at once suffered and inflicted. From afar she would master the master and with the same blow (in fact 'the same thing') that produced his desire, kill him" (89). Derrida derides this woman for practicing a simple reversal of hierarchical value, and insists that *Woman*—one presumes he means the affirmative woman here—would not pursue such a reversal because it would "only deprive her of her powers of simulation" (61). It is odd that Derrida isolates reversal as a negative strategy here, since he has described his own enterprise as a practice of reversal and displacement, implying that both logics are necessary in the deconstruction of phallogocentrism.[12] Derrida clinches the feminist's fate in this all too familiar formulation:

They too are men, those women feminists so derided by Nietzsche. Feminism is nothing but the operation of a woman who aspires to be like a man. And in order to resemble the masculine dogmatic philosopher this woman lays claim—just as much claim as he—to truth, science, objectivity in all their castrated virility. Feminism too seeks to castrate. It wants a castrated woman. Gone the style. (65)[13]

In opposition to his "feminine" operation, Derrida defines feminism as "nothing but the operation of a woman who aspires to be a man"; feminist discourse, apparently, does not enjoy the heterogeneity, the "style" of the philosopher-woman's discourse. In this glib dismissal, Derrida vacates the feminist space; and with the feminist safely out of the way, he goes on to inscribe the feminine as a figure of male desire.[14]

I want to dwell for a moment on the logic which leads Derrida to banish the feminist from his "feminine" textual world, since it is with this move that we can see why Derrida's text fails to take gender into account. The first problem with Derrida's characterization of feminism is that he evaluates it as a new law, seeking a new center; he characterizes feminism, in short, within the terms of an exclusively masculine history of discourse, a history that feminism itself has helped to deconstruct. As Nancy Hartsock points out, if women and other minorities came to inhabit the "center" of theory and social systems, the center would probably cease to look like a center; while Derrida might be an "inheritor of the disembodied, transcendent voice of reason," minority writers and feminists have always occupied a marginal position in relation to this voice and its discourses (Hartsock, 200–201). To theorize feminism as just another "ism"—or, worse, simply as the flip side of an outmoded humanism—amounts to ignoring gender and conflating women once again into some universal "mankind." Gender is first of all an ideological system that produces subjects in relation to discursive and social practices.

Within a certain conceptual, or semiotic, framework, the feminist might indeed be a "man"; if we assign exclusively to "man" the prerogative of subjectivity and enunciation, then the feminist would be placed this side of a sexual difference conceived as the difference between subject (man) and object (woman). Or, to put it more plainly, the feminist would be a "man" insofar as s/he usurps the (masculine) place of enunciation and, worse, that she dares to speak about gender, that is, about men and women, with the slightest assurance of her own authority. It is the assumption of authority that disqualifies the "feminist" from participating in the elaboration of the "feminine," according to Derrida. I will confine my remarks, then, to the fact that the "feminist" speaks about gender and thus threatens to undermine Derrida's project of mapping out a "feminine" textual space and claiming it as his own.

In making the terms "man" and "woman" interchangeable by "freeing" them of their ideological bases in sociality, Derrida displaces these terms from their position in gender as ideological representation, thus ignoring their differential values within social hierarchies. Subjects gendered male and female have different investments in discourse, as well as different relations to the hegemony of discourses. In short, the two terms, "man" and "woman," are *not* interchangeable nor can they be; to posit them as such means to ignore "experience," the process by which subjects are constituted through interaction with discourse and sociality in gender-specific terms. The feminist, this time without quotation marks, threatens to bring the question of gender to bear on Derrida's discourse; by doing so, she would have the power to deconstruct his ideologically motivated construction of femininity as a purely textual operation, accessible to men and women alike, but ultimately, the privilege of the man. As I insisted earlier, the ideological motivation in question can be read as a desire to retain hegemony over the representational space; by constructing the feminine as a space that can be occupied by the masculine, Derrida re-places woman as the ground of man's self-representation. The feminist threatens to short-circuit this process—in part because she, like the "dogmatic philosopher," wants to speak about "woman's femininity, female sexuality," and female subjectivity—and thus must be disqualified from participating in the elaboration of a "new" feminine space.

Derrida's descriptions of the reactive feminist assign her a certain agency: she plays, she mocks, indeed, she speaks; and, again, this is part of her threat to a system which would declare agency taboo. The affirmative dissimulatress, on the other hand, is unrelentlessly passive: she "will not be pinned down" (55); she "is recognized and affirmed as an affirmative power" (97) (one presumes) by Nietzsche and Derrida. He argues that woman "takes so little interest in truth, because in fact she barely even believes in it, the truth, as regards her, does not concern her in the least" (63). To argue that man's truth does not concern woman is to place her *safely* outside the place of enunciation and subjectivity; it amounts to placing women outside of discourse, in an alien, even if, utopian space. This space, as elaborated in *Spurs,* is a place of passivity and silence. As Alice Jardine points out in her reading of Derrida, the hymen and other privileged Derridean (feminine) effects are connoted as "nonexistent, invisible, and overwhelmingly passive" (188). But even in this passive figure of woman, there remains something threatening, a "trace," if you will, of her "reactive" sister. Derrida's language in *Spurs* often reproduces traditional metaphors of the feminine, metaphors which suggest that it is the masculine desire to control a threatening feminine power, even while admitting an attraction to it: "A woman seduces from a distance. In fact, distance is the very element of her power. Yet one must beware to keep one's own distance from her beguiling song of enchantment" (49). What we have here is a "new" feminine figure that reproduces such metaphorical configurations as woman=enigma="chasm"—a new version of an old signifying chain based on woman's (negative) difference from man. In a discourse which would attempt to demystify an oppositional sexual difference, the woman becomes re-mystified as other of man, "non-identity, non-figure, simulacrum" (49).

Woman's distance is, first of all, distance from man; as the other of man, "non-figure, non-identity, simulacrum," woman remains the ground of a representation based on *the* sexual difference. Since the Other is constructed from the hegemonic perspective, indeed since the Other is a function of that perspective; then the hegemonic perspective can incorporate that Otherness into itself. It is Derrida's appropriation of the Other (woman) that Irigaray has in mind when she characterizes Derrida's "spurring operation" as a penetration. While the Other must be kept at a distance, it must also remain within the control of the One—the same or the masculine, in Irigaray's terms. As both threat to and ground of man's (self)representation, woman as Other must be kept "always at a distance. Not exactly at hand, but well in sight... Giving and taking back again the dream of their compliantly offered sails" ("Veiled Lips," 105). For Irigaray, though, the distance in/of woman is more specifically a distance from herself, her body, and the maternal. In "Veiled Lips," she mimics Derrida's discourse in *Spurs* in order to deconstruct the figure of woman as distance, and as simulacrum of man, and obliquely asks the question: For *whom* is this woman affirmative? Whom does she affirm?[15] The answer unfolds as Irigaray posits Athena, a "man's woman," as the figure of affirmative dissimulation. For me, "Veiled Lips" raises another question in relation to *Spurs:* Against whom does the feminist "react"? What is at stake in enforcing a seemingly binary division between "affirmation" and "reaction"?

Irigaray: Mimicry, Contradiction, and the Subject of Feminism

The speaker in "Veiled Lips" might be said to react against the discourse of man in order to demonstrate the desire which mobilizes this discourse. We will remember Derrida's characterization of the feminist as she who "mocks man" by playing around with *his* truth. Derrida implies that the feminist always operates by instating a new order of truth, in opposition to man's truth, a new law with woman at the center; in other words, according to Derrida, feminist reaction does not carry within itself even a trace of affirmation. Irigaray's discourse problematizes this either/or characterization of woman/feminist by practicing a simultaneous reaction and affirmation. As such, it would fall within the range of a feminist praxis theorized as a doubled discourse, a notion finding increasing currency in feminist theory and other theories of marginality.[16] It is the "performance" staged by Irigaray's text that interests me here; as de Lauretis writes, "to perform the terms of the production of woman as text, as image, is to resist identification with that image. It is to have stepped through the looking glass" (*Alice Doesn't*, 36).

In "Veiled Lips," Irigaray steps through the looking glass and finds that the affirmative woman is still on the other side; or, rather, that she *is* the looking glass designed to redouble man. Her reading of Nietzsche-with-Derrida offers an interpretation of affirmative dissimulation as a version of the masculine imperative that woman specularize man. Irigaray suggests that women have always been asked to redouble men, that "woman's exile from herself entails her inexhaustible mimesis/mimicry for the father's benefit" (107). She theorizes a different feminine mimic, and insists that she remains "elsewhere," even as she might replay the master's desire. Woman always "sub-sists" even in her role as simulacrum of man; "If she deceives, it is because the phallic display does not amount to her, cannot show her" (115). What differentiates Derrida's "feminine operation" from Irigaray's "feminist operation"—as I would like to call it—is this elsewhere which remains through woman's dissimulation. To put it in slightly different terms, this feminist operation reacts to the terms of a masculine representation of woman; Irigaray pushes this representation to its limits and thus foregrounds its constitutive contradictions. At the same time, she affirms the production of a feminist discourse which can never be reduced to a simple mimicry of the father's discourse. The "style" of her discourse—to evoke Derrida—is what precludes a simple reinscription of the feminine within masculine parameters; her performance in "Veiled Lips" can be characterized as an oscillation that never quite rests in affirmation or reaction. One component of this style is a self-conscious awareness of what it means to speak as a gendered subject, from both within and without the dominant ideology of gender.

In positing Athena as the figure of affirmative dissimulation, Irigaray deconstructs the masculine desire at stake in Nietzsche-Derrida. Her reading of Athena is anchored in Aeschylus's *The Eumenides,* and refers beyond *Spurs* to Nietzsche's writings about Greek tragedy in *The Birth of Tragedy* and other texts.[17] A brief synopsis of the play will help to illuminate why Irigaray chooses Athena as the figure of the affirmative woman. Clytemnestra has murdered her husband Agamemnon, which act, in turn, motivates the son Orestes to murder the mother. The Furies have been pursuing Orestes, urging that he pay for his matricide. Apollo, in order to settle the score once and for all, and to put an end to the feminine havoc being wrought by the outraged Furies, sends Orestes to Athena for judgment. What is ultimately at issue in Athena's decision is whether to grant priority to marital ties by seeing Orestes's matricide as a justifiable action in response to Clytemnestra's murder of her husband; or to grant priority to maternal-blood ties by refusing to excuse the murder of a mother by her son. In order to rule in favor of Orestes, Athena argues:

> There is no mother anywhere who gave me birth, and,
>   but for
> marriage, I am always for the male with all my heart,
>   and strongly
> on my father's side. So, in a case where the wife has
>   killed her
> husband, lord of the house, her death shall not mean
>   most to me. (737–740)

Earlier, Apollo has appealed to Athena's predisposition in favor of the male with what has to be the most tidy displacement of the maternal in the whole of Western discourse: "The mother is no parent of that which is called/ her child, but only nurse of the new-planted seed/ that grows. The parent is he who mounts" (658–660). So it is that, *du-même-coup,* the nascent patriarchal order overrules the maternal and celebrates the male-identified Athena as the legend of feminine power. Predictably, the play ends by Athena domesticating the Furies; "Femininity redoubles the burial of the mother with that of the chorus. In order that Zeus, 'the god of speech,' prevail" ("Veiled Lips," 100).[18]

I want to draw attention to the way Irigaray is using the term "femininity" in this comment. Far from positing an essential feminine—outside the ideology of gender—Irigaray is locating femininity as a masculine construction in "Veiled Lips." She takes woman as text, as does Derrida, but only in order to deconstruct the terms of that text's production. Her performance in this text reads against Derrida's privileging of the feminine by demonstrating what is at stake in this "new," purportedly radical inscription of woman as affirmative dissimulatress. Athena-woman is affirmative of and for man; she is "a manifestation of the father's idea of feminine power. Appropriating the mother's power, swallowing it up, introjecting it, he engenders, produces this daughter who (only) gives herself for that which she is not: a simulacrum assumed by the God to help him in his work" (102). In this case, the "God" is Nietzsche-Derrida, and the "work" is the deconstruction-cum-"femininization" of philosophy. Athena, the "woman" who identifies with the law of the father, enables the gods to regain control over the social space temporarily disrupted by the feminine Furies. Because she legislates against the Furies and the mother, Athena enables the father to retain hegemony over the space of production. We can see this appropriation of maternal production in *Spurs,* as Derrida celebrates Nietzsche as mother: "One might imagine Nietzsche, who was so easily moved to tears, who referred to his thought as a pregnant woman might speak of her unborn child, one might well imagine him shedding tears over his swollen belly" (65).[19]

Derrida's renegotiation of the masculine space of representation depends on displacing the woman's body and her desire *as* a woman. For Irigaray, this displacement finds its legend in Athena as "the dissimulation of horror, masking the wound, covering up the difference of values" (102), the "man's woman" who conceals the "mark" of her femaleness and thus becomes "affirmative." In describing Athena as the "dissimulation of horror," Irigaray teases out a certain thread in Nietzsche's discourse on woman, one that would link him to the Freudian phallocratic tradition: "When we love a woman, we easily conceive a hatred for nature on account of all the repulsive natural functions to which every woman is subject...nature seems to encroach on our possessions, and with the profanest hands at that" (*Gay Science,* 122; quoted in Irigaray, 107). While this comment in no way speaks for the whole of Nietzsche's speculations on woman, it nevertheless indicates his placement of the feminine within a masculine parameter. Irigaray insists on the systemic and strategic construction of femininity in masculinist discourse, both Nietzsche's and Derrida's: "With the patriarchal order, femininity forms a system. Dissimulation of woman in the thought of the father. Where she is created fully-clothed and armed. Veiled, her beauty concealed" (99). The production of woman as dissimulatress, especially as elaborated by Derrida, can thus be read as a patriarchal ruse designed to recontain a threatening feminine within the masculine space of representation; femininity is desexualized, then appropriated by the masculine in order to mark its self-representation with heterogeneity. This operation both depends on and produces what Irigaray calls "the neutrality of femininity" (98). Thus, Irigaray unveils, if you will, what Derrida's text keeps under wraps: it is in service to the masculine that femininity becomes veiling dissimulation. Woman is produced in order to specularize man and is thus put into circulation according to the logic of a "hom(m)osexual" economy. A desexualization of woman returns the feminine to the masculine; or, more to the point, recontains the feminine in the masculine as universal point of view.

It may be that what emerges in Irigaray is simply another metaphor of woman which, thus, reproduces the masculine logic that leads Derrida to posit woman as distance and as affirmative dissimulatress. Her discourse raises problems for feminist theory, rather than offering solutions, as many commentators on her work have noted. But, in my view, this is precisely what is valuable in Irigaray's work: in foregrounding the difficulty in speaking "as a woman" within the frame of an explicitly masculine construction of woman, Irigaray enacts the contradictions between Woman and women. Irigaray affirms as she reacts, to stick with Derrida's terms; the woman who emerges in her discourse plays at dissimulation and mimicry—but also remains elsewhere, in a kind of reversal/displacement that is politically motivated. She insists that "one must assume the feminine role deliberately. Which means already to convert a form of subordination into an affirmation, and thus to begin to thwart it" (*This Sex*, 76). Domna Stanton questions the political efficacy of Irigaray's position here:

> Despite the seductiveness of Irigaray's logic, the repetition of masculinist notions and images of the feminine does not necessarily have a ludic or subversive impact that points to an elsewhere. The adoption of the mimetic function, traditionally assigned to woman, may freeze and fixate the feminine at the mirror stage, rather than lead to a difference beyond the same old binary plays. (172)

While Stanton admits that Irigaray recognizes this problem, she concludes that Irigaray's self-consciousness is ultimately lost in an identification with the feminine as defined by the masculine. This identification can result in "an enduring confinement within the parameters of the dominant discourse" (172). Although I agree with Stanton's characterization of the risks Irigaray takes, I am not so convinced that her self-consciousness gets lost in identification. In "Veiled Lips," at least, Irigaray does point to a subversive elsewhere beyond the parameters of the dominant discourse; indeed, I would argue that her discourse already enacts that elsewhere. This elsewhere cannot be described in representational or spatial terms; like subjectivity, it is not a product, but a process. I would characterize this process as an oscillation between mimicry of the master's desire and a feminist deconstruction and argue that such a process produces a different kind of textual subject. What Stanton neglects in her reading of Irigaray is the question of textual desire, what her texts *perform* as well as what they may or may not "conceptualize." In re-playing the desire of Nietzsche-Derrida, in demonstrating that woman-Athena is affirmative of and for man, Irigaray rewrites a certain master narrative in order to subvert it from within. The speaker in "Veiled Lips" approximates what de Lauretis theorizes as a subject of feminism, a subject in discourse characterized by "the movement in and out of gender as ideological representation," a "movement back and forth between the representation of gender (in its male-centered frame of reference) and what that representation leaves out or, more pointedly, makes unrepresentable" (*Technologies*, 26).

Irigaray's text simultaneously demonstrates that Derrida's construction of woman is in service to masculine self-representation, and posits the possibility of a feminine self-representation. Although I find that Irigaray's text succeeds in exploring an elsewhere, a space characterized by a movement in and out of gender as ideological representation, her use of the term "feminine" is problematic. When she speaks as a subject gendered female, Irigaray counteracts the Western construction of femininity as silent passivity; more to the point, she foregrounds the contradiction implicit in "speaking as a woman" within this Western tradition. But her desire to theorize a "feminine" space implicates her in the same kind of logic for which I have been criticizing Derrida. The "feminine" cannot be elaborated outside its historic cultural construction, and although Irigaray is aware of this, her discourse often hovers on the edge of the kind of metaphysical reversal Stanton critiques in her work. Celebrating a feminine multiplicity in opposition to masculine unity or sameness will not get us very far; but this tendency on Irigaray's part is less evident in "Veiled Lips" than it is in some of her other texts.[20]

Independently of Irigaray's reading of Athena, Gayatri Spivak, in her reading of the "double displacement of woman" in Derridean discourse, comes to this conclusion: "Women armed with deconstruction must beware of becoming Athenas, uncontaminated by the womb, sprung in armor from the Father's forehead, ruling against Clytemnestra" ("Displacement," 174). I read this comment as a warning to beware the possibly seductive appeal of a discourse which celebrates the feminine as the deconstructive lever *par excellence* while simultaneously recontaining that feminine within masculine parameters. In other words, Derrida's *Spurs* contains women within Woman in the interests of masculine self-representation. Faced with the postmodernist scepticism about such concepts as subjective agency, experience, and sociality, feminist theorists have two options: to accept an exclusively discursive construction of sexual differences, which amounts to a displacement of gender as ideological representation; or, to bring the possibility of a different, that is female, subjectivity to bear on these discourses as a critical tool. Deconstruction, like any other discourse, is itself open to deconstruction.

What Derrida's conceptualization of the feminine leaves out is the possibility of a female subjectivity; that is, the possibility that Woman might not amount to women. The "space" of the "elsewhere" of discourse can be located in the gap between Woman and women, the contradiction experienced by female subjects attempting to speak as women. Technologies of gender, to use de Lauretis's phrase, place Woman outside discourse, as both ground and object of representation, but never as the subject of discourse; this metaphysical conception of Woman, still persisting in Derridean discourse, exists in ideology. But women, speaking subjects gendered female, are outside this ideology of gender, precisely as the subjects who cannot be theorized within the frame of a metaphysical construction of Woman. The subject of feminism, then, enacts the contradiction between Woman and women; she is *simultaneously* inside and outside the ideology of gender. Unlike Derrida's affirmative woman, placed outside of man's truth in a non-place, the subject of feminism does not occupy a utopian space, "unconcerned" with man's truth and his construction of the feminine; on the contrary, this subject occupies a double position in relation to hegemonic discourses and sociocultural practices. This position is not stable; indeed, it is more like a process than a fixed position.

Angela Carter's novels employ a doubled feminist perspective by performing a movement between the "inside" and the "outside" of normative gender constructions, includ-

ing the construction of Woman as Other to Man's self—
whether that Other be denigrated or celebrated. For Carter,
denigration and celebration of Woman as Other are both
masculinist strategies within patriarchal cultures, whereby
Man secures his hegemony over the places of enunciation.
Woman, whether revered or reviled, is spoken through dominant representational practices, whereas women are prohib-
ited from speaking. To speak, or write, as a woman means
to enact the double relation of women to dominant representational practices. For Carter, this entails practicing the double strategies of mimicry, parody, and masquerade. Each of
these performative strategies negotiates between the terms
of a series of oppositions: construction/deconstruction of
"natural" sexual difference; compliance/resistance to the
ideologies of gender difference as offered through hegemonic discursive systems; and, inscription/subversion of the fit
between Woman and women, between metaphorical figures
constructed according to the logics of a desire encoded as
masculine and social subjects who position themselves
through processes of self-representation. Like Irigaray's
strategy of mimicry, Carter's parodies and masquerades
point to an "elsewhere" of discourse, what de Lauretis refers
to as the "chinks and cracks" in dominant representational
practices. That elsewhere is the space of radical critique that
exceeds the performance of mimicry or parody, and gets the
text, and its readers, off the fence of what Linda Hutcheon
calls the "political ambidexterity" of postmodernist parody.[21]

The Anti-hero as Oedipus:
Gender and the Postmodern Narrative

The Infernal Desire Machines of Doctor Hoffman chronicles
a revolution in the relationship between reason and unreason
in which Dr. Hoffman—a renegade philosopher, whose theoretical framework echoes Nietzsche, Derrida, and others—has
declared a war on reality, in order to liberate desire; he is
intent on exploring and materializing the "obscure and con-
troversial borderline between the thinkable and the unthink-
able" (22). Eschewing binary and linear logic, Hoffman

attempts to find the "loopholes in metaphysics" (212), rewriting the *cogito* to read: "I DESIRE, THEREFORE I EXIST" (211). Against the law of the city fathers—represented by the Minister of Determination who "is not a man but a theorem, clear, hard, unified and harmonious" (13)—Hoffman is "disseminating" "lawless images" (12). The Doctor is attractive in his ability to think beyond binary oppositions, to read the world in ways not wholly dependent on a logic which would repress the unconscious in a hegemony of logocentrism. But, early in the novel, something sinister enters into the textual mapping of the Doctor's effects. In an absurd confrontation between Hoffman's Ambassador and the Minister, the former speaks for seduction and the latter for coercion; however, the two figures come closer together as the Ambassador describes the Doctor's terms for capitulation: he wants "absolute authority to establish a regime of total liberation" (38). The language here foregrounds the idea that the Doctor's liberatory schema is complicit in the same will to power that the Minister clings to.[22] The Minister, a representative of "logical positivism" (194) speaks for a humanist epistemology that cannot countenance contradiction in its systems. The Doctor speaks for a posthumanist epistemology where contradiction rules and where rationality has been put radically into question. Yet, the two systems are quickly seen to be complicit in the same ideological agenda: they both position Man as an imperialist subject whose desire gives free reign to exploitation and domination.

Desiderio, a postmodern Oedipus, is sent to destroy the doctor; but his quest is complicated by the fact that everything he sees and experiences turns out to be an emanation of his desires. The world across which Desiderio moves is literally a construction: the Doctor's desire machines have disrupted "reality" to the extent that any epistemological certainty has become impossible. Objects, people, landscapes, and even time are subject to the whims of the desire machines which are generating "eroto-energy" as a force in opposition to rational knowledge. This eroto-energy causes each subject to perceive and experience the world according to the logic—or, illogic—of his/her desires. Since we see everything through Desiderio's eyes, we are immersed in his desires and forced to experience them along with him. All of Desiderio's "experiences," thus, are constructions of his desire. In reading this text, we are constantly aware that desire is, indeed, the "motor force" of narrative, as Peter Brooks would have it; and, further, that the "engine" behind the narrative, like the male "eroto-energy" Dr. Hoffman's revolution unleashes, is hostile to women.[23] Desiderio's desire participates in the fantasy of colonization that, simultaneously, marks the Doctor's and the Minister's projects for "liberation"—this despite his ambiguously claimed membership in a a colonized group, due to his being "of Indian extraction" (16). Desiderio's discursive self-positioning throughout the narrative is dependent on his negation of the various exotic and erotic "others" his desire invokes. Against these others, he claims the "unique allure of the norm" (101).

Despite the fact that Desiderio's narrative is anything but a traditional quest story, its structure follows pretty closely the form of that story: sent to seek and destroy the diabolical Doctor, Desiderio gets sidetracked and, in fact, seduced to the Doctor's side through the mediation of his daughter, Albertina. While his pursuit of the elusive woman disrupts his primary quest—a quest that originates through the imperative of a stern father figure—he nevertheless finally finds the Doctor, and it appears that he will get a bonus for his trouble: possession of Albertina. Finding himself duped, however, by Albertina—who turns out to be even more diabolical than her father—and his "physicality thwarted by metaphysics" (204), he kills them both, and returns to his city of origin, a hero. Like Oedipus, he has rid the city of its pollution and, also like Oedipus, must pay the price of his new knowledge: "I knew I was condemned to disillusionment in perpetuity," he reminisces. "My punishment had been my crime" (220). While culture's master narratives are losing their authority in this deconstructing textual world, the power relations embedded within white capitalist patriarchy remain intact. Desiderio begins his quest from the "thickly, obtusely masculine" city that "settled serge-clad buttocks at vulgar ease as if in a leather armchair" (15)—a city whose "smug, impenetrable, bourgeois affluence" is achieved at the expense of "indigenous" peoples whose names have now become "unmentionable" (16). At the end of his journey, instead of finding the disruption he expects through the Doctor's liberatory projects, Desiderio finds a "chaste, masculine room...with a narrow bed and a black leather armchair...and a magazine rack containing current numbers of *Playboy, The New Yorker, Time,* and *Newsweek*" (199). Woman, in Desiderio's narrative, as in the classical quest story, occupies a range of traditional object positions: she is a fetish, a foil, the exotic/erotic object awaiting the hero at the end of his quest, but never a subject. She is, like Derrida's "affirmative woman," an object put into circulation according to the logic of male desire. As object of the male gaze, she is subject to regulation, exploitation and violence.

Desiderio's narrative is, then, an exaggerated form of the mythical quest plot that de Lauretis identifies with the prevalence of Oedipus as paradigm in patriarchal culture. It is exaggerated in that Carter brings to the surface what often remains underground in male-centered fictions: the trajectories of desire whereby Woman becomes merely a foil or a "prize" in the stories of male subjectivity. For her part, Carter sees the primacy of the Oedipus story in culture's master narratives and would seem to agree with Laura Mulvey's observation that "sadism demands a story," and perhaps vice versa.[24] Speaking to the prevalence of erotic violence in representation and other social practices, Carter invokes Oedipus. Acts of violence, she writes,

> ...reawaken the memory of the social fiction of the female wound, the bleeding scar left by her castration, which is a psychic fiction as deeply at the heart of Western culture as the myth of Oedipus, to which it is related in the complex dialectic of imagination and reality that produces culture. Female castration is an imaginary fact that pervades the whole of men's attitude towards women and our attitude to ourselves, that transforms women from human beings into wounded creatures who were born to bleed. (*The Sadeian Woman,* 23)

The Infernal Desire Machines of Doctor Hoffman reinscribes this transformation, complete with erotic violence unleashed. Oedipal narrative not only keeps woman "in her place," but does so in order to safeguard male subjectivity from the "bleeding wound" of difference she represents. This text brings to the surface the violent excesses of the transformation of women into Woman by exaggerating the complicities between desire and domination in Western culture's master narratives.

The Infernal Desire Machines of Doctor Hoffman mimics male-centered fictions in a particularly ingenious and telling way. In this text, Carter assumes the mask of maleness, using Desiderio as the only locus of narrative voice and desire—a gendering of the "I" that the reader cannot forget for one moment. Desiderio is the architect, or author, of a narrative of sexual exploitation and violence—a quasi-pornographic writer who enlists an array of misogynist sentiment and fantasy. In this novel, Carter is playing with a tradition of pornographic fiction she describes in *The Sadeian Woman,* a tradition marked by the appropriation of a woman's voice to speak for male sexuality:

> Many pornographic novels are written in the first person as if by a woman, or use a woman as the focus of the narrative; but this device only reinforces the male orientation of the fiction. John Cleland's *Fanny Hill* and the anonymous *The Story of O,* both classics of the genre, appear to describe a woman's mind through the fiction of her sexuality. This technique ensures that the gap left in the text is of just the right size for the reader to insert his prick into, the exact dimensions, in fact, of Fanny's vagina or O's anus. Pornography engages the reader in a most intimate fashion before it leaves him to his own resources. (15-16)[25]

In *The Infernal Desire Machines of Doctor Hoffman,* Carter appropriates a man's subjectivity to describe the fictions of his sexuality, but does so self-consciously; that is, the text foregrounds the problematics of gendered address by deliberately framing the female figures within the text, as well as the woman reader, as figments of a masculine imaginary. In containing women within a figure of Woman, Carter demonstrates how Woman is trapped *inside* gender. But, her strategic engagement with fictions of male subjectivity simultaneously demonstrates what it means to be *outside* hegemonic representations of gender, dismantling them from the margins. This text does, in fact, inscribe a "hole" or gap; but it signifies an absence, rather than a presence. While Woman is everywhere present in this novel, women are conspicuously absent.

How, then, does a text that seems so violently to foreclose on female subjectivity be read as a feminist critique of narrative structures? Or, to put it in slightly different terms, if Carter's text details the dangerous economies of male desire lurking behind narrative and representation, does it simply reinforce the power of these economies, thus closing off the possibility of changing them? How can one tell the difference between construction and deconstruction?[26] Linda Hutcheon, for one, wonders if it is possible to tell the difference at all. She claims that postmodernist artistic practices both use and abuse history, tradition, representation, humanist ideology, and so on. Through parody, the texts of postmodernism *inscribe* in order to *subvert* the master narratives of Western culture, a practice that results in what she calls the "political ambidexterity" of postmodernism. She writes: "Postmodernism knows it cannot escape implication in the economic (late capitalist) and ideological (liberal humanist) dominants of its time. There is no outside. All it can do is question from within" (*Poetics,* xiii). However, Hutcheon notes that perhaps women have more to win, than to lose, from critique of the politics of representation; and, further, that feminist postmodern practice would have little to gain through a "legitimation" of that which it critiques.[27] In other words, feminist postmodernist parody has a political stake in disrupting representations of woman, and such disruptions are marked by the desire to change these representations. The feminist postmodernist text

...parodically inscribes the conventions of feminine representation, provokes our conditioned response and then subverts that response, making us aware of how it was induced in us. To work it must be complicitous with the values in challenges; we have to feel the seduction in order to question it and then to theorize the site of that contradiction. Such feminist use of postmodern tactics *politicize desire* in their play with the revealed and the hidden, the offered and the deferred. (*Politics*, 154, my emphasis)

Carter's text does, indeed, politicize desire, and does so by playing with the conventions of pornographic address, a strategy that Hutcheon notes in other feminist texts. Carter foregrounds the text's enunciative apparatus by making explicit the complicities between desire and domination. Throughout all of Desiderio's adventures, his subjectivity is guaranteed by his objectification of women—of all races, classes, and sexual orientations—who are never, in this text, "fully human" (73). They are "erotic toys," mutilated bodies, phallic mothers, castrating Amazons who are all punished for the crime of being female. Except, that is, for Albertina, the Doctor's daughter, who is punished, to be sure—in a gang rape by a group of Centaurs; but she is also the supreme object of desire, the "inexpressible woman" (13) who takes different shapes according to the logic of Desiderio's desire. Because of the mechanisms of identification built into a first-person quest narrative, this text seems to address its readers as male: as subjects who can enjoy, along with Desiderio, the triumphs of his desire. As feminist theorists of narrative film have suggested, when a woman reader approaches such a text, she may well find herself engaged in a split identification: the narrative positions her to identify with the (male) protagonist by various mechanisms, such as first-person narration as the locus of desire; while, by virtue of her gender, she may also feel identification with the female or feminine forces in the narrative.[28] The overt masculinization of the narrative in Carter's text, however, serves to subvert the mechanisms of identification that support the successful narrativization of violence against women. Carter's mimicry of pornographic narrative—an exaggerated form of all narratives mobilized by male desire—confronts the issue of gendered address head-on by placing the woman reader in an impossible position. There is, quite simply, *no place* for a woman reader in this text; and that no place foregrounds the hom(m)osexual economy Carter is mimicking in it.

The text, then, paradoxically addresses its reader as *feminist* by de-naturalizing the processes by which narrative constructs differences—sexual, racial, class, national—according to the twin logics of desire and domination; that is, it invites the reader to occupy a position not sanctioned by Desiderio's narrative itself but, rather, a position on the outside of that narrative. Carter's text offers this outsider position through a disruption of identification in a number of ways. First, and most obvious, is the fact that, because Desiderio is so clearly complicit in his adventures—which include a number of rapes and female mutilations—a reader who identifies with him will uncomfortably share in his complicity. Second, because the text makes explicit the economies of male desire behind representations of women, the reader does not so easily get seduced into identification—either with Desiderio, or with the female figures he encounters (constructs) on his journey. In other words, there is no illusion of "reality" in this text which might mask the fact that Desiderio's desire is the motor force of the narrative, and we are, thus, constantly aware that none of his constructions of women are "natural." The text demonstrates how Woman is *produced,* rather than simply represented, in narratives of male desire and subjectivity. Finally, Carter makes explicit the "underside" of narrative and history through the use and abuse of pornographic narrative conventions. This "underside"—the mechanics of desire and pleasure as they function beneath the violent and de-humanizing fictions of masculinist pornographic narrative—is brought to the surface and, thus, problematizes the identification that is necessary in order for pornography to do its "work."[29]

The text contains a number of explicit references to pornographic representation, including a couple of scenes straight out of the pages of the Marquis de Sade, and a "Peep Show," where very familiar representations are de-familiarized by being framed with ironic titles. If the text is pornographic, it is what Carter calls "pornography in the service of women." She speculates, in *The Sadeian Woman,* that a political "pornographer would not be the enemy of women, perhaps because he might begin to penetrate to the heart of the contempt for women that distorts our culture even as he entered the realms of true obscenity as he describes it" (20). The use of the masculine pronoun here, always gendered in Carter's work, foregrounds, I think, the reasons behind her appropriation of male subjectivity in her novel. Because, according to Carter, pornography is representation by and for men, her intervention into the politics of representation must be, as Linda Hutcheon puts it, from the inside. Yet something of the "outside" of this representation remains in the novel, a critical perspective akin to the one Luce Irigaray claims as that which remains through women's mimicry. The text refuses to guarantee a voyeuristic or narcissistic position for its readers—male and female—because its metafictional strategies continuously disrupt the "pleasure" such positions traditionally afford. Take, for example, this description of the female figures who people the Sadeian "House of Anonymity" that Desiderio visits:

> Each was as circumscribed as a figure in rhetoric and you could not imagine they had names, for they had been reduced by the rigorous discipline of their vocation to the undifferentiated essence of the idea of the female. This ideational femaleness took amazingly different shapes though its nature was not that of Woman; when I examined them closely, I saw that none of them were any longer, or might never have been, woman. All, without exception, passed beyond or did not enter the realm of simple humanity. They were sinister, abominable, inverted mutations, part clockwork, part vegetable and part brute. (132)

Desiderio's confusion here marks the contradictions Carter sees in the construction of Woman through pornographic narrative. Are these figures women or Woman? Both and neither, it would seem, as Desiderio is forced to confront his complicity in the de-humanization of the objects of his desire. This passage is more like literary criticism than it is like pornography: here, Carter deconstructs representations of women as the machines of male pleasure, bringing to its logical conclusion the ideology of pornography that reduces agents to mere functions. Such a reduction removes sexuality and erotic domination from the social world and makes the "pursuit of pleasure" into "a metaphysical quest" (*The Sadeian Woman*, 16). Carter aims in *The Infernal Desire Machines* to show how "sexual relations between men and women always render explicit the nature of social relations in the society in which they take place" and how, "if described explicitly, will form a critique of those relations" (*The Sadeian Woman*, 20).

Carter's critique of desire as domination works through a literalization—or de-metaphorization—of the structures of male fantasy underlying traditional, and not so traditional, quest narratives, including the kind of quest narrative that I read against the grain of Derrida's *Spurs* in the first part of this chapter. The notion of woman as "ideational femaleness" that "can take amazingly different shapes" in Carter's text resonates thematically with the philosophical trend chronicled by Jardine in *Gynesis*. Hoffman is a figure intent on liberating the repressed of culture, on exploring the margins of philosophy and reason—precisely, the "feminine" disorder that complements masculine order. At the end of the novel, we learn that the Doctor believes in the "inherent symmetry of divergent asymmetry" modeled on the "intercommunication of seed between male and female all things produced" (213), and represented, predictably, by his daughter Albertina. This woman-figure, like Irigaray's Athena, speaks the word of the father and makes that word flesh. The "divergent asymmetry" to which the Doctor refers is gender difference and Albertina's gender fluidity throughout the novel serves, not to blur the boundaries of sexual difference in order to liberate us from the tyranny of absolute division by gender, but to perpetuate the whole metaphysical apparatus as it works around the question of sexual difference. The fact that Hoffman's metaphysics are *openly* based on sexual difference does not significantly differentiate them from the old system against which he is working; as in Derrida's appropriation of the feminine in a new narrative of sexual difference, here we see a female object put into circulation according to a male desire to control representation. The "inherent symmetry" turns out not to be a symmetry at all; the male figures in the text retain power over the female, and put this power into play as Hoffman's "liberation of desire" results in increased objectification of, and sexual violence against, women. As Alice Jardine suggests, there tends to be a congruence between valorizations of the "feminine" as the repressed or "unnameable," and increased narrativization of violence against women in male-authored fictions.[30]

That Albertina Hoffman is as malleable as an ideational femaleness makes of her a fetish object. The blurring of "reality" and "fantasy" in this text, in fact, works by a fetishistic logic that makes of woman a tool of man's pleasure and self-representation. The mechanism of fetishism in classic Hollywood narrative is what leads Laura Mulvey to claim that "sadism demands a story," and to argue that that story entails the disavowal of the threat of castration represented by the woman in the narrative. Carter's novel actively engages with the fetishistic economy that Mulvey identifies in order to show how the "bleeding wound" of female castration sets off the trajectories of male desire for domination. A brief digression back into Derrida, via Freud, is in order here in that it will allow me to suggest how fetishism, like Oedipal narrative, places woman in the middle of male crises as a space across which the subject must travel in order to safeguard his subjectivity and self-representation. For, in spite of Alice Jardine's claim that "the crisis in the discursive itineraries of Western philosophy...involves first and foremost a problematization of the boundaries and spaces necessary to their existence, and this, in turn, involves a disruption of the male and female connotations upon which the latter depend" (71), a metaphorical version of this ideological representation of gender still obtains in the privileging of woman as a solution to that discursive crisis. As Mary Ann Doane points out, investigations of woman always mask a more pressing question for male subjectivity, "What signifies man?": "The claim to investigate an otherness is a pretense, haunted by the mirror-effect by means of which the question of the woman reflects only the man's own ontological doubts" ("Film and the Masquerade," 74-75).

Jardine suggests a causal logic behind Derrida's, and others', move toward the "feminine," and that logic has more than a slightly Freudian ring to it: "in the search for new kinds of legitimation, in the absence of Truth, in *anxiety* over the decline of paternal authority, and in the midst of spiraling diagnoses of Paranoia, the End of Man and History, 'woman' has been set in motion both rhetorically and ideologically" (36, my emphasis). I highlight *anxiety* in her comment in order to suggest that the inscription of woman in modernity's texts can be read as a paranoid reaction which reproduces a certain castration scenario in relation to the death of the paternal metaphor, or the crisis in culture's master narratives. Because that crisis explicitly has to do with the loss of phallic privilege, it seems almost inevitable, given the fact that our cultural imaginations are dominated by Freudian problematics, that a certain anxiety would follow in its wake. The "solution" to this crisis is metaphorically akin to what Freud describes as the fetishist's solution to the problem of sexual difference.[31] The rhetoric of *Spurs,* with its emphasis on a simultaneous veiling/unveiling as the woman's operation, replicates Freud's discourse on the fetish.[32] Woman is a metaphor constructed according to a male desire reminiscent of the fetishist's desire to simultaneously affirm and disavow the threat to his narcissism that the woman represents, a threat evoked in the absence of paternal authority and the privilege of the phallus. In *Spurs,* the feminine is thus what Judith Roof calls a decoy, in that she functions to mask the text's hom(m)osexuality by representing a sexual difference which, ultimately, serves only to facilitate an exchange between men.[33] Derrida's text inscribes "*women's role as fetish-objects,* inasmuch as, in exchanges, they are the manifestation and the circulation of a power of the Phallus, establishing relationships of men with each other" (Irigaray, *This Sex,* 183). She is also a decoy in the sense that this figure draws attention away from what I am reading as the male philosopher's desire to retain the phallic privilege, including the privilege of subjectivity. As Shoshana Felman observes in another context, "ironically enough, femininity itself turns out to be metaphor of the phallus" (24–25).

In explaining fetishism, Freud highlights its status as an operation of undecidability: the construction of the fetish represents "both the disavowal and the affirmation of...castration" ("Fetishism," 156). The both/and logic of the fetish would undermine the notion of castration as truth-effect in that a fetishist can have it both ways: by constructing a fetish, he maintains that woman is both castrated and not castrated, and thus alleviates his own castration anxiety while retaining his belief in woman's lack. Fetishism, in Freud, serves to maintain the subject's belief in a sexual difference based on presence/absence; and, since the fetish "is a substitute for the woman's (the mother's) penis" (152), what is at stake in the fetishist's desire is the priority (or transcendence) of the phallic value. For any reader familiar with Derrida's discourse, it will come as no surprise that the fetishist's logic seems particularly appropriate to describe the deconstructive enterprise. What is attractive for Derrida in the fetish is that its construction "rests *at once* on the denial and on the affirmation, the assertion or the assumption of castration. This at-once, the in-the-same-stroke, the *du-même-coup* of the two contraries, of the two opposite operations, prohibits cutting through to a decision within the undecidable" (*Glas,* 210ai).[34] The fetish joins other privileged Derridean figures of oscillation and undecidability in having the power to undo oppositional thinking and the dialectic. In his reading of Freud's "Fetishism," Derrida foregrounds "the double bond and the undecidable mobility of the fetish, its power of excess in relation to the opposition (true/nontrue, substitute/nonsubstitute, denial/affirmation, and so on)" (*Glas,* 211ai).

What Derrida elides in his reading of Freud's text is the male narcissism at stake in fetishism. Freud writes:

> What happened, therefore, was that the boy refused to take cognizance of the fact of his having perceived that a woman does not possess a penis. No, that could not be

true: for if a woman had been castrated, then his own possession of a penis was in danger; and against that there rose in rebellion the portion of his narcissism which Nature has, as a precaution, attached to that particular organ. [The same Nature, one presumes, that has been "less kind to women."[35]] In later life a grown man may perhaps experience a similar panic when the cry goes up that Throne and Altar are in danger, and similar illogical consequences will ensue. ("Fetishism," 153)

Clearly, Throne and Altar, as paternal signifiers, are in danger in contemporary critical discourse—even if deliberately so. It is my contention that the crisis in masculine subjectivity within these discourses has led to a fetishization of woman as a substitute for the missing phallus. Indeed, in *Spurs,* we can see the narcissistic investment at stake in privileging a woman-fetish; this figure allows the male philosopher to disavow his participation in phallogocentric systems while simultaneously saving himself from the fear of castration. The woman, as woman, remains a threatening figure in *Spurs;* it is only when she is constructed as a fetish—that is, as a substitute for the phallus—that she is "affirmative." Woman, as woman, is outside this economy; or, rather, she/we is/are trapped within its narrative, "framed" by its male-centered construction of sexual difference.

In Carter's text, Oedipus/Desiderio creates a fetish object, in the person of Albertina, a figure marked by undecidability. Like Derrida's woman-figure, Albertina is nearly impossible to pin down; she assumes numerous different identities, experiences gender fluidity, and takes any form that Desiderio's desire imposes on her. He seeks her as his "Platonic other, [his] necessary extinction, [his] dream made flesh" (215) and, as such, she can take any form; she is an idea, not a woman—or, more precisely, she is Woman, rather than *a* woman. As our protagonist himself comes to realize, she "was inextricably mingled with [his] idea of her and her substance was so flexible she could have worn a left glove on her right hand" (142). This woman-object serves as a decoy to mask the real object of desire—the father cum-phallus-cum "Master." What actually circulates in hom(m)osexual economies, then, is not the woman, but the phallus represented by the woman. As Gayle Rubin observes in her analysis of Freud and Levi-Strauss, the interfamily exchange of women coincides with another, intrafamily, exchange: "in the cycle of exchange manifested by the Oedipal complex, the phallus passes through the medium of women from one man to another.... In this family *Kula* ring, women go one way, the phallus goes another.... It is an expression of the transmission of male dominance. It passes through women and settles upon men" (192). Desiderio himself eventually realizes that "perhaps the whole history of my adventure could be titled 'Desiderio in Search of a Master.' But I only wanted to find a master...so that I could lean on him at first and then, after a while, jeer" (190). Albertina's role here is to mediate between Desiderio and Hoffman, just as the affirmative woman's role in *Spurs* is to mediate between Derrida and Nietzsche.

Desiderio is literally fatherless: his mother, a prostitute, conceived him through her work in the Indian slums of the city. Thus, not only has his mother deprived him of a present father, but also, forced him to carry the "genetic imprint" of this lost father "on his face" (16). And, while he disclaims his Indian heritage in his life before Hoffman's revolution, this repressed material gets released once the desire machines start their work. Thus it is that Desiderio finds himself "adopted" by a family of "River people" in an adventure that plays out his ambivalence toward his mother's actions and his father's race. During his time with the river people, Desiderio's colonialist imagination is given full scope, as he constructs this isolated society as "ex-centric": primitive, naive, living with "a complex, hesitant but absolute immediacy" (71).[36] Not surprisingly, this way of life is encoded as "feminine": the River People don't "think in straight lines," but in "subtle and intricate interlocking circles"; concepts are relational, rather than absolute, opposites existing in "a locked tension"; the written form of their language is "beautiful," but "utterly lacking in signification" (75); and so on. Their society is "theoretically matrilinear though in practice all decisions devolved upon the father"

(80). Because everything that happens to Desiderio is an emanation of his desires, we can read in this episode a nostalgic return to the "feminine," to his (absent) mother and the threat that this return evokes.

That threat, of course, is castration, and Desiderio's adventure with the river family replays the Freudian family romance in a new, although still recognizable, way. It is assumed that he will become the husband of one of the clan's daughter, Aoi, whom Desiderio consistently refers to as an "erotic toy" (86). In preparation for her marriage, Aoi's grandmother has manipulated her clitoris over the years, until it approximates a penis. Desiderio cannot help approving this practice: "[I]t was the custom for mothers of young girls to manipulate their daughters' private parts for a regulation hour a day from babyhood upwards, coaxing the sensitive little projection until it attained lengths the river people considered both aesthetically and sexually desirable" (84). What is important here is not so much this practice itself, but Desiderio's interpretation of it; from his male-centered frame of reference, the women are aspiring to masculinity.[37] His desire to masculinize the women amounts to a fetishistic desire to endow his "erotic toy" with a penis. He leaves the river people, reluctantly, after it becomes clear that the father is about to make good on the threat of castration—but not, however, until he succeeds in sleeping with the mother. It is this experience which prompts Desiderio to remark, "Indeed, I was growing almost reconciled to mothers" (85).

Desiderio's desire constructs women as phallic in order to alleviate his anxieties over his own masculinity, evoked by the absence of his father. We have Mamie Buckskin, a "freak" in a circus who is trapped within a conventional narrative from classical Hollywood Westerns. Mamie, Desiderio tells us, "was a paradox—a fully phallic female with the bosom of a nursing mother and a gun, death-dealing erectile tissue, perpetually at her thigh" (108). We have the tribe of Amazons on the coast of Africa who are much more threatening, the destructive mother of male fantasy, with a vengeance. The massive black cheiftain who presides over this tribe, a figure of racist fantasy, tells Desiderio and his companions about why he has chosen women to be his warriors—that is, after all "capacity for feeling" has been excised from them through clitorodectomy:

> Why, you may ask, have I built my army out of women since they are often held to be the gentler sex? Gentleman, if you rid your hearts of prejudice and examine the bases of the traditional notions of the figure of the female, you will find you have founded them all on the remote figure you thought you glimpsed, once, in your earliest childhood, bending over you with an offering of warm, sugared milk.... Tear this notion of the mother from your hearts. Vengeful as nature herself, she loves her children only in order to devour them better and if she herself rips her own veils of self-deceit, Mother perceives in herself untold abysses of cruelty as subtle as it is refined. (160)

Like the female figures in the House of Anonymity, these women "have passed far beyond all human feeling" (160), which is, of course, where both the cheiftain and Desiderio want them. They are not "human" because they have been dehumanized and it is the logic of Desiderio's desire that evokes these destructive, cannibalizing women. While the cheiftain, and Desiderio, thus, debunk one myth of femininity, they replace it with another: the all-good mother gives way to her opposite, both of whom are constructions of cultures where motherhood, whether revered or reviled, is the a priori condition of femaleness.

This adventure, like the episode with the River People, clearly shows how desire and domination are complicit and points to what I am reading as the text's inscription and subversion of a colonialist mentality. From here, Desiderio and Albertina move on to visit a tribe of centaurs who are evoked through a Western fantasy of "primitive" cultures. The complex religious mythology that governs the centaurs' lives is merely a translation of Christian mythology, complete with a genesis story, a Christ figure, resurrection, and salvation. As Brian McHale points out, Carter "has constructed an Africa wholly derived from European fantasy. She populates its coast with cannibal tribesmen straight out of party jokes, comic-strips, and slapstick comedy; while in the interior she places centaurs, in effect suppressing indigenous mythology in favor of an imported European myth. This is imperialism of the imagination, and Carter knows it; indeed, her purpose is to foreground it and expose it for what it is" (55). McHale further notes that these African figures are all "reifications of European desire"—especially since they are the figments of Desiderio's imaginary. But what McHale does not note is the continuity of violent misogyny we can discern throughout all of these adventures, a misogyny that is as much a part of an imperialist imagination. The centaurs, for example, "believed that women were only born to suffer" (172), and, thus, "the females were ritually degraded and reviled" (176). Desiderio, while not exactly applauding this orientation to sexual difference, respects this culture for elevating the "virile principle" to such a degree. He watches, "indifferently," while Albertina suffers a gang rape by the centaurs, later observing that "even the rape had had elements of the kind of punishment said to hurt the giver more than the receiver though I do not know what they were punishing her for, unless it was for being female to a degree unprecedented among them" (181). Later, when the centaurs understand that Albertina is Desiderio's mate, "and therefore [his] property" (182), they apologize to him for their "punishment" of Albertina's "crime." To put the finishing touches on this construction of femininity, Carter has Albertina suggest that the centaurs were an emanation of her desire, not Desiderio's, and that the gang rape was "dredged up and objectively reified from the dark abysses of [her] unconscious" (186).

The quest plot that structures *The Infernal Desire Machines of Doctor Hoffman* is a contorted version of Oedipal narrative that Carter uses to foreground the ideological stakes in this kind of story. Because Desiderio's adventures represent a direct expression of his desire—both conscious and unconscious—the text serves as a commentary on the gendering of that desire as masculine. This novel is an indepth exploration of male subjectivity in narrative, and the construction of sexual difference along binary and often violent lines; as such, it foregrounds the problematics in reading as a woman. Yet Carter systematically disrupts the pleasure of the text by foregrounding the enunciative apparatus behind its inscriptions of desire. If the pleasure of the text is dependent on identification with Desiderio who, after all, has been produced as a "war hero" by History, that pleasure is continuously disrupted by Carter's insistence on what that official History leaves unspoken: the complicities between desire and domination. Desire, in this text, ultimately destroys both its subject and its object. For, although Desiderio emerges intact from his adventures, Carter deprives him, at the last minute, of his "climax": he fails, after all, to find either a worthy master-father, since Hoffman turns out to be a "hypocrite," a "totalitarian of the unconscious"; or the object of desire, since Albertina must be killed in order for Desiderio to fulfill his mission and become a "hero." Desiderio, in turn, deprives his imagined reader of that climax, as well, breaking the pattern of narrative dénouement which would ensure the pleasure of the text through the release of tension, modeled, as Peter Brooks and others seem to assume, on male sexuality: "See, I have ruined all the suspense. I have quite spoiled my climax. But why do you deserve a climax, anyway?" (208). But the pleasure of this text resides elsewhere, an "alternative thrill," as Laura Mulvey would say, "that comes from leaving the past behind without rejecting it...or daring to break with normal pleasurable expectations in order to conceive a new language of desire" ("Visual Pleasure," 8). That thrill, in Carter's text, comes from the negotiation of seduction by and resistance to narrative forms and their production of gender.

In Linda Hutcheon's terms, the text "seduces" its readers into certain constructions of Woman, through its use of traditional conventions of first-person quest narrative. These conventions ensure that Man's self-representation is achieved through his objectification, appropriation, and exploitation of feminine figures: Self can only be realized in opposition to others. But Carter's exaggeration and literalization of these conventions serves to deconstruct the processes by which narrative engenders the subject as male through a violent negation of female subjectivity. Unlike Hutcheon, who implies that construction and deconstruction cancel each other out, and thus, leaves postmodern parody floundering in "political ambidexterity," I have argued that this double strategy in Carter's text carries a sharp ideological critique that is not neutralized by the fact that the text does, in fact, represent Woman in all too traditional ways.[38] On the contrary, it is through Carter's strategic engagement with various master narratives of Western culture that her critique of the politics of representation emerges. While this text presents many difficulties for a feminist reading, those difficulties foreground the stakes in pursuing such a reading. Carter is no idealist, not one to take a utopian leap beyond normative representations of Woman to some uncontaminated representation of women; rather, her text inscribes, in order to subvert, representations that produce women as Woman.

In *Nights at the Circus,* Carter takes on the claustrophobic enclosure of Woman within narratives of male desire and practices a deconstruction of the very terms on which that enclosure depends: masculinity and femininity. In my analysis of this text, I will draw on feminist film theory in order to argue that Carter's text genders spectacle and spectator as feminine and masculine, terms that do not denote a one-to-one correspondence with what Carter calls one's "official gender." They are, instead, "produced very precisely as...position[s] within a network of power relations," as Mary Ann Doane puts it ("Film and the Masquerade," 87). While masculinity and femininity are generally produced discursively as a difference between subject and object, *Nights at the Circus* disrupts this production by assigning agency to the (feminized) spectacle, making of her, simultaneously, a spectator. That "simultaneously" is important to my argument here, as I will read Carter's novel not as a utopian fiction of femininity or female subjectivity, but as a narrative that *strategically* engages the contradictions between Woman and women. For Carter, the "notion of a universality of human experience is a confidence trick and the notion of a universality of female experience is a clever confidence trick" (*The Sadeian Woman,* 12). Moreover, the latter is a politically motivated ruse which obscures a socially constituted female subjectivity and sexuality under a blanket of myth; notions such as the eternal feminine, the goddess, the benevolent or destructive mother, the virgin, the whore, and even the "affirmative woman," are all "consolatory fictions" which mask the real power relations that obtain between man and his others.[39] Carter creates a carnivalesque world of "ex-centricity" where difference reigns. On the one hand, Carter's ex-centric circus performs a deconstruction of falsely universal and homogenous notions of identity and culture; on the other hand, the text demonstrates how marginality and difference can be appropriated by the dominant culture and made into a commodity.[40] The spectacles in *Nights at the Circus*—the cast of "freaks," women, clowns, etc.—are produced as powerless within the terms of a dominant culture that engender the object of the gaze as feminine; but they also produce themselves as social subjects, agents who turn the gaze on themselves and on their position in relation to that dominant culture.

Difference as Spectacle:
Deconstructing Mythologies of Gender

In an article on theorizing the female spectator, Mary Ann Doane describes a process of deconstruction akin to what Irigaray calls mimicry: a self-conscious re-enactment, by women, of the place traditionally assigned to Woman within narrative and other discourse. She calls this strategy masquerade, and reads in it a subversion of the classical opposition between male spectator and female spectacle.[41] A brief discussion of this article will set the stage for my reading of *Nights at the Circus,* since Doane's theory has much in common with Carter's strategic engagement in official narratives of gender difference. While Doane's analysis is rooted in a certain specificity of filmic narrative and imaging, it is translatable into literary narrative to the extent that, in both media, woman signifies object to man's subject, image to his look—such is certainly the case, at least, in Carter's text. Doane focuses on the ways in which Woman, in classical narrative cinema, occupies the place of passive image, and on how this positioning "reinforces the dominant system of aligning sexual difference with a subject/object dichotomy. And an essential attribute of that dominant system is the matching of male subjectivity with the agency of the look" ("Film and the Masquerade," 77). She goes on to discuss the genesis of this dichotomy, and argues that woman has been aligned with the image because, as Irigaray has noted, she has come to represent proximity rather than distance. While man gazes, from a distance, at Woman as image, Woman "is the image" (78). It is this distance between the image and the look, or between "the visible and the knowable," that leads the male subject to fetishism, in order to safeguard his subjectivity, associated, here, with the agency of the look (80). For the female spectator, or reader, things are slightly more complicated. She can either identify with the masculine agency of the gaze and enjoy a kind of "transvestite" subjectivity; or she can, masochistically, identify with the image.[42] There is, however, another alternative, one theorized by Doane as playing the masquerade.[43]

Masquerade, Doane argues, is a mode of "flaunting femininity," of a woman producing *herself* "as an excess of femininity" (81). Doane suggests that, since patriarchal culture constructs femininity as masquerade in the first place, self-consciously assuming that position can lead to its deconstruction. She writes:

> The masquerade, in flaunting femininity, holds it at a distance. Womanliness is a mask which can be worn or removed. The masquerade's resistance to patriarchal positioning would therefore lie in its denial of the production of femininity as closeness, as presence-to-itself, as, precisely, imagistic. The transvestite adopts the sexuality of the other—the woman becomes a man in order to attain the necessary distance from the image. Masquerade, on the other hand, involves a realignment of femininity, the recovery, or more accurately, simulation, of

the missing gap or distance.... The masquerade doubles representation; it is constituted by a hyperbolisation of the accoutrements of femininity. (81–82)

Mary Russo notes a further distinction between transvestitism and the masquerade by suggesting that, for the male transvestite who masquerades as a woman, femininity as mask "is a take-it-or-leave-it proposition; for a woman, a similar flaunting of the feminine is a take-it-*and*-leave-it *possibility*. To put on femininity with a vengeance suggests the power of taking it off" (Russo, 224). The masquerade, conceived as a double strategy of acceptance and denial of femininity, is, thus, a means toward subverting all notions of a "natural" femininity. If one can both take it and leave it, then gender becomes a performance rather than an essence.

Yet the question arises as to what the masquerade of femininity is actually masking. There are several possible answers to this question. First, and least satisfactory because it comes from a masculine perspective, is the idea that the woman is masking her lack of a phallus by making herself into a fetish object—an operation that, thus, she performs for the benefit of the male subject for whom femininity is a threat. Second, the masquerade might be conceived as hiding some "ontological femininity" that exists *prior* to the performance of femininity, a being that pre-exists a doing. Such a reading leads us to see masquerade "as a denial of a feminine desire...regularly unrepresented by the phallic economy" (Butler, 45). The problem here is slightly more complicated than in the first answer because the notion of an ontological feminine desire *outside* of a phallic economy cannot be of much help in thinking about the masquerade as unfolding *inside* that economy. For, clearly, the masquerade engages with a phallic construction of femininity, even if it can be seen to disrupt that construction in some way. In any case, if we were to accept the notion of an ontological feminine desire, as Luce Irigaray, perhaps, does, we would be left with a seemingly unconstructed—and untheorized—femininity as somehow "natural" to individuals sexed female. The most satisfactory answer to the question of what the masquerade masks is *nothing*—not the nothing that women are granted within a phallic psychoanalytic conception of sexual difference but, rather, a no-thing in the sense that there is no feminine being prior to the performances of gender, whether those performances be through masquerade or any other (self)representational strategy. As Judith Butler puts it, we might then conclude that the masquerade "may be understood as performative production of a sexual ontology, an appearance that makes itself convincing as a 'being'"—with the consequence that "all gender ontology is reducible to a play of appearances" (47).[44]

Masquerade, then, is a strategy for self-representation that disrupts the very thing that it apparently inscribes: the reduction of women to a normative representation of Woman. As such, it de-naturalizes gender, while suggesting how it is that women become subjects by enacting the contradictions between normative representations of Woman—as image-object offered for the male gaze—and women as agents of self-representations. I would like to take Doane's analysis of the masquerade, the gaze, and the female spectator one step further and suggest a further connection between these three problematics. For, although Doane's article is centrally concerned with the gaze as indicative of subjectivity, she does not analyze the status of the gaze in the masquerade, nor does she take up the question of the female spectator in relation to that gaze. It is clear enough that the woman, in masquerading her femininity, is deliberately displaying herself for the male gaze; but what of her gaze? She is, it would seem, gazing at herself, at least metaphorically, if not literally. Because Doane's article never quite takes that step, she is almost forced to conclude that it is impossible to theorize the female spectator—as masquerader, or any other thing—without recuperating her within masculine systems of looking or reading. However, it seems reasonable to posit, at least provisionally, that innertextual mechanisms can provide models for extratextual processes, and it is this tact I am taking here. What is particularly valuable in Doane's formulation is the notion that it is possible to disrupt culturally constructed positions of masculinity and femininity by turning them on themselves. I would take it further and suggest that, in the masquerade, the woman is appropriating the masculine position by actively turning the gaze on herself in a reversal of gender positions that leads to the displacement of gender ontologies. This is precisely what Carter does in *Nights at the Circus* and her masquerader also turns an active gaze on the male spectator, and in the process, causes quite a bit of discomfort. It is in this sense that the female subject in this text is both spectacle and spectator and, thus, the text plays out de Lauretis's contention that only re-enacting the contradictions between Woman and women does a woman become a subject (*Alice Doesn't*, 186).

This text is structured around a dual protagonist, one female and one male: Fevvers, the famed circus *aerialiste,* and Walser, an American reporter. The text begins by setting up a conventional relation between these two figures: Fevvers, the "object of learned discussion and profane surmise" (8) *appears* to be the representative female object of discourse, who will be pursued by the male reporter. The novel begins with Walser trying to get at the "truth" of Fevvers's story and her identity. He hopes to "expose" her for what she really is, and this desire motivates him to follow her all over the world. Thus, it begins with a parody of the kind of "seek and destroy" narrative that is so popular in classic Hollywood cinema: the feminine enigma must be "solved," or the troubling female presence must be eradicated.[45] Her slogan "Is she fact or is she fiction?" (7) is an advertising ploy she uses to attract audiences and to sustain the enigma of her difference—Fevvers is nothing if not a shrewd businesswoman—but Walser takes it seriously as a question. In a sense, then, she deliberately positions herself in the "woman's place" demanded by narratives of sexual difference; but, she appropriates, for her own purposes, the enigma of femininity. Fevvers's mark of difference is not only her female body; it is also the enormous wings she sprouted from her back when she was a child. But she is also "all woman," and as such, becomes vulnerable to various and ingenious modes of male exploitation, variations on a metaphor of penetration, the most prevalent of which is gazing.

Fevvers's career begins with her posing as Cupid—"a tableau vivant" at the age of seven in Ma Nelson's whore house. Here, Fevvers tells Walser, "I served my apprenticeship in *being looked at*—at being the object of the eye of the beholder" (23). Her winged body represents an exaggerated difference, and she plays it to the hilt, flaunting her "freakish" femininity. Walser seems to sense her masquerade, her open invitation to be looked at, when he wonders: "in order to earn a living, might not a genuine bird-woman—in the implausible event that such a thing existed—have to pretend she was an artificial one?" (17). Take away the "bird" from "bird-woman" and what you have is the notion that a "genuine" woman, in order to take an active subject position, must pretend to be "artificial"—a woman masquerading as an idea of woman. That "idea" of woman originates in a masculine desire to contain women, and Carter's text plays on the significations of that idea. For Walser, Fevvers's "meaning" resides in her position as "symbolic woman." He, thus, imposes his desire on her, interpreting it as her own: "She owes it to herself to remain a woman, he thought. It is her human duty. As a symbolic woman, she has a meaning, as an anomoly, none" (161). What would be threatened by Fevvers's being an anomoly—that is, a "real" bird woman, rather than a woman masquerading as a bird-woman—is the entire representational system, based on a binary sexual difference, that Walser needs to make sense of the world. What he really means is that she owes it to *him*—and all he represents in terms of phallocratic privilege and power—to remain a symbolic woman, not some anomoly that might signify a kind of "third sex." Walser, at least for the first part of the novel, stands in for the male spectator who "thrilled, as always to the shop-soiled yet polyvalent romance of the image" (107).

Fevvers not only turns her own gaze on herself, producing herself as its object, but also turns it on Walser. The text does not simply reverse masculine and feminine positions by granting Fevvers the agency of the look; rather, it also works to displace this gendered opposition by the both/and logic which marks Fevvers's self-representation.[46] We can see this most clearly through Walser's response to Fevvers's gaze, which is a confusing and disarming sense of gender ambiguity: "She fixed Walser with a piercing, judging regard, as if to ascertain just how far she could go with him.... It flickered through his mind: Is she really a man?" (35). At another point, as she narrates her own story to him, she gives him "the touch of an eye like sudden blue steel," an act that makes Walser cringe: "Walser *wilted* in the blast of her full attention" (78, my emphasis). The word "wilted" evokes an emasculation of Walser, caused by Fevvers's appropriating the agency of the look from him. Doane points out that, in films where women appropriate the gaze, Woman is "constructed as the site of an excessive and dangerous desire. This desire mobilizes extreme efforts of containment and unveils the sadistic aspect of narrative" ("Film and the Masquerade," 83–84). That look signifies castration and, within masculinist fictions, the bearer of that look must be punished, usually by death. In Carter's take on this dynamic, however, Walser and the reader are left to experience the full discomfort of Fevvers's look, the consequence of which is Walser's temporary inability to *write:* to take hold of Fevvers's narrative and put it in his own terms. Indeed, Walser feels himself "at the point of prostration. The hand that followed their dictations across the page obediently as a little dog no longer felt as if it belonged to him. It flapped at the hinge of the wrist" (78). He is, as it were, emasculated by Fevvers's gaze, and loses the power of the speaking subject.

Fevvers's appropriation of the gaze signifies her control over her narrative, just as, in classic Hollywood cinema, the woman's position as object of the gaze ensures that she remain powerless. She and Lizzie take turns narrativizing Fevvers's life, and again, the language Carter uses to describe this control suggests a certain amount of aggression on their parts: "Lizzie fixed Walser with her glittering eye and seized the narrative between her teeth" (32); and, "Fevvers lasooed him with her narrative and dragged him along with her" (60). Yet these "masculine" moves, while they might "de-feminize" Fevvers in iconographical terms, do not render her any less a woman. Or, more precisely, while her active gaze and narrative control signal gender disruption to Walser—he had not bargained for an enigma who spoke back—she does not, thus, position herself as masculine. She disrupts the singularity of masculine/feminine positions by representing herself as both spectacle and spectator, and forcing Walser to do the same.

In Carter's terms, Fevvers is a type of Mae West figure who perpetrates a "superior kind of double bluff" on her audience. According to Carter, West always "selected theatrical and cinematic roles of women whose work entailed sexual self-display" and used these roles to "invert the myth of female masochism." In Carter's analysis, West comes to signify a woman who practices a masquerade of femininity, playing on male fears of the predatory woman: "She made of her own predatoriness a joke that concealed its power, whilst simultaneously exploiting it" (*The Sadeian Woman*, 61).[47] In contradistinction to West, Carter places Marilyn Monroe, whom she calls, along with Sade's Justine, a martyr to be used by "connoisseurs of the poetry of masochism"—among whom she numbers Norman Mailer.[48] Monroe is, in Doane's terms, the woman who is the image, without maintaining any distance from it—or, as Carter puts it, the woman who is "always more like her own image in the mirror than she is like herself" (63). In *Nights at the Circus,* Carter places a Monroe figure, Mignon, against the West figure, Fevvers, and thus foregrounds the difference between two different kinds of spectacle. Mignon has silently suffered has career as spectacle, her exploitation in various "profit schemes" devised by calculating men. In the narrative of her life, Mignon consistently "assumed a woman's place—that of the cause of discord between men; how else, to these men, could she play any real part in their lives?" (150). While Mignon hides behind the "victim's defence of no responsibility" (139), and thus insures her own martyrdom, Fevvers takes full responsibility for engineering herself as spectacle and, thus, resists victimization.

Fevvers prefers to remain a "freak," that is, to play her part as spectacle in order to avoid being reduced to an "idea of woman." Indeed, toward the end of the novel, after a

series of misadventures that threaten to rob her of her difference, her "freakish" femininity, she fears that she is "becoming woman": "Fevvers felt that shivering sensation which
always visited her when mages, wizards, impresarios came
to take away her singularity as though it were their own
invention, as though they believed she depended on their
imaginations in order to be herself. She felt herself turning,
willy-nilly, from a woman into an idea." More importantly, it
is Walser's gaze that threatens to effect this transformation:
"She felt her outlines waver; she felt herself trapped forever
in the reflection of Walser's eyes" (289–90). I will return to
the dénouement of the narrative later, but for now, I want to
make the point that the location of the gaze has everything
to do with whether Fevvers feels herself to be an active subject or a symbolic woman. Fevvers's masquerade enables
her to distance herself from an "idea of woman," and thus,
like the other circus performers, experience "the freedom
that lies behind the mask, within dissimulation, the freedom
to juggle with being" (103).

The arch dissimulators in the text, however, are clowns, not
women—although the "officially" male clowns occupy a feminized position. They are "ex-centrics," outsiders, marginalized
figures whom we see from the "underside." The clowns, and
indeed the entire cast of characters in Carter's circus, are outsiders in several senses. They are outside the social sphere of
privilege, bordering on the "inhuman"; and they are outside of
themselves. As "freaks," they are in the position to cross limits and boundaries; what ties them to the world, of course, is
language. The extent of these characters' mastery of discourse, the degree of their ability to represent themselves in
opposition to how the wider culture represents them, is an
index of their ability to work through their exploitation. On
one end of the spectrum is Mignon, who has been rendered
silent by her production as feminine spectacle. On the other
end is Buffo the Clown, who declaims on various philosophical topics, including "dissimulation," the veil/mask, and "the
nature of plus." Buffo, on the one hand, tends to value what
he calls his "fingerprint of authentic dissimilarity," his dis-
guise; he tries to see it as "a genuine expression of [his] own

autonomy." He claims autonomy in free choice: "and so my face which is not mine, and yet I chose it freely" (122). When Walser—in many ways an *insider*—first puts on the clown's makeup, he "experienced the freedom that lies behind the mask, within dissimulation, the freedom to juggle with being, and, indeed, with the language which is vital to our being, that lies at the heart of burlesque" (103). But, this "freedom" is somewhat deceptive, as Walser himself learns. Buffo begins to wonder about his "choice," about the consequences of creating "ex nihilo, another self who is not me." He asks: "What am I without Buffo's face? Why, nobody at all. Take away my make-up and underneath is merely not-Buffo. An absence. A vacancy" (122). The clowns, mostly dwarves, enact a symbolic repetition of the site of their marginalization. As not-man—even though "male"—as "castrated" man, they mime violence as castration. Like Fevvers's masquerade of femininity, then, the clowns' self-representation includes an exaggeration of the terms by which masculinity is produced. They thus parody what it means to be "official" men, performing a de-naturalization of gender.

The carnivalesque world of Carter's text is not, as Linda Hutcheon suggests, simply "the pluralized and paradoxical metaphor for a decentered world where there is only ex-centricity" (*Poetics*, 61). Rather, this marginalized world exists only in relation to the centers of cultural power. As Judith Mayne warns those who would privilege the carnivalesque—or the ex-centric—as an a priori disruption of the dominant culture, there is a problem in the "assumption that the mode of carnival is by very definition radical, posited from outside the dominant order rather than from within it.... Such enthusiastic celebration of carnival obscures the extent to which the carnival may exist as a safety valve, as a controlled eruption that guarantees the maintenance of the existing order" (40).[49] Carter heeds this warning by showing not only the underside of the carnival spectacle—the perspective of those who are oppressed by their position of marginality in relation to the dominant culture; but also by showing that the carnival is implicated in the commodification of difference. Such an implication need not cancel out the circus performers' subversive parody of the dominant culture. On the contrary, Fevvers's masquerade and the clowns' mimicry strategically engage with that dominant culture, producing the carnival as "a site of insurgency, and not merely withdrawal" (Russo, 218). The discourse of carnival, including masquerade and mimicry, then, is another example of the double strategy of self-representation that is my concern here. As Mary Russo claims, carnival is dialogic, in Bakhtin's terms, because "the categories of carnivalesque speech and spectacle are heterogeneous.... [T]hey contain the protocols and styles of high culture in and from a position of debasement. The masks and voices of carnival resist, exaggerate, and destabilize the distinctions and boundaries that mark and maintain high culture and organized society" (218).

Carter's text takes us through many positions of "debasement," focusing on the "underside of spectacle" (126). Fevvers's vocation as spectacle takes her to various places where "wholly female" worlds are assembled and contained solely for the pleasure of the male gaze and other forms of penetration. From Ma Nelson's "academy"—where the stereotypical figure of the kind-hearted whore is complicated by radical socialist tendencies—Fevvers moves on to Madame Schreck's "museum of woman monsters" to become the "Virgin Whore."[50] With the exception of Ma Nelson's, these enclosures are all extremely claustrophobic, signifying a concerted effort by the powerful to isolate and imprison the powerless. The women who people Schreck's subterranean museum, the darker side of Ma Nelson's and its logical successor in the grammar of male desire, are "slaves and prisoners" kept in a "sort of vault or crypt constructed with wormy beams overhead and nasty damp flagstones underfoot, and this place was known as the 'Down Below,' or else, 'The Abyss'" (61)—a fantastical geography of the female body, according to a masculine perspective. This description suggests the kind of "feminine" closeness to itself that, according to Doane's analysis, has characterized Woman in representation, and kept women from the privilege of self-representation. It also suggests the mixture of horror and desire that characterizes male constructions of the female body within Western discursive traditions, an attitude represented here by the fact that Walser, on hearing about this "abyss," feels "revulsion" and "enchantment" simultaneously (69). Here, Fevvers is one among many "tableaux vivantes," arrested images of various "perversions" of femininity assembled for penetration by the male gaze. As Fevvers remarks, the men who visit Madame Schreck's do not hire the use of the women's bodies, but rather, "hire the use of the idea of [them]" (70).

Such is the desire of Mr. Rosencreutz, who arranges to buy Fevvers from Madame Schreck in order to seduce/ coerce her into aiding in a bizarre ritual that exemplifies the appropriation of the "feminine" for male purposes: he wants to suck out of her body her "mysterious spirit of efflorescence" and thus, "release him[self] from the bonds of the material" (79). Rosencreutz follows a detailed, and recognizable, iconography of masculinity and femininity, constructing a narrative around Fevvers as fetish. In order to save himself from the threat of her sexuality—which he describes as the "female part, or absence, or atrocious hole, or dreadful chasm, the Abyss, Down Below, the vortex that sucks everything dreadfully down, down, down where Terror rules" (77)—he fetishizes her as a figure that has more than a little in common with Derrida's "affirmative woman." He "apostrophises" Fevvers—that is, addresses his remarks to her as if to an "imaginary or absent person" (*New American Heritage Dictionary*): "Queen of ambiguities, goddess of in-between states, being on the borderline of the species...reconciler of opposing states through the mediation of your ambivalent body," and so on (81).

Fevvers is to be his "rejuvenatrix" (82); his plan is to sacrifice her in order to incorporate her femininity into himself. Commenting on her captor's gold medallion, Fevvers "sees the light": "So that was the signification of the gold medallion! The penis, represented by itself, aspires upward, represented by the wings, but is dragged downwards, represented by the twining stem, by the female part, represented by the rose. H'm. This is some kind of heretical possibly Manichean version of neo-Platonic Roisicrucianism, thinks I to myself; tread carefully, girlie!" (77). This medallion embodies what Carter calls the "elementary iconography [from which] may be derived the metaphysics of sexual difference—man aspires; woman has no other function but to exist, waiting. The male is positive, an exclamation mark. Woman is negative. Between her legs lies nothing but zero, the sign for nothing, that only becomes something when the male principle fills it with meaning" (*The Sadeian Woman*, 4). Fevvers resists this positioning, in part because she maintains an ironic distance on male constructions of her. She is more than willing to play the part of feminine spectacle for fun and profit, but it is another thing entirely to relinquish control over that spectacle.

All of the novel's "wholly female worlds" are designed to keep women outside history, to keep them from "experiencing their experience as experience."[51] By this phrase, Carter means a critical perspective on one's experience, an analysis of experience that will lead to change. Fevvers has this historical sense, a consciousness of her place in history that allows her to analyze her experience, unlike many of the other women in the novel. She sees herself as the living metaphor of the New Woman, "child of the new century, the New Age in which no women will be bound to the ground" (25). Her wings will carry her into the twentieth-century, where she will be an active participant in history, rather than a passive recipient of it. Carter, however, takes an ironic stance on Fevvers's desire to be the avatar of a new mythology because, like all mythologies, it is so much "consolatory nonsense."[52] This irony becomes most apparent in the self-consciously conventional ending of the novel. Through a series of misadventures, Fevvers is beginning to lose her beauty, her talent, and her difference. Her wings have become mere, even troublesome, appendages, and her whole identity is brought into question. What she lacks is "that silent demand to be looked at that had made her once stand out" (277); as Lizzie warns her, "You're fading away, as if it was only always nothing but the discipline of the audience that kept you in trim" (280). A spectacle without an audience is no spectacle at all, and Fevvers's carefully worked out self-representation through masquerade threatens to break down. Yet something else is going on here, for it is the gaze of the now beloved and lost Walser that Fevvers needs to safeguard her identity and/as her difference. Indeed, when Walser returns, his gaze makes Fevvers "whole" again (285). Is Carter, then, at the last minute, returning her narrative to a conventional love story, complete with an all too familiar ideology of gender? I would like to suggest that, having set Fevvers on the course of a conventional love story, despite the very unconventional elements in it, Carter takes the opportunity to comment on the demands of such a story on the female subject of it.

Indeed, Lizzie's warning to Fevvers leads the two into a discussion of the institution of marriage, and its place in the conventions of narrative, prompted by Lizzie's suspicions that it's really the loss of Walser that is destroying Fevvers. Lizzie ironically comments: "The Prince who rescues the Princess from the dragon's lair is always forced to marry her, whether they've taken a liking to one another or not. That's the custom. And I don't doubt that custom will apply to the trapeze artiste who rescues the clown. The name of this custom is a 'happy ending'" (281). And, despite the fact that the gender roles are reversed in this narrative dénouement, the result is the same: women, once again, continue to become Woman. Yet Lizzie, always the materialist, draws Fevvers back from this becoming Woman by pointing to the woman with a baby who occupies the cottage where they are awaiting Walser's return: "This tableau of woman in bondage to her reproductive system, a woman tied hand and foot to that Nature which your physiology denies, Sophie," Lizzie remarks, using Fevvers's pre-spectacle name, "has been set here on purpose to make you think twice about turning from a freak into a woman" (283). And, in fact, when Walser does arrive, Fevvers begins another narrative performance. They begin the interview anew, and this time, Fevvers will tell her own story, in her own terms.

Nights at the Circus plays fast and loose with mythologies of difference, pushing official narratives of gender to their limits in order to dismantle them. Female subjectivity in this text is not some romanticized notion of a specifically feminine way of being in the world; rather it is a relation of gender, subjectivity, and experience to systems of power, including discourse. Carter's turn of the century novel—straddling both the twentieth and twenty-first centuries—serves as a corrective to the theoretical fictions that sustain modernity's new interest in the "feminine." Such fictions remain in service to the hegemonic perspective and would, one imagines, be labeled by Carter as "consolatory fictions." "If women allow themselves to be consoled for their culturally determined lack of access to modes of intellectual debates," Carter writes, "they are simply flattering themselves into submission (a technique often used on them by men)" (*The Sadeian Woman*, 5). To place woman in an Utopian space outside of history, discourse, and "man's truth"—to evoke Derrida— means, at the very least, to obscure the real effects of gender in favor of a new myth; at the worst, it means to ensure business as usual in the realms of power and knowledge. Another kind of strategy is necessary if feminist women are to rewrite culture's master narratives, or install ourselves as subjects of any narrative. My argument about Carter's appropriation of the masquerade for the purposes of subversion—in contrast to what I see as Derrida's ultimately conservative appropriation of (feminine) dissimulation—is meant to suggest one such strategy.

All of the texts I've discussed in this chapter participate in the construction of gender; indeed, any text—feminist, anti-feminist or "post-feminist"—that represents woman constructs gender, even through its deconstruction. Carter's work is akin to Irigaray's, when the latter takes the position of questioning subject in order to interrogate the gender ideology at the foundation of phallocentric discourse. She writes: "I am going to make an effort—for one cannot simply leap outside that discourse—to situate myself at its borders and to move continuously from the inside to the outside" (*This Sex*, 122). This effort enables Irigaray to explore the contradictions between Woman and women, to speak as a subject gendered female without being resorbed in the space allotted to the feminine within Western discourses. It is also the effort that characterizes Carter's novels, although in radically different ways. To assume the doubled perspective of feminist theory, simultaneously inside and outside gender as ideological representation, means to question the construction of Woman without ignoring the cultural productions of women, or the material effects of that representation. To do so, we need to reopen the question of subjectivity as "our" question and not "theirs," to paraphrase Spivak again. As Nancy Hartsock puts it, "we know we are not the universal man who can assume his experience of the world is the experience of all" (205). The crisis in masculine subjectivity, as elaborated in the new master narratives of philosophical and literary discourse, is precisely that: man's crisis. Which is not to say, as Derrida does, that it should not "concern" us; rather, it should concern us precisely to the extent that the crisis in masculinity leads subjects gendered male to recontain women (and especially *feminist* women) within Woman in order to maintain the male hegemony over discursive spaces.

A politically indifferent, ahistorical privileging of "woman" or the "marginal" results in an impasse that can do little but deconstruct the history of Western thought as a male "mistake"; such a privileging fails to consider the politics of enunciation, the fact that not all subjects speak from the center, and that not all subjects have had the luxury of *choosing* to occupy the margins. If women and other inhabitants of the margin remain *spoken by* hegemonic discourses, rather than speaking, the privileging of a posthumanist indeterminacy—as opposed to a humanist certainty and self-presence—can do little to enable that speaking. In other words, in order for a deconstruction of "identity" to take us beyond the politics of a white, male humanism, we need to articulate the complex relations between marginality and centrality in such a way as to prevent the re-containment of the marginal voice as the "difference" within the hegemonic. Minority discourse theorists have recently begun to work towards just such an articulation.

In an article entitled "Ethnic Identity and Post-Structuralist Differance," R. Radhakrishnan argues for a theory of "radical ethnicity" constituted across the intersection of ethnic identity and the poststructuralist concept of radical indeterminacy; this intersection can both "historicize and situate the radical politics of 'indeterminacy'" and "situate the politics of empowerment as a transgression of the algorithm of 'identity'" (199). Radhakrishnan's argument for a transgression of identity politics is not simply a recognition that poststructuralist thought, as articulated by such white "masters" as Derrida, has rendered the concept of identity naive or passé; rather, he suggests that to posit ethnicity as an identifiable entity amounts to the same apolitical move as situating pure "differance" in the minority subject or text. Addressing the politics of "post," he writes: "The constituency of 'the ethnic' occupies quite literally a 'pre-post'-erous space where it has to actualize, enfranchize, and empower its own 'identity' and coextensively engage in the deconstruction of the very logic of 'identity' and its binary and exclusionary politics" (199).[53] I will now turn to a reading of Gayl Jones's deconstructive fictions of black womanhood and trace the processes by which they perform a transgression of (humanist) identity politics while simultaneously theorizing a subjective agency for black women. The protagonists of these novels speak against a history of being spoken by discursive systems which depend on essentialist notions of gender and race for their coherence. Through their strategic engagement in discourses of sexism, racism, and colonialism, these textual figures work toward a self-representation that deconstructs normative representations of the black woman.

"We're all consequences of something": Cultural Mythologies of Gender and Race in the Novels of Gayl Jones

Critical reception of Gayl Jones's two novels, *Corregidora* (1975) and *Eva's Man* (1976), has been ambivalent, at best. Feminist critics, in particular, have tended to stay away from these two troubling texts.[1] Written in the 1970s' climate of "identity politics," these texts seem to stubbornly defy that context because they work to dismantle the humanist paradigm of singular and definitive identity.[2] Criticism of these novels has tended toward evaluation, and even condemnation, on the one hand, and attempts to force the texts into a humanist tradition, on the other hand.[3] This response is not all that surprising, since the novels actively work to generate radical contradiction; what is surprising is that Jones's critics do not read the production of ambivalence as a textual strategy.[4] Far from stranding the black woman in the politically paralyzed position of victim doubly oppressed, Jones's novels work to dismantle the social structures and discourses that necessitate that positioning of the black female subject. The protagonists of these novels have no access to anything as stable and fixed as "identity," a position that they can unproblematically occupy; rather, they attempt to speak their subjectivity both within and against the discourses which place them in positions marginal to subjectivity. Jones's protagonists, Ursa Corregidora and Eva Medina Canada, do not step "outside" sexist and racist representational structures, in order to forge an "identity" uncontaminated by them; such an utopian move would do nothing to dismantle the representational and social structures that enforce the marginality of minority subjectivities. Rather, Ursa and Eva oscillate between inside and outside, writing in the margins of hegemonic discourses in order to forge a self-representation which is neither independent of, nor reducible to, normative representations of the black woman as wholly "other." This double movement inscribes identity as a process by which the black woman as subjective agent resists becoming "naturalized" into a singular and essential position.

Jones's two novels work against a humanist "identity politics" by showing the production of the black woman within hegemonic discourses to be a colonialist strategy for containing the "other" in a space constructed according to the desires and needs of the hegemonic "self." The idea that identity is a product, rather than a process, has as its corollary the humanist idea that gender and race are essences. If gender and race are conceived in the realm of being, then they become irreducible facts of identity that place gendered and racial subjects—read: women and non-whites—in singular positions in relation to hegemonic ideologies. Such singular positioning makes it possible for minority subjectivity to be regulated by the dominant social group whose self-representations are not "marked" by gender and race. Cultural constructions of the black woman, for example, have worked to stabilize a heterogeneous social group in order that that group can be contained as the difference necessary for the coherent self-representation of the dominant group. Humanist ideologies purport to *represent* already constituted subjectivities and social groups when, in fact, they actively work to *produce* these subjectivities, to place black women, for example, in a stable, and thus recuperable, space. As Abdul JanMohamed and David Lloyd argue, humanist theories—of literature and subjectivity—have been "structurally blind" to minority perspectives, but have been able to recuperate these perspectives through the ideology of pluralism JanMohamed and Lloyd call the "great white hope of conservatives and liberals alike"; that is, the humanist ideology whereby individual minority texts can be recuperated into the "universalizing project" of humanism as examples of the ethnic "essence" against which the hegemonic perspective defines itself (9).[5] To posit ethnicity—or femininity—as difference *tout court* means to negate any differences within ethnicity and gender; it means to reduce minority subjectivities to a monolithic Other and to disempower the marginal voice as, precisely, a function of an equally monolithic center.

If normative representations of Woman function to contain women within a singular and essential space outside of subjectivity, then normative representations of the black woman as racial and sexual other further exacerbate that containment. Yet at the same time, race complicates the production of Woman/containment of women nexus, for, within white patriarchal cultures, the black woman is produced in contradistinction to the white woman, as well as in opposition to the black man. To become a woman, for Gayl Jones's protagonists, is not the same process as it is, say, for Doris Lessing's Martha Quest. Indeed, as I argued in my reading of Lessing's *Children of Violence,* the black woman—Martha's "invisible sister"—becomes the body on which the white woman displaces her fears of becoming Woman, signified as total lack of access to cultural and political power. A similar displacement operates in the discourses on American slavery that I will analyze in order to contextualize my reading of Jones's deconstruction of mythologies of gender and race. For, within these discourses, the black woman becomes the linchpin of a representational system based on gender and racial difference, the zero-degree figure against which all other differences are measured. Both *Corregidora* and *Eva's Man* engage with this representational system, tracing its coherences and its fissures in order to theorize an identity politics that can account for the processes by which subjectivity is constituted through self-representation. For the protagonists of these novels, that self-representation entails strategically inscribing, in order to subvert, discourses that place the black woman in an essentialized position. The identities that emerge from this negotiation—between speaking and being spoken—are unstable and provisional but, nevertheless, empowering.

Jones's two novels theorize what R. Radhadkrishnan calls a "radical ethnicity" to the extent that they situate the black female subject in a position of indeterminacy, and coextensively work to empower that subject.[6] On the one hand, this indeterminacy is a function of the historical situation of the black woman, the fact that her "identity" has been buried beneath the hegemonic construction of her as doubly Other—that is, the lack of any determinate identity for the black woman describes a politically motivated strategy that has foreclosed on the possibility of her subjectivity, or, indeed, her "humanness." On the other hand, this indeterminacy can be used as a tool in forging another subjectivity and "identity" that escape "capture" or appropriation by the hegemonic perspective in its efforts to define itself. Both *Corregidora* and *Eva's Man* deconstruct what Hortense Spillers calls the "overdetermined nominative properties" that have been used to describe, and constrain, Afro-American womanhood in historically specific ways. Spillers writes: "Embedded in bizarre axiological ground, [these nominative properties] demonstrate a sort of telegraphic coding; they are markers so loaded with mythical prepossession that there is no easy way for the agents buried beneath them to come clean" (65). It is to this "telegraphic coding" that I now turn in order to consider the ways in which American culture has made it impossible for the black woman, as agent, to "come clean."

Black Female Essence: Slavery and the Cultural Production of the Black Woman

The sexual politics that inform Jones's novels stem from an historically constituted discursive construction of the black woman and the black man. This construction originates in a colonialist discourse on U.S. slavery, and must be understood as an extension of the hegemonic—that is, white male—perspective's self-representation. From its inception in the seventeenth century, this discourse of colonialism has constructed "Negro" as the sign of difference; from slave traders' travelogues, to proslavery arguments, the discourse on the "commercial deportation"[7] of African peoples and their place in the American system positions the "Negro" as Other to white. This strategy has served to naturalize the exploitation and oppression of the Afro-American community, within slavery, and on into the twentieth century. In what follows I will be using the terms "the black woman" and "the black man" to describe discursive constructions, the indefinite article signifying the essentializing strategy of positing race as a visible and irreducible sign of difference. Within this discursive economy, the black Other can be differentiated by gender, but the differentiation originates in the hegemonic perspective and thus can be understood as dependent on the essential opposition of white and non-white. The construction of sexual difference within the racial Other has responded to the needs of the hegemonic perspective in historically specific instances. The female "captive body," to use Hortense Spillers's phrase, is at times "ungendered," which is to say, not gendered in any way recognizable by the white cultural perspective; at other times, the slave is engendered as a woman in order to make possible particular brands of exploitation. Jones's exploration of the racial and sexual mythologies originating in slavery embraces the black experience both in the United States and in Brazil. I will turn to the Brazilian experience in my discussion of *Corregidora*, as it is in that novel that Jones deals with the specificities of the slavery experience in that country.

As feminist historians have demonstrated, the discursive construction of black womanhood exists in a complex relationship to the lived reality of black women's lives, a relationship summed up by Deborah Gray White's conclusions about the image of the black female slave produced in the discourse on slavery in the antebellum South.[8] White focuses on the image of Jezebel as a white male fantasy, and argues that the image of a libidinous and promiscuous black woman "was nurtured by the conditions under which slave women lived and worked" (33). Southerners observed scantily clad women, a condition they themselves enforced, and concluded that these women were "naturally" lascivious. The fact that the female slave's reproductive capabilities became a matter of public discourse, that female slaves were openly discussed and advertised as "good breeders," served to further entrench the image of the black woman as a purely sexual, and thus animal, being. Once these women were categorized as "breeders," it was only a small step for the masters to conclude that their female slaves were readily accessible as sexual partners. The discursive and social positioning of the black female slave as sexual and "immoral" object becomes a strategy for safeguarding the position of the white male master as exempt from "moral" responsibility. If sexual accessibility and willingness are a "natural," constitutive quality of the black woman, then the white masters could absolve themselves from charges of immorality. The documents of slave traders and owners attest to the prevalence of the mythological construction of the black woman as the repository of a sensual animality unmitigated by "moral," or even "human," values. And, as White points out, this construction works by the cyclical reasoning that served to "naturalize" this ideological construction of the black woman: "The conditions under which bonded women lived and worked helped imprint the Jezebel image on the white mind, but traders and owners also consciously and unconsciously created an environment which insured female slave behavior that would fulfill their expectations" (33–34). In creating the Jezebel image, masters submitted the black female slave to the exigencies of a foregone conclusion; if the black woman was "naturally" lascivious and promiscuous, then her behavior could be understood within the interpretive frame established to mask her humanity, and to inscribe her difference from the hegemonic group—in this case, the white woman.

As White points out, all of the Southern pro-slavery arguments, and the documents of slave traders in Africa and the U.S., construct the black woman as Jezebel in contradistinction to the purity of Southern White Womanhood. Putting White's argument in slightly different terms, the black woman was constructed as Other to the white; that is, she was made to bear a difference—in body—from the white woman.[9] The paranoia about white womanhood gave the construction of the black woman added fuel; in order to differentiate their "own women" from what they perceived to be a sexuality out of control, these white men displaced all their fears of female sexuality onto the black woman. The common currency of black immorality—usually ascribed mainly to black women, who "corrupted" black and white men alike—led Southerners to argue that the existence of the black woman in their world actually served to *protect* white womanhood. White writes:

> Proponents of this line of reasoning actually celebrated the societal stratification that made black women available but put white women out of reach. Northerners, they argued, debased the civilized; they defamed the white prostitute, cut her off from the hope of useful and profitable employment, immured her in a state of depravity. By contrast, Southern white women were kept free and pure from the taint of immorality because black women acted as a buffer against their degradation (38–39).[10]

This kind of argument was shortlived, however, due to the pressure exerted by Northerners concerned about the decadent morality on Southern plantations. In response to Northern criticism, slavery apologists created a figure in contradistinction to Jezebel: Mammy, the asexual maternal slave. In this move, we can see the resilience in the cultural construction of the black woman; that is, how the hegemonic perspective effectively had the power to rewrite the black woman's experience in response to the exigencies of the moment. The change in focus from Jezebel to Mammy marks a shift in the hegemonic perspective on the black woman, not a shift in the lived experiences of the female slave. Indeed, as White points out, "many Southerners were able to embrace both images of black women simultaneously and to switch from one to the other depending on the context of their thought" (46). Just as Jezebel served to inscribe the black woman's difference from the white woman, Mammy, too, was a figure originating in the ideological construction of white womanhood. At a time when the "cult of domesticity" was at its height, the "cultural uplift theory" of slavery was able to embrace the black woman—as Mammy—in relation to the ideal of white womanhood.

The discursive construction of the black woman was not without its effects on the representation of the black man. Because of the binary machinery at work in the discourse of racial domination, sexual difference is put into play in much the same way as is racial difference. Michele Wallace points out that in slavery, "the business of sexual and racial definition, hideously intertwined, had become a matter of balancing extremes" (138). The discourse of slavery in nineteenth century America participates in what Abdul JanMohamed calls the "Manichean allegory" that obtains in all discourses of colonialism and inscribes a set of hierarchical binary oppositions: "a field of diverse yet interchangeable oppositions between white and black, good and evil, superiority and inferiority, civilization and savagery, intelligence and emotion, rationality and sensuality, self and Other, subject and object" ("Colonialist Literature," 63). Although JanMohamed does not invoke gender here, the racial oppositions he cites can be seen to operate in the inscription of sexual difference, as feminist theorists have made clear.[11] What is interesting about the "balancing extremes" that Wallace notes in the context of U.S. slavery is the ways in which the construction of the black woman carried with it a "complementary" construction of the black man; and the ways in which the white master's self-representation depended on a complementary representation of the black Other. Wallace writes:

> Every tenet of the mythology about [the black woman] was used to reinforce the notion of the spinelessness and unreliability of the black man, as well as the notion of the frivolity and vulnerability of the white woman. That white was powerful meant that black had to be powerless. That white men were omnipotent meant that white women had to be impotent. But slavery produced further complications: black women had to be strong in ways that white women were not allowed to be, black men had to be weak in ways that white men were not allowed to be. (138)

Thus, the white "man's fear of woman's emasculating sexual powers" (White, 61) produced the black woman as

Jezebel, and at the same time, produced the black man as emasculated. Since these fears of female sexuality were displaced onto the black woman, the white man could be free of the fear of emasculation by, similarly, displacing it onto the black man. We can see how this discursive network had its effects in the material lives of slaves, and how what Wallace calls the "hideously intertwined" business of racial and sexual definition functioned in the black experience under slavery and the discursive construction of that experience. For example, Jacqueline Jones suggests that slave masters used the figure of Jezebel—a cultural construction masquerading as a natural essence—to keep male slaves in a position of vulnerability. She notes that slave holders used the rape of black wives as a form of humiliation, a way to emasculate the male slaves. Usurping the black man's right to "his own woman" was one way for the white man to simultaneously exercise his absolute power over the bodies of his slaves, and to rob male slaves of any power to either protect those bodies or to "possess" them.[12] J. Jones implies that sexual exploitation of black female slaves, a practice that was naturalized by the identification of the black woman with Jezebel, was used as a method of sowing dissension in the slave quarters and, thus, perhaps, preventing the kind of community unity necessary to successful rebellion.[13] But the black woman was made to bear the effects, if not the responsibility, for her own exploitation; as J. Jones writes, "it would be naive to assume that the rape of the black wife by a white man did not adversely affect the woman's relationship with her husband; her innocence in initiating or sustaining a sexual encounter might not have shielded her from her husband's wrath" (38).

Another common form of humiliation, according to J. Jones's reading of slavery documents, was making a man do "women's work" as punishment:

A limited amount of primary evidence indicates that men actively scorned women's work, especially cooking, house cleaning, sewing, washing clothes, and intimate forms of childcare.... Some slaveholders devised forms of public humiliation that capitalized on men's attempts to avoid these tasks. One Louisiana cotton planter punished slave men by forcing them to wash clothes; he also made chronic offenders wear women's dresses. (38)

This "feminization" of male slaves is a literalization of the Sambo persona: the construction of a weak, emasculated black man in opposition to the omnipotent white. This strategic representation not only degrades the black man, but works through an implicit devaluation of woman—both black and white; indeed, the ascription of femininity to the male racial Other serves to exaggerate his difference from the white male self. The reconstruction of the black experience under slavery from a black perspective in the mid twentieth century had as its main impetus the desire to humanize the black slave, but most often took the form of "remasculinizing" the black male and concurrently "putting black women in their proper 'feminine' place" (White, 22).

White argues that Stanley Elkins's groudbreaking book[14] effectively erases the black woman from the history of slavery in two ways: first, by focusing solely on the male experience of Samboism; and, second, by unproblematically placing the black woman in the frame of the white representation of "femininity"—a construction of the female slave's experience that has little reference to her lived experience.[15] Elkins argues that Sambo was not just an image, but rather, an accurate description of the reality of the black slave's life; the white master had such total power over his slaves, that they were reduced to a childlike dependency. Elkins thus began a debate in which (male) historians were concerned to reassert the ideal of black masculinity which had been damaged by the feminine idea associated with Sambo. Since women are not "supposed" to be assertive or aggressive, the conclusions Elkins reached were that (at least implicitly) it is the black man who had to "bear the burden of the insult" to the race (White, 20). When Elkins's work became cultural currency— in part, in relation to the Black Power movement—this pro-masculinity ideology became central.[16] White writes: "If the stage Elkins set for the debate over slavery reemphasized the femininity of the race, those who did most of the debating were bent on defeminizing black men, sometimes by emphasizing the masculine roles played by slave men, sometimes by imposing the Victorian model of domesticity and maternity on the pattern of black female slave life" (21). White concludes: "The male slave's 'masculinity' was restored by putting black women in their proper 'feminine' place" (22)—a place that the black woman never occupied under slavery, except in the narratives constructed by hegemonic groups.

The "divide-and-conquer" strategy that enabled the disruption of the slave community has as its analogue in the mid to late twentieth century the myth of the "Black matriarchy." Rooted in slavery, this myth assigns to black women a power that they simply did not enjoy. Because of the economic bases of slavery, the mother-child bond enjoyed prominence over the husband-wife bond, or the father-child bond (White, 159)—a state of affairs that has led historians to conclude, erroneously, that the black female slave was placed in a position of dominance. But, as Dorothy Sterling points out, "matriarchy implies power. The slave woman had no power over husband, children, or even her own body. All power flowed from her master and his male deputies, the overseer and the driver" (37). Nevertheless, this myth found added fuel in the form of the infamous "Moynihan Report" that, published in 1965, ascribed the failure of black American "manhood" to his emasculation at the hands of the black woman.[17] No longer Jezebel or Mammy, the black woman becomes Sapphire: "a domineering black woman who consumes men.... Sapphire emasculates men by the aggressive usurpation of their role" as head of the family (White, 165–66).

Sapphire's power is a destructive one, not the productive power of the woman who seeks to safeguard her own rights within a racist society; she "is depicted as iron-willed, effectual, treacherous toward and contemptuous of Black men, the latter being portrayed as simpering, ineffectual whipping boys" (Bond and Peery, 116).[18] While White argues that Sapphire is not a "sexual persona," she is, in fact, simply an extension of Jezebel; "Moynihan's thesis of black woman as a castrater of males,"[19] makes it clear that power and sexuality are irrevocably linked. As damaging as the figure of Sapphire has been to the black male ego, the myth of the black matriarchy has obscured the real power relations that obtain in a racist culture. As Robert Staples points out, this myth originates in and serves the interests of the hegemonic group in American culture; the myth is a prime example of what Malcolm X called "making the victim a criminal."[20] Staples argues that "it has been functional for the white ruling class, through its ideological apparatus, to create internal antagonisms in the black community between black men and black women to divide them and to ward off effective attacks on the external system of white racism" (15).[21]

Feminist scholars have echoed Staples's sentiments here, but have also stressed the ways in which the black woman has been explicitly *blamed* for the so-called emasculation of the black man. In 1969, in response to the debate over the Moynihan report, Jean Carey Bond and Patricia Peery warn against taking Moynihan at his word by focusing on the strategic value of the Report in sustaining white male dominance:

> [Moynihan] and his gang postulate that Black society is matriarchal, and that Black women have been the primary castrating force in the demise of Black manhood. The casting of this image of the Black female in sociological bold relief is both consistent and logical in racist terms, for the so-called Black matriarch is a kind of folk character largely fashioned by whites out of half-truths and lies about the involuntary condition of Black women. The matriarchal fairy tale is part of a perennial tendency among whites to employ every available device in *their* ongoing effort to demasculinize the Black male. (116)

Thus, what Michele Wallace calls the resurgence of "black macho" during the Black Power Movement can be read as a response to what the hegemonic perspective was busily defining as the demasculinization of the black man. Wallace suggests that this response signifies an unquestioning acceptance of the terms of racial oppression as devised by a white perspective, the black man's acceptance of Moynihan's, and others', suggestion that "the existence of anything so subversive as a 'strong black woman' precluded the existence of a strong black man or, indeed, any black 'man' at all" (31). As Hortense Spillers points out, the possibility of a *different* masculinity or femininity—different, that is, from these terms' construction within white culture—never occurred to Moynihan. Spillers argues that the Report "suggest[s] that black males should reign because that is the way the majority culture carries things out" (66), and quotes from Moynihan: "It is clearly a disadvantage for a minority group to be operating under one principle, while the great majority of the population...is operating on another."[22] "Blaming" the mother, or the daughter, for this "pathological" state of affairs, to use Moynihan's term, "becomes an aspect of the African-American female's misnaming," and simultaneously functions to "freeze" the "Ethnic"—here, "ungendered"—"as a scene of negation" (Spillers, 66).

Thus, gender differentiation within the ethnic Other remains the prerogative of the hegemonic perspective. During slavery, the production of sexual difference was based on economic imperatives. Spillers argues that slaves remain "ungendered" in the limbo of deportation; the chronicles of slave ships include no gender differentiation, except a *quantative* one—that is, female slaves were differentiated from male only to the extent that they occupied slightly less space on the ships (72). Gender difference is subsumed under the larger difference of human and non-human:

> First of all, their New-World, diasporic plight marked a *theft of the body*—a willful and violent...severing of the captive body from its motive will, its active desire. Under these conditions, we lose at least *gender* difference *in the outcome,* and the female body and the male body become a territory of cultural and political maneuver, not at all gender-related, gender-specific. (Spillers, 67)

It is not until the captive slaves reach the "domestic" arena of plantation life that they become gendered, and here comes into play what Angela Davis calls the "expediency [that] governed the slaveholders' posture toward female slaves: when it was profitable to exploit them as if they were men, they were regarded, in effect, as genderless, but when they could be exploited, punished and repressed in ways suited only for women, they were locked into their exclusively female roles" (6). The Moynihan Report, similarly, enforces a gender differentiation originating in, and serving the interests of, the white male perspective that can only see difference as aberration and desires to displace blame for that aberration away from itself. The binary machinery at work here becomes a strategy for "naturalizing" cultural forces, not least of which is culturally and historically sanctioned "othering" of ethnic subjectivity, a strategy that has always already (over)determined the sexual politics within ethnic communities.

Corregidora: *Black Female Subjectivity and*
the Politics of Heterosexuality

The complex, binary symbolic network I have sketched out here is the target of a radical critique in Gayl Jones's novels. Because the narrative of *Corregidora* unfolds both in slavery and post-slavery time, Jones is able to represent a continuity in the cultural construction of the black woman, akin to the representation of this continuity in the historical texts I have discussed above. In *Eva's Man,* Jones plays with the discursive inscription of the Jezebel-Sapphire figure in contemporary American culture in ways which evoke the *historical* construction of black female experience. I am calling Jones's engagement with hegemonic representational structures a *deconstruction* because the texts work both with and against the language of that hegemony and bear out Henry Louis Gates's suggestion that "only a black person alienated from black language-use could fail to understand that [black people] have been deconstructing white people's languages and discourses since that dreadful day in 1619 when [they] marched off the boat in Virginia" (34). Minority discourses, as Gates implies, always exist in a dialogic relation with majority discourses, so that when a black subject speaks, she carries within her enunciation the echoes of the languages which have worked to oppress her. Mae Henderson takes this suggestion further in pointing to the specific "deconstructive function" of black *women's* texts: "to interpret or interpenetrate the signifying structures of the dominant [white and male] and subdominant [black and male and/or white and female] discourse in order to formulate a critique and, ultimately, a transformation of the white and male symbolic order" (34). Black women's writing, then, can be seen as a dialogue with both hegemonic and "ambiguously (non)hegemonic" discourses.[23] For Jones, this dialogism evokes an uneasy relationship between the black female subject and the discourses of white patriarchy that have determined black heterosexual relations in complex and troubling ways.

The inscription of black heterosexual relations in these two novels works to deconstruct the binary representational politics that place the black woman in an impossible position. As a victim of white male sexual exploitation, she has been made responsible for a sexuality that is, at once, the fantasy of the white male constructed in opposition to white femininity, and a threat to the black male's masculinity. At once Jezebel and Sapphire, the black woman has had no control over her self-representation; her "identity" has been constructed within a representational paradigm that assigns to Black and Woman a timeless essence that exists in opposition to both the White Woman and the Black Man, and that supports the hegemony of the White Man. The exploration of the heterosexual contract as a relation of male owner to female property in *Corregidora* takes on added force because of the historical experience of U.S. slavery; while the white woman has also been historically constituted as the property of the white man, the black woman has more literally been reduced to object status in that she has had the historical experience of being defined as "chattel" with no human rights. Jones's two protagonists, Ursa Corregidora and Eva Medina Canada, work to carve out spaces in which to speak their subjectivities, spaces constituted across the gaps in dominant discourses and subdominant discourses, especially narratives, that define them as objects. These texts practice what Teresa de Lauretis characterizes as "a movement between the (represented) discursive space of the positions made available by hegemonic discourses and the space-off, the elsewhere of those discourses: those other spaces that exist...in the margins...of hegemonic discourse and in the interstices of institutions" (*Technologies,* 26).

For Ursa, writing in the margins of hegemonic discourses means negotiating between her mothers' past, and its pre-written future, and her present. Ursa's narrative in *Corregidora* practices the double strategy R. Radhakrishnan describes as an articulation that "has to invoke two temporalities: that of oppression, memory, and enforced identity, and that of emergence after the 'break,' the counter-memory, and heterogeneous difference" (211). Ursa must negotiate between these two "temporalities" in order to speak her subjectivity in a mode that is neither defined solely as "enforced identity" or as "counter-memory," but is constituted in their intersection. What remains consistent in these two temporalities is a reduction of black female subjectivity to an essence located in the body and subject to a biological determinism. By having Ursa's discourse oscillate between a repetition of her mothers' stories, and a narrative of her own experience, Jones constructs a tale that demonstrates the ways in which the specificity of Corregidora's mastery gets translated into the present, in the form of a heterosexual contract based on man's complete mastery over, and ownership of, women's bodies. In order for Ursa to represent herself as subject, she must become adept at reading normative representations of the "self" that is required by the master narratives of white, patriarchal cultures. As Mae Henderson points out, black women writers "have encoded oppression as a discursive dilemma, that is, their works have consistently raised the problem of the black woman's relationship to power and discourse" (24). Thus, the "self-inscription of black women requires disruption, rereading and rewriting the conventional and canonical stories, as well as revising the conventional generic forms that convey these stories" (30). Ursa's reading, and her self-inscription, serve to denaturalize the discursive processes by which the black woman is positioned as non-self—not white and not male—and the ideologies that produce the black woman as body.

At the beginning of the novel, Ursa has been pushed down the stairs by her jealous husband, Mutt, and has "lost her womb." Ursa's "losing her womb" is the site of an overdetermined set of meanings in the text; her "accident" takes on more than ordinary, present significance in the context of the past that has made the substance of her life: descended from three generations of the Brazilian slave owner Corregidora's concubines, Ursa has been told that she must "make generations" in order to "give evidence" because when "they did away with slavery down there they burned all the slavery papers so it would be like they never had it" (9). In the absence of a written record, the Corregidora women believe that they must speak through their bodies in the form of producing children to whom they can pass on the story of Corregidora. Ursa has been fed the story of Corregidora from birth almost as a substitute for any other kind of nourishment: "I was made to touch my past at an early age. I found it on my mother's tiddies. In her milk" (77). She sees the history of Corregidora's women as "days that were *pages* of hysteria" (59; my emphasis), and asks, "What's a life always spoken, and only spoken?" (103). The problem Ursa sees with this life "only spoken" is that her mothers are passing down an already written script, a record that transcribes Corregidora's desire, but not their own. In Corregidora's narrative, black women occupy the position of body and, thus, they are spoken by him, and unable to speak themselves.

In one sense, Ursa's mothers perpetuate Corregidora's control over their bodies in their insistence that "making generations" is the only mode of expression available to them; in their belief that they can only speak with their bodies, they reproduce the construction of female subjectivity as sexuality. More importantly, they allow Corregidora to retain control over the place of enunciation by keeping him firmly in the center of their reconstructions. Ursa remembers her Great Gram's stories—always the same story, with minor variations, repeated over and over—and ponders: "It was as if the words were helping her, as if the words repeated again and again could be a substitute for memory, were somehow more than the memory. As if it were only the words that kept her anger" (11). Ursa perceives Great Gram's stories as a kind of automatic recitation over which she has no control; her narrative functions independently of her agency. As Ursa gradually comes to realize, Great Gram and Gram *have* no control over their pasts and their discourse, despite what they see as their power to "give evidence" of the horrors they experienced under Corregidora's sexual slavery. The Corregidora women are all trapped within a narrative that can only represent them through the lens of the master's desire. Ursa must learn to read this narrative against the grain, in order to envision a different desire that has been marginalized through the women's adherence to Corregidora's script.

Ursa's second husband Tadpole suggests that the obsession with "making generations" continues Corregidora's enslavement of their bodies: "Procreation. That could also be a slave-breeder's way of thinking" (22). Ursa, however, proposes another reading: "No, because it depends on if it's for you or somebody else. Your life or theirs" (23). Between Tadpole's comment and Ursa's answer, Jones inserts one of the italicized passages which proliferate throughout the text and, in this case, transcribes Great Gram's narrative. Here, the essentialized difference between the white woman and the black within Brazilian slavery comes into focus as Great Gram tells Ursa about Corregidora's wife's failure to produce her own "generations": "Naw, she couldn't do a damn thing. Naw, she didn't give him nothing but a little sick rabbit that didn't live but to be a day old.... Naw, she couldn't do a damn thing" (23). According to Great Gram, the only "thing" a white woman can do is to provide babies; but the black woman's body in Brazil had a slightly different function. Tadpole is wrong about the function of procreation within Brazilian slavery; it was the white woman who was responsible for providing children, as heirs, while the black woman functioned almost entirely as a sexual partner whose reproductive capacities would be more of a threat than an asset to her function as prostitute. As Great Gram says, Corregidora had "lands, and slaves and things, but he didn't hardly use nothing but the womens. Naw, he wasn't the first that did it. There was plenty that did it. Make the women fuck and then take their money" (23). As Carl Degler points out in his comparison of slavery in Brazil and the United States, slave women were used more as prostitutes than as "breeders," mostly because the international slave trade continued in Brazil throughout the tenure of slavery, and eradicated the need for the slave population to reproduce itself.[24]

The prostitution of the black female slave was openly encouraged in Brazil, in contrast to the more surreptitious prostitution in the United States. Degler points out that many a slave owner made his living entirely by selling the bodies of his female slaves, but the overall justification for, and effect of, this practice was the same as in the United States: to protect white women from male lust, while allowing white men a constant sexual outlet. Roger Bastide argues that miscegenation, as practiced in Brazil,

> ...effectively reduces a whole race to prostitutes. For just as the middle classes of Europe created prostitution in order to shield their daughters from the lubricity of the male, so the whites spare their own women by chan-nelling their desire towards the condemned race.... Underlying sexual relationships between different colours is this most terrifying of prejudices, which sentences a whole race to immorality in order to preserve the virgini-ty of the women of the other race. (11)[25]

But, as Angela Davis points out, the rape of black women by white men during slavery cannot be seen simply as an effect of the cultural construction of the white woman as a figure who must be protected from male lust; the "institutionalized pattern of rape," rather, can be understood as a "weapon of domination, a weapon of repression, whose covert goal was to extinguish slave women's will to resist, and in the process, to demoralize their men" (23–24).[26] As Jones makes clear in *Corregidora,* the prostitution of female slaves in Brazil amounts to an institutionalized practice of rape.[27] Like the Jezebel figure in U.S. slavery, the *mulata* slave in Brazil was constructed as a "naturally" "immoral" and promiscuous being. And, like her sister in the antebellum South, the Brazilian *mulata* was functional to the politics of racial domination: "all the legendary and folklore materials which can be collected in regard to the asserted extraordinary qualities of the woman of color—especially the *mulata,* as sexual companion—are no more than pure rationalizations of the accessibility of the *mulata* to seduction by the white."[28]

The specificity of black women's experience under Brazilian slavery informs Jones's novel, as does the history of U.S. slavery and the cultural construction of the black woman. Corregidora's "coffee bean woman" is a version of what Bastide calls the "Dusky Venus" whose erotic powers were touted by the slave owners who exploited these women's bodies, both for their pleasure and profit. Just as in U.S. slavery, the cultural construction of the black woman as Jezebel or Dusky Venus places the black man in a vulnerable position, a figurative emasculation that too often becomes a literal castration. The white master, not the black female slave, is responsible for this complementary construction of the black man, and Corregidora is obsessed with asserting his difference from his black slaves. He is careful to prohibit sexual relations among his slaves, a strategy that reinforces the property status of *his* women. Great Gram tells the story of a mulatto slave "who looked more like a white man than [Corregidora] did, so I just think he wont any excuse to get rid of him.... Anyway, he wouldn't let me see him, cause he said a black man wasn't nothing but a waste of pussy, and wear me out when it came to other mens.... He said he didn't want no waste on nothing black" (124). The fact that Great Gram was "just talking" to this man can do nothing to sway Corregidora; as a black woman, she is "naturally" promiscuous, and can only talk "with her thighs." Despite the distance between Corregidora and Mutt, they share in this construction of the black woman: Jones suggests that Mutt's obsession with safeguarding "his woman" from the gaze of other men, and the fact that he cannot view her singing as an expression of her mind as well as her body, participates in the same proprietary impulse as that exhibited by Corregidora.

Mutt resents Corregidora's hold over Ursa, not because it keeps her locked in an oppressive past with no hope for liberation, but because it militates against his own possession of her. He complains: "Ain't even took my name. You Corregidora's, ain't you? Ain't even took my name. You ain't my woman" (61). Michele Wallace's analysis of the ways in which the historical experience of slavery has influenced contemporary black heterosexual relations seems appropriate to the relationship between Mutt and Ursa: "[the black man's] actual gripe must be, at least in part, that the black woman, his woman, was not *his* slave, that his right to expect her complete service and devotion was usurped. She *was,* after all, the white man's slave" (23).[29] Mutt's almost pathological jealousy, predicated on his construction of Ursa as sexual object, is targeted at her singing. But it is not her singing *per se* that Mutt disapproves of; it is his perception of her performance as an open sexual invitation to the men in the audience that prompts him to violence. Mutt's anger is rooted in his conviction that Ursa is his property and, thus, should be safely off limits to all other men. But Mutt is not listening to Ursa's songs; his perception of her as a kind of Jezebel figure makes him assume that she is inviting men into her body, when in fact Ursa's songs are more about "closing" than "opening" her body: "I felt uncomfortable singing...any song that had anything to do with opening up. I still sang the song about the tunnel closing tight around the train and the one about the bird woman who took this man on a long journey, but never returned him" (152). Ursa deconstructs Mutt's reduction of her discourse to an emanation of her body, by writing a song that plays with the trope of female expression as "speaking the body": *"O Mister who come to my house You do not come to visit You do not come to see me to visit You come to hear me sing with my thighs You come to see me open my door and sing with my thighs"* (66–67).

Ursa's narrative throughout the novel links Mutt with Corregidora, and demonstrates the ways in which the men in her own life have foreclosed the possibility that she might want to be *her own woman,* and not "theirs." Ursa's memories of Mutt get all mixed up with the stories of Corregidora, and the two men occupy interchangeable positions in her dreams. When Mutt says "Your pussy's a little gold piece.... My little gold piece" (60), he echoes Corregidora. The fact that the narrative also gives these words to Tadpole suggests that both Mutt and Tadpole are versions of Corregidora. It is not important whether or not they all "really" say these things; the significance in the repetition is that Ursa makes the connection, and does so in the process of her reading the present as implicated in the past. While it is true that Ursa's obsession with Corregidora tends to paralyze her in the present, and that Mutt and Tadpole do try to help her overcome this paralysis; it is also true that they, too, are responsible for perpetuating Corregidora's sexual slavery. Mutt, at one point, even tries to prostitute Ursa, in an act that is as *self*-deprecatory as it is degrading to Ursa. Frustrated by Ursa's refusal to give up her work, Mutt vows to go to the club and auction her off: "'That's what I'm gon do,' he said.... 'One a y'all wont to bid for her? Piece a ass for sale'" (159). When Mutt decides not to do this, it is not Ursa he is thinking of, but rather his great grandfather—an ex-slave who bought his wife's freedom, only to have her "repossessed" when he fell into financial difficulties. Mutt explains: "It wasn't on account of you, it was on account of my great-grandaddy. Seeing as how he went through all that for his woman, he wouldn't have appreciated me selling you off" (160).

This detail about Mutt's family history, as well as the details about the male slaves on Corregidora's plantation, makes it clear that Jones places Mutt's behavior in the historical context of racial oppression which has left him powerless. But while this context can help explain how he treats Ursa, it cannot justify his reduction of her to a "piece of ass"—more specifically, *his* piece of ass. Ursa's narrative represents her struggle to attain control both over the place of enunciation and over her own body and sexuality, to write in the margins of Corregidora/Mutt's discourse, in order to "give evidence" through a form of expression that disrupts two different versions of male constructions of woman as sexual object. Since she can no longer "make generations," Ursa determines to rewrite the story of Corregidora's "coffee bean woman," Great Gram, because "Everything said in the beginning must be said better than in the beginning": "I'll make a fetus out of grounds of coffee to rub inside my eyes. When it's time to give witness, I'll make a fetus out of grounds of coffee. I'll stain their hands." (54) Ursa's desire here is to unmake Corregidora's "coffee bean woman," in order to remake her; to give birth to a woman who would not be always already engendered by Corregidora's legacy. Her fantasy of rubbing the coffee grounds inside her eyes suggests her desire to see the world and history anew, to subvert the hold Corregidora has over the construction of that history: "I wanted a song that would touch my life *and* theirs. A Portuguese song, but not a Portuguese song. A new world song. A song branded with the new world" (59). Ursa's desire to revise the narrative in which her mothers are trapped is not a desire to forget the past. Ursa cannot simply step "outside" sexist and racist representational structures, in order to speak a story uncontaminated by them; rather, she must oscillate between inside and outside, writing in the margins of Corregidora's narrative. This double strategy will allow Ursa to negotiate between Corregidora's essentialist representation of the black woman as sexual object and what that representation leaves out, the possibility that the women can represent themselves as subjects.

Throughout the text, Ursa questions the reduction of women to sex—a questioning precipitated by Great Gram's stories about Corregidora, her own experience with Mutt, and her attempt to come to terms with the fact that she can no longer make the generations that she has been compelled to believe is her entire *raison d'être*. As Jones's critics have pointed out, this is a vicious circle in which the Corregidora women themselves are complicit. What these critics have consistently ignored, however, is Ursa's analysis —indeed, her deconstruction—of the ideology that reduces a woman to her sex. Ursa oscillates between acceptance and critique of this ideology in a textual movement which suggests that Ursa both does and does not see herself from within the framework of this cultural construction of woman. She speaks, as Caren Kaplan would put it, "in the interstices of masculine culture, moving between use of the dominant language and a form of expression and specific versions of experience based on [her] marginality" (187).[30] Ursa mimics the language of Corregidora and Mutt, and their construction of black womanhood as itself marginal to subjectivity; Ursa speaks *as* sexual object, and thus deconstructs the narratives that place her in this position:

> Maybe it's just that a man can't stand to have a woman as hard as he is. If he couldn't support her in money, he'd be wanting to support her in spirit. And what if I'd thrown Mutt Thomas down those stairs instead, and done away with the source of his sex, or inspiration, or whatever the hell it is for a man, what would he feel now? At least a woman's still got the hole. Look, nigger, I still got my hole. Finger-pop it. (40–41)
>
> *Are you mine, Ursa, or theirs?* What he would ask. What would I ask now? Do you want to see me? Naw, I don't want to see you, I want to screw you…. But it's your fault all my seeds are wounded forever. Let me in between your legs. It ain't a pussy down there, it's a whole world. Talking about *his* pussy. Asking me to let him see his pussy. The center of a woman's being. Is it? No seeds. Is that what snaps away my music, a harp string broken, guitar string, string of my banjo belly strain in my voice. (45–46)

Here, Ursa not only questions Mutt/Corregidora's construction of woman as a "hole" that exists to be filled according to man's desire, but also her mothers' belief that a black woman's reproductive capacity must be the "center" of her being. Both constructions of the female subject—or, better, object—are predicated on a kind of biological determinism that forecloses the possibility that the "center of a woman's being" might not be determined by her body. The contradiction between her mothers' beliefs and Mutt's desire places Ursa in limbo; while the Corregidora women tell Ursa that her center is her womb, Mutt tells her it is her "pussy." This limbo becomes even more pronounced when she is no longer able to "make generations." But both versions of female destiny or essence amount to the same thing. Mutt's view reinforces Corregidora's; as I argued above, it was the female slave's "hole," not her womb, that was of value to her Brazilian master.

In a certain sense, then, the desire to "make generations" subverts Corregidora's definition of black female sexuality, and indicates that the Corregidora women are, in fact, taking their sexuality into their own control. This becomes clear through Ursa's mother's experience; she, in effect, takes control and only sleeps with Martin because she wants to "make generations." She tells Ursa: "Like my body or something knew what it wanted even if I didn't want no man. Cause I knew I wasn't lookin for none. But it was like it knew it wanted you. It was like my whole body knew it wanted you, and knew it would have you, and knew you'd be a girl" (114). However, Mama's use of the pronoun "it" here to signify her body suggests that she is not really in control of her sexuality; her ascription of desire to her body as an "it" separate from her, implies that she is not a sexual, subjective agent in this transaction. Like her mothers', her body is not under her own control, although it appears that Mama is determining her own "center." Whether Ursa sees herself as a "hole" or a "womb," the result is the same; both cultural constructions reduce her subjectivity to a bodily force that functions independently of her agency. Ursa finds this "centering" of her identity inadequate to describe "what snaps away [her] music"; Ursa sees that her body is a part of her expression, but not the (w)hole.

Because of the contradictions Ursa experiences between her status as object and her desire as subject, she suffers from a kind of sexual paralysis. The novel's critics, however, have tended to focus on the crippling effects of Ursa's mothers' discourse as an explanation of this paralysis, and have ignored the fact that Mutt participates in foreclosing the possibility of a sexual subjectivity for Ursa. Janice Harris, for

example, argues that the contradictions implicit in the Corregidora women's stories are what place Ursa in an impossible position: "But making generations is making love; and
there is the crippling contradiction in the message Ursa has
been nursed upon. Ursa is taught to make love in order to
keep alive an historical tale of rape. She is bred up to make
generations to carry on a saga of the brutality of man to
woman, owner to property, master to slave" (2). But Ursa is
not alone in carrying on the "saga of the brutality of man to
woman"; Mutt's attitude toward her perpetuates the relation
of "owner to property, master to slave" independently of her
agency. Ursa senses the contradictions in her mothers' message, but also realizes that what these women have to say
needs to be said—only differently. She needs to find a form
of enunciation that keeps these contradictions in suspension,
and finds it in the blues: "*What do the blues do for you?*
They help me to explain what I can't explain" (56). What
Ursa can't explain is the ambivalence she senses in her
mothers' relation to their master, and in her own relations
with men: "All those blues feelings.... What do they say
about pleasure mixed in the pain?" (50).[31] Here, Ursa
echoes her father's question about Corregidora, as related to
her by her mother: "I think what really made them dislike
Martin was because he had the nerve to ask them what I
never had the nerve to ask.... How much was hate for Corregidora and how much was love" (131).

Martin's question carries some authority in the text, particularly because it is spoken by Ursa's Mama when finally
enjoined to tell her own story; but to give priority to Martin's
insight means to disallow the women's construction of their
own experience, and to obscure the power relations operative
in that experience. Despite the fact that Corregidora retains
hegemony over the place of enunciation, Great Gram and
Grandmama's desire to articulate their experience of oppression responds to a real need to "give evidence," to prevent
the erasure of their history. To "blame" Great Gram and
Grandmama for perpetuating Corregidora's mastery—and to
"blame" Ursa for Mutt's obsession with owning her—as many
of Jones's critics do, means to absolve both Mutt and Cor-

regidora of responsibility. Keith Byerman notes that Ursa has used her hatred for both Corregidora and Mutt in a way that makes her complicit in her own victimization; "the hatred of domination and oppression itself becomes obsessive," and thus leads Ursa to perpetuate the vicious circle begun by Corregidora (178). Melvin Dixon goes one step further and argues that Mutt's violence against Ursa enables her "to free herself from the pattern of *mutual* abuse implicit in the pledge [to make generations] itself" (239), and thus effectively validates the novel's male voices, at the expense of the female voices. In a certain sense, Dixon is right; that is, the consequences of Mutt's violence, the fact that Ursa can no longer "make generations," frees her from the necessity of perpetuating the hold Corregidora has over the women in her family. But the fact that Mutt's act causes Ursa to "lose her womb" itself "gives evidence" of what the male characters in the novel cannot recognize: the fact that their attitudes toward Ursa also work to perpetuate a kind of sexual slavery.

While the question of the women's complicity in their own oppression is indeed central to the text, it is complicated by the power relations intricated in both the past and present experience Jones chronicles. *Corregidora* explores the Hegelian master/slave dialectic as it describes a pattern of mutual dependency between master and slave, but goes beyond Hegel in foregrounding the ways in which his formulation naturalizes a dynamic that, in the black woman's experience, can better be explained by socioeconomic relations. In Alexander Kojève's reading of Hegel, he stresses the ways in which the "slavish" consciousness can transcend the deadlock of the master/slave dialectic by his power to transform natural objects into commodities for the master's consumption. While the master has all the "real power" in the relationship, this power is productive only to the extent that it forces the slave to *work;* and, because the master has access to this productivity only through the mediation of his slave, he lacks the power to realize what Kojève describes as "the *sine qua non* of historical progress," the ability to transform the natural world and to make history (23). Kojève concludes that "thus, in the long run, all slavish work realizes not the Master's will, but the will—at first unconscious—of the Slave, who—finally—succeeds where the Master—necessarily—fails. Therefore, it is indeed the originally dependent, serving, and slavish Consciousness that in the end realizes and reveals the ideal of autonomous Self-Consciousness and is thus its 'truth'" (29–30).

One problem with Hegel's account, in its emphasis on the process by which the slave "outmasters" the master, is that it depends on the slave transforming natural objects into commodities to satisfy the master's desire. The dubious benefits of a deferred "transcendence" are complicated within the economics of literal slavery, where the slave has no hope of transforming history without *first* transforming the economic system that defines the black slave as "chattel," on the same level as "livestock" or even household possessions.[32] The deferral here has much in common with the nineteenth century American Christian doctrine of self-denial as a path toward "salvation," as exemplified in Harriet Beecher Stowe's Uncle Tom. The ideology that assigns to the "meek" slave the future transcendence over the master in an indefinitely deferred promise of "paradise" can be read as a weapon in the justification of the slaves' oppression, as well as an ideology that protected the white population from the threat of slave insurrections. Hegel's idealistic reading of the powers of slavish consciousness cannot take into account the fact that, in U.S. slavery, for example, the slave was considered as herself a "natural object" in two senses: she was "closer to nature" than the master's race, and she was an object that the master owned by legal and "natural" right. This problem becomes even more pronounced when sexual exploitation is taken into account: What happens when the slave *herself* is the object desired by the master? While Hegel demonstrates that the master's desire is always mediated by the slave, and vice versa, he makes no provision for analyzing a kind of slavery that produces the slave as *object* for the master's consumption. This is the experience of slavery described by Jones in *Corregidora,* and the impasse in which the Corregidora women find themselves—their inability to "transcend" slavish consciousness—might be explained by the fact that they have had to produce *themselves* as objects for consumption. In this sense, we could read Ursa's desire to get beyond this impasse as a desire to *work:* to transform the Corregidora women's object status into subjectivity.

Abdul JanMohamed, in an article on colonial discourse, politicizes Hegel's dialectic by focusing on the ways in which this theoretical construct gets translated into a politics of domination, both in the socioeconomic arena and in representation.[33] The colonialist, as master, has the political power to subjugate the native, and thus is

> ...able to compel the Other's recognition of him and, in the process, allow his own identity to become deeply dependent on his position as master. This enforced recognition from the Other in fact amounts to the European's narcissistic self-recognition since the native, who is considered too degraded and inhuman to be credited with any specific subjectivity, is cast as no more than a recipient of the negative elements of the self that the European projects onto him. ("Colonialist Literature," 66–67)

But, since the master's desire is mediated through the native/slave, he suffers an alienation that results in violence against the Other on whom he has projected his own negative qualities. What JanMohamed calls the "fetishization of the Other," "the process of substituting natural or generic categories for those that are socially or ideologically determined" (67), is precisely what happens in Hegel's account of the master/slave relation and in the nineteenth century discourses on U.S. and Brazilian slavery; if one social group is always already constituted as master, another group "naturally" falls into the category of slave.

It is the "naturalness" of these binary categories that is the target of Jones's critique in *Corregidora*. In the last scene of the novel, we see Ursa play out the possibility of reversing the master/slave positions, and of claiming a potential power as victim of sexual exploitation. This scene transpires between Ursa and Mutt, but once again, the distinctions between Mutt and Corregidora get blurred, as Ursa admits,

"It was like I didn't know how much was me and Mutt and how much was Great Gram and Corregidora" (184). Ursa and Mutt have returned to each other after several years of being alone. As Ursa takes his penis in her mouth, she replays an imagined scene between Great Gram and Corregidora, thinking:

> It had to be sexual, I was thinking, it had to be something sexual that Great Gram did to Corregidora. I knew it had to be sexual: "What is it a woman can do to a man that make him hate her so bad he wont to kill her one minute and keep thinking about her and can't get her out of his mind the next?" In a split second I knew what it was, in a split second of hate and love I knew what it was, and I think he might have known it too. A moment of pleasure and excruciating pain at the same time, a moment of broken skin but not sexlessness, a moment just before sexlessness, a moment that stops just before sexlessness, a moment that stops before it breaks the skin: "I could kill you." (184)

Ursa's power in this scene indicates a temporary reversal of the master/slave relation, but does not break the circuit of oppression/victimization that marks Jones's presentation of heterosexual relations. Although Ursa recognizes Mutt's vulnerability, metaphorically rendered by the threat of castration, this scene locks the male and female agents into the circular pattern of a master/slave dialectic with no hope for escape. Keith Byerman argues that Jones presents heterosexual love as a dialectical relation structured by the "paradox of desire"; "men are obsessed with women even though they know their obsession makes them vulnerable." For Byerman, this paradox "is precisely the power that women have over men" (179), an explicitly sexual power that raises the specter of both Jezebel and Sapphire. Byerman suggests that, for Jones, this is the "natural" state of affairs, and thus fixes the male and female agents in a kind of timeless essence based on the complementarity of gendered positions. Where some critics see this last scene as a "catharsis" or a resolution of the conflicts that have structured the novel,[34] I read it as more of a stalemate—a logical, if unsatisfactory, conclusion to the text's exploration of racial and sexual mythologies. Ursa might play the part of Jezebel or Sapphire in this scene, but that is the only part available to her within the network of binary representational politics within the text. Jones does, indeed, flirt with these cultural constructions of the black woman—more in *Eva's Man,* than in *Corregidora;* but she does so in order to deconstruct them by focusing on the power relations that necessitate the placement of the black woman in these positions.

The mutual dependence between master and slave—both literal and figurative—is not a "natural" state of affairs; rather, it is a justification for a history of racial and sexual exploitation that Jones critiques, not endorses. What Mutt and Ursa play out in this last scene is an historically determined exchange, not an isolated or purely personal one. At the end of the novel, Ursa asks: "But was what Corregidora had done to *her,* to *them,* any worse than what Mutt had done to me, than what we had done to each other, than what Mama had done to Daddy, or what he had done to her in return?" (184). The desire that mobilizes this question is not the desire to attribute blame, as indicated by the fact that Ursa does not answer it. Rather, this question resounds back through the text as a final comment on the sexual and racial politics that lock the black woman—and the black man—in a complex symbolic network that denies them agency in their situational specificity. The complicity between Ursa and Mutt in this scene parallels *Corregidora*'s complicity in cultural mythologies of gender and race. That is, as in Carter's deconstructive fictions, Jones's text inscribes in order to subvert dominant representational paradigms that construct gender and race as essences. Despite the deadlock implicit in this last scene—represented by Ursa's compliance with the very heterosexual contract she has worked to displace through her narrative—her rereading of the discursive systems that have positioned the black woman in a space outside of subjectivity stands as a powerful critique of those systems, a critique that sets the stage for the more radical displacements that operate in *Eva's Man.*

Eva's Man: *Excess as Subversion*

Eva's Man begins with the *fait accompli* of what Ursa only fantasized about: Eva Medina Canada is in a prison asylum for poisoning, then castrating Davis Carter. She takes the victim's insight into the vulnerability of the oppressor to its logical, if perverse conclusion. The details of the events leading up to Eva's act are murky, at best; while some critics argue that Eva was kept as a prisoner for five days in the hotel room, I would argue that this is only one of several competing interpretations the novel offers. The narrative of *Eva's Man* is composed of dreams, memories, interrogation scenes, and exchanges between Eva and her cell-mate Elvira; it is a narrative originating in Eva's consciousness and is fragmented and disjointed. As Jones remarks in an interview, Eva is an unreliable narrator who takes control over her story, but does not put the pieces of the puzzle together for us.[35] The narrative resists unity, and the reader is left to soak up Eva's experience, just as Eva's consciousness throughout her life is presented as a kind of sponge, soaking up the scenes she has witnessed and participated in. Unlike the Corregidora women, however, Eva exercises a certain control over her narrative; while Great Gram and Grandmama speak in a kind of automatic repetition beyond their agency, and are unable to change the narrative of their history, Eva's narrative actively shapes her history so that others' representations of her are displaced by her self-representation.

The fact that all of Eva's memories and dreams address sexual exploitation of women has led the novel's critics to see Eva's act as the logical—if extreme and violent—reaction to the overwhelming pattern of male domination of women's bodies which describes her experience.[36] In my view, however, this impulse places those critics on the side of the authorities who attempt to explain Eva, to unify her story, in order to provide her narrative with a closure that the novel itself resists. The authorities with whom Eva comes into contact—including the police, the court officers, the psychiatrists and the press—attempt to pigeonhole Eva within the parameters of their discourse, to (re)place her firmly in a predetermined position as chaotic dehumanized Other to the "rational," fully human Self. Eva is more subversive than the novel's critics have given her credit for; in resisting cooptation into authoritative discourse, Eva's story follows its own logic and, like the blues, *expresses* rather than *explains* her experience.[37] Eva is a character who, in Jones's terms, "invents herself"[38] in a narrative performance that resists recuperation into a discourse which would attempt to ascertain her position in relation to itself. Her refusal to explain her act (her*self*) is one of two subversive strategies Eva practices; the other is her excessive identification with mythological figures of black womanhood. Like Ursa, Eva's subjectivity is constituted through contradiction; she writes across the gaps in hegemonic discourses, moving fluidly inside and outside these discourses, in a doubled narrative movement that puts into play the contradictions between her objectification and her subjectivity. This subjectivity is not a fixed identity—essential, singular, determinate, coherent; Eva's subjectivity is a process of multiple identification with different discursive constructions of the black woman that functions to dismantle those constructions. While various discourses work to recontain Eva in an essential Otherness, and thus to reduce the threat she represents, Eva's narrative works against this kind of recuperation. She remains in a position of excess in relation to hegemonic discourse, not as its essential Other, but as a subjectivity that threatens the coherence of the discursive systems that depend on her marginality. Eva does not, then, move from margin to center; rather, she "remain[s] on the borders of discourse, speaking from the vantage point of the insider/outsider" (Henderson, 36).[39]

Various authority figures in the novel attempt to explain Eva's crime by fitting it into a ready-made model. These official figures incessantly enjoin Eva to talk about her past because they are convinced that this past must be the key to her recent action. As Eva admits, however, her memories are sometimes fabrications; her narrative weaves remembered experiences with fantasies that, in significant ways, comment critically on those experiences. It is not always possible to discern if Eva is "telling the truth" or not; she is playing games with her listeners—both diagetic and extradiagetic—challenging them and us to make sense out of her story. Eva tells the reader, at the beginning of her narrative, how her questioners want to hear about "things that don't even have to do with what I did.... Sometimes they think I'm lying to them, though. I tell them it ain't me lying, it's memory lying. I don't believe that, because the past is still as hard on me as the present, but I tell them that anyway. They say they're helping me. I'm forty-three years old, and I ain't seen none of their help yet" (5). Eva plays the game, but makes up her own rules as she goes along, resisting the straightforward interpretations these official speakers want to impose on her. As her cell-mate Elvira observes, the authorities need to see her as crazy, to explain her in this way "cause it's easier for them if they keep on thinking it. A woman done what you done to a man" (41). The most "rational" explanation of Eva's behavior would be to see her murder, then castration, of Davis as a logical reaction to a personal history of sexual exploitation and abuse.[40] While Eva's memories and thoughts might indeed lead us to this explanation, the novel warns us against such an easy answer. When Eva is in a session with one of the various "Dr. Frauds" in the prison, it becomes clear that this explanation of her behavior can be given little validity. Here is the exchange between Eva and the psychiatrist:

> "You know what I think," the psychiatrist said. "I think he came to represent all the men you'd known in your life."
> "Who?"
> "I got *something* out of you," he said. He was proud of himself. (81)

Eva resists this explanation by asking the question "Who?", a question that represents her refusal to be assimilated into the discourse that would rationalize her behavior. This particular "Dr. Fraud" has a predetermined narrative in which he hopes to insert the "Eva" who is necessary to that narrative's coherence. She refuses this predetermined positioning by questioning the appropriateness of that narrative to her experience and, thus, refuses to play the pyschiatrist's game. The psychiatrist's response and Eva's reaction to it, moreover, foreground what is at stake in trying to get an explanation out of her: it is his success, rather than Eva's health, that the psychiatrist is interested in.[41] After a long session of psychological badgering toward the end of the novel, Eva speaks the words that I read as a warning to the reader, as well as to the psychiatrist: "Don't explain me. Don't you explain me. Don't you explain me" (173). All of the answers offered by the psychiatrists are attempts to appropriate Eva's story in order to fit it into a neat little pattern; Eva's greatest act of defiance is to refuse all such patterns. The psychiatrist, like the other representatives of the judicial machinery brought into play by Eva's act, is titillated by what Eva has done. The fact that his name is Smoot, the name of the first male to have "messed" with Eva, causes her to chuckle in a recognition of the psychiatrist's complicity in the structures of sexual domination her act has brought into question.

While Eva's silence does, in one sense, place her in the margins of hegemonic discourse, as a disempowered subject—or, rather, *object*—of discourse, she speaks from those margins by weaving her own narrative that follows its own logic. On the other hand, Eva's narrative situates her squarely in the center of hegemonic discourses when she mimics the cultural constructions of black woman as essential Other, as pure and dangerous sexuality; she subverts these representations by *exceeding* them, and thus denaturalizing and defamiliarizing them. Her acting upon Ursa's fantasy can be read as a mode of excess that serves to critique the cultural construction of black female sexuality: In literally castrating Davis, Eva claims a power that mythologies of race and gender have always assigned to women, at least metaphorically. Throughout the text, Eva identifies with three mythological female figures who have in common one thing: they hold a deadly power over men. Eva's identification with Medusa, the Queen Bee, and Eve literalizes the metaphorical construction of the black woman as a victim of her own excessive sexuality who, in turn, victimizes men.[42] These figures all represent *for* the hegemon-

ic perspective a devouring female sexuality that both originates in, and feeds, male fears, including the fear of the
devouring mother. We can see this fear at work in the myth of
the black matriarch that has been taken up by black sociolo-
gists and psychologists.[43] Eva inscribes this male fear of the
maternal in thinking, "A man sucking milk from her breasts.
He is sucking blood" (131). This death-dealing "she," deliberately unidentified by Eva, plays on mythologies of black womanhood, as the novel asks the question: What would happen if
the mythologies were enacted literally? Eva mimics these
mythological constructions with a vengeance, as it were.

Eva's Man engages in the "feminine" operation of
mimicry, theorized by Irigaray, but with certain key (political) differences. Irigaray's formulation is, arguably, grounded
in an ethnocentric orientation toward "woman" that cannot
begin to account for the situational specificity of women
from different cultural locations. For Irigaray:

> To play with mimesis is thus, for a woman, to try to recov-
> er the place of her exploitation by discourse, without
> allowing herself to be simply reduced to it. It means to
> resubmit herself—inasmuch as she is on the side of the
> "perceptible," of "matter"—to "ideas," in particular to
> ideas about herself, that are elaborated in/by a masculine
> logic, but so as to make "visible," by an act of playful rep-
> etition, what was supposed to remain invisible: the cover-
> up of a possible operation of the feminine in language. It
> also means "to unveil" the fact that, if women are such
> good mimics, it is because they are simply resorbed in
> this function. They also remain elsewhere. (This Sex, 76)

When Irigaray argues that "mimicry" is the position "historically assigned to the feminine," she is referring to the idea
that women have always been required to "specularize" men;
that is, the feminine position has historically been constituted
as a "bad copy" of the masculine. The feminine, "within discourse," has always been "defined as lack, deficiency, or as
imitation and negative image of the subject" (78). Eva's
experience seems to support this characterization of the fem-

inine, and its function in hegemonic discourse: like Ursa, Eva has been defined as a "hole" to be filled by man, as an object that can only experience subjectivity by proxy, as it were. As I will argue, Eva does, indeed, take up a position of mimicry in her literalization of the metaphors which have defined woman, and specifically, black woman, and she also "remains elsewhere" in what Irigaray calls a "disruptive excess" (78). This excess, however, is not a "sexual pleasure" vaguely posited in opposition to a masculine logic, although Eva's excess does work to deconstruct the logic of masculine desire; indeed, the black woman has had a very different discursive relationship to the "feminine" than the white woman, and Irigaray's formulation can be critiqued on these grounds.[44] Eva's excess is more accurately described as the process of "a paradoxical movement between minor and major"—or margin and center—in "a refusal to admit either position as final or static" (Kaplan, 189). The "elsewhere" of Eva's mimicry is a place of power.[45]

Homi Bhabha deploys a similar theoretical construct in his argument about how mimicry can disrupt colonial power and authority, focusing on race rather than gender.[46] For Bhabha, colonial discourses are always ambivalent because, like the fetishist's logic,[47] they rest on a simultaneous recognition and disavowal of "native" difference. To put this in simpler terms, the colonial project is divided against itself in that it has two contradictory aims: to construct the "native" as Other by a dehumanization that facilitates appropriation; and to construct the colonized population as subject of/to the "civilizing" force of·European rule. We saw this process at work in *Children of Violence,* particularly in relation to Martha's comments about her "invisible black sister" who is, in Bhabha's terms, "a subject of a difference that is almost the same, but not quite" ("Of Mimicry and Man," 126). These contradictory aims produce a "discursive system split in enunciation that, in turn, constitutes a dispersed and variously positioned native who by (mis)appropriating the terms of the dominant ideology, is able to intercede against and resist this mode of construction."[48]

Thus, Bhabha works against an analysis which would

posit colonial discourses and authority as unitary, and as a mode of "autocolonization" against which resistance would be extremely difficult, if not impossible. While the colonialist desires a mimicry on the part of the native, it is possible for that mimicry to destabilize the very power and authority it is meant to secure. Bhabha writes:

> Mimicry is, thus, the sign of a double articulation; a complex strategy of reform, regulation, and discipline, which 'appropriates' the Other as it visualizes power. Mimicry is also the sign of the inappropriate, however, a difference or recalcitrance which coheres the dominant strategic function of colonial power, intensifies surveillance, and poses an immanent threat to both 'normalized' knowledges and disciplinary powers. ("Of Mimicry and Man," 126)

Bhabha's focus, in my view, is more on the internal disruptions of colonial discourse—its self-deconstructing authority—than on the subversive possibilities of a "native" mimicry, of, as Benita Parry puts it, "returning the look of surveillance as the displacing gaze of the disciplined" in order to "menace" colonial authority (41).[49] Still, the idea that the colonized can intervene into the terms of his/her construction as other, and (mis)appropriate those terms for subversive purposes is entirely relevant to what I am arguing here. Eva's mimicry takes the terms of a culturally sanctioned marginalization and turns them against the authority of a colonizing power.

In his focus on the gaze and his invocation of fetishism, Bhabha's theory of colonial mimicry has more than a little in common with the theory of feminine masquerade that I discussed in my reading of Angela Carter. Eva's performance, as mimicry of the cultural construction of black womanhood in my terms—or, the terms of colonial appropriation in Bhabha's—is a kind of masquerade that serves to disrupt the very representations it mimics.[50] By actively turning the gaze on herself, by inviting her "official" audience to see her as the spectacular and negative image of their own singularity, Eva effectively forces a disruption of the coercive power of those who place her under surveillance. This kind of strategy, according to Abdul JanMohamed, is paradigmatic of "the negation of negation as a form of affirmation" in minority discourse. JanMohamed argues that, in a racist society, there is always a *struggle* over black subjectivity because it is in the interests of the hegemonic group to retain control over that subjectivity. In a reading of Richard Wright's *Black Boy,* he argues that this double negation works by Wright "establishing a specular relation with society's attempt to negate him; he turned himself into a mirror that reflected the negation back at the hegemony" (247). Jones pursues a similar strategy. Although Eva's mimicry, in some sense, serves to perpetuate her cultural marginality—in that she simply takes up the position that is provided for her within hegemonic discourses, the position that gives those discourses coherence by virtue of her exclusion from them—it can also serve to deconstruct those discourses. It is, as Bhabha suggests, "at once resemblance and menace" ("Of Mimicry and Man," 127). If Eva "has imprisoned herself in the debilitating stereotypes of Queen Bee, Medusa, and Eve long before she is locked away for her crime," as Melvin Dixon argues (245), her literalization of these metaphors stands as a critique of the cultural construction of black womanhood.

These metaphors are double-edged in that, while they reduce woman to an excessive sexuality to be "serviced" by men, they also carry within them the potential to disrupt the discourses of male domination.[51] As Eva sits in her prison cell, she thinks back to her experience, and transcribes the discourses which enforce the cultural construction of woman as Jezebel, in language deployed by both men and women. She remembers a conversation with Mama and Miss Billie, about the latter's daughter, that situates woman as a figure of voracious sexual appetite. Jones transcribes this conversation without comment, but then inserts one of the italicized passages which function as indices of Eva's fabricated intervention into her memories:

"Yeah, well, all I hope is she ain't let him had none, cause once she let him get some, she ain't gon rest till he get some more."

"Naw, once they done it, they ain't satisfied till they done it again."

"Yeah, that's what I'm worried about," Miss Billie said.

"You let me do it once."

"I ain't gon let you do it no more."

"When you gon let me fuck you again, Eva?"

"You didn't fuck me before." (15)

What is significant in the conversation between Miss Billie and Mama is the blurring of sexual agency between gender positions; while the man "gets it," it is the woman who "lets" him "have" it. In Mama's reply, the pronoun "they" functions to confuse these two positions, and to raise the question of whose satisfaction is at stake here, the man's or the woman's. Mama and Miss Billie's representation of heterosexual relations, thus, places the two agents in a mutual complicity based on the notion that both the man and the woman are insatiable, their sexuality out of control. This is the dialectical representation of heterosexuality we saw in *Corregidora*. But the italicized passage, indicating Eva's intervention into the discourse, disrupts the vicious circle of mutual complicity, and serves as a negation of the ideological construction of the black woman that gives this narrative its coherence. If Eva can refuse to participate, much as she refuses to explain herself, then she cannot be "blamed" for arousing a sexual desire that, then, comes back to exploit her.

Another of Miss Billie's statements circulates through the text, and this time, Elvira intervenes by asking an unauthorized question: "'Once you open your legs, Miss Billie said, it seem like you cain't close them.'...[Elvira] looked at me hard. 'What about once you close them?' she asked" (15–16). This question is as unauthorized as is Ursa's question about Great Gram's desire in *Corregidora;* it articulates the possibility that women might have control over their own sexuality, whereas Miss Billie's and Mama's construction of female sexuality— enforced by the male voices in the text—situates it as a force that women can't control, and that makes them responsible for satisfying the male desire that they have evoked. Elvira keeps asking this question throughout the text, until Eva finally says, "Once you close your legs, you keep them closed" (142). Before Eva can come to this conclusion, however, she must work through her experience, rewriting it as she sees fit, in order to consider fully the consequences of this dialectical conceptualization of heterosexual relations—that is, the notion that women are complicit in provoking male desire, and thus only get "what they ask for." Eva remembers when she was seventeen and her cousin Alfonso tells her "You too old not to had the meat" (58), and keeps courting her, expecting her to sleep with him, and then chiding her for being "hard" when she refuses. Since sexuality is an arena of power relations in Jones's texts, such statements must be understood within the context of a potential violence and exploitation. This man is the same one who beats up his wife regularly, in what one (male) observer sees as their "working some kind of blues ritual" (131). If the "blues ritual" suggests the mutual complicity of husband and wife, it also suggests that it is the husband who wields the real power in the relationship—as we have seen in *Corregidora*. Alfonso shares with Miss Billie and Mama the assumption that women are responsible for making men vulnerable to their sexuality, and the assumption that a woman represents a "hole" to be filled with "the meat." Eva soaks up this mythology, and begins to identify with the figure who embodies this contradiction: the Queen Bee.

The Queen Bee is a character from Eva's childhood whose legendary power over men receives two different interpretations. Her story is that any man who loves her finds an untimely and bizarre end. The first interpretation, the one endorsed by Davis, is that she is guilty of luring men with her eyes—shades of Medusa—and then causing their deaths. The second, the one endorsed by Eva, is more sympathetic to the Queen Bee, who ended up killing herself after falling in love, in order to save the man from what she saw as his unavoidable destiny. Eva interprets the Queen Bee by saying "She must've been sucked hollow. She must've had nothing left"—to which Davis replies: "Naw, those men kept bringing it to her. She must've sucked them hollow. That's why they died. Cause *they* had nothing left" (73–74). Davis's interpretation is predicated on the construction of woman as a "hole" that exists only to be filled up by a man, while Eva's interpretation assigns to the Queen Bee the humanity—and desire—that Davis would attempt to deny her. In killing Davis, Eva literalizes the metaphor of the Queen Bee; in doing so, she challenges the ideology that has produced woman as a lethal force in the first place. Keith Byerman suggests that she is an example of characters who "become grotesque either by being victims who personify and exaggerate their society's obsessions or by resisting its conventions, sometimes by carrying them to their logical and violent extreme." Byerman argues that such grotesques can either reinforce cultural hegemony or resist it through exploring alternatives to domination (171); I would argue that Eva does both simultaneously—that is, she resists *through* her excessive and exaggerated identification with hegemonic constructions of black womanhood.

As the history of discourses on black sexuality demonstrates, the cultural construction of the black woman is *complemented* by a cultural construction of the black man. We see this complementarity in *Corregidora,* in Jones's exploration of the the dialectic structured around female vulnerability and male power, which can be turned—at least provisionally—into female power and male vulnerability. In *Eva's Man,* Jones goes further in what I see as a deconstruction of this dynamic, and its bases in the historical construction of black sexuality—both female *and* male. The Queen Bee is the figure that most closely describes this dialectical relation based on the mythological construction of black sexuality as an insatiable force. Eva's cousin Alfonso is a caricature of a black man who is as "obsessed with his genitals as the white man" has been throughout history (Wallace, 73). This obsession, of course, originates in white fears of black male sexuality as an animal virility unmitigated by "moral" values, and has as its historical consequence the institutionalized lynching of black men who were, more often than not, framed on rape charges.[52] The myth of the black rapist has as its complement the myth of the black woman as Jezebel. Thus, Eva learns from her mother and Miss Billie that women have an insatiable appetite for sex, and that men are reducible to their genitals. The young Eva, who has internalized this dualistic representation, sees Mr. Logan—a threatening male figure—as a human phallus: "I was scared of him after what Miss Billie said. I kept expecting something white to come out of him" (19). As Gerda Lerner points out, "the myth of the black rapist...is the twin of the myth of the bad black woman—both designed to apologize for and facilitate the continued exploitation of black men and women."[53] Because of the binary mechanisms at play in the construction of sexual difference, an "oversexed" black male is needed to complement an "oversexed" black female—and both cultural constructions are necessary to the production of racial difference. In this case, the inscription of racial difference overshadows that of sexual difference, as the black subject is produced by the dominant discourse as essential Other to the hegemonic self. Because of the power of discourse to construct human experience, it is not surprising that these myths have had material effects on the Afro-American community.

Michele Wallace argues that the black man learned to use this white fear as a road to power; writers such as Richard Wright began "to present the white nightmare, Black Macho, as a vehicle of liberation" (73).[54] The consequences of this literalization of the "white nightmare of black sexuality" on the black woman are severe, and Wallace cites black male sexism as a force that has militated against the liberation of the black community as a whole. While it might appear that Wallace is displacing the blame for racist stereotypes onto the black man, her analysis must be understood within the context of her critique of white domination; she argues that the black movements of the 1960s were unable to see the ways in which their promotion of a certain black (male) image reinforced the white power structure, since the Black Power Movement tended to embrace a white-centered representation of black sexuality.

Jones's representation of black male sexuality critiques this construction, while seeming to accept it; just as Eva represents an excessive identification with cultural constructions of black womanhood, Alfonso represents Black Macho unleashed. Since Jones is more interested in exploring the effects of these cultural constructions on the black community, than in explicitly finding their origins in the white psyche, critics have often chided her for being too hard on the black man. I would argue that both Eva and Alfonso are "grotesques," in Byerman's sense of the word; but, like Wallace, Jones is more interested in exploring the sexual exploitation of the black woman than in looking at the victimization of the black man—an interest perhaps stemming from black historians' silence on this question. Nevertheless, *Eva's Man* contains exaggerated representations of black male sexuality and works to deconstruct the complementarity—or the dialectical relation—between cultural constructions of black manhood and womanhood. Eva's excessive behavior disrupts the equilibrium of the dialectic that Jones has shown to subtend the heterosexual contract in *Corregidora* by pushing it to its limits.

Jones remarks that, because all the men in the text assume Eva is a whore, "she begins to feel she is, and eventually associates herself with the Queen Bee and the Medusa symbol. I put those images in the story to show how the myths or ways in which men perceive women actually define women's characters" (Tate, *Black Women Writers*, 96). At the beginning of the novel, Eva clearly indicates that the representatives of authority and domination are *producing* her as Medusa; "Elvira said they had my picture in [the newspaper] and my hair was all uncombed and *they had me looking* like a wild woman" (3, my emphasis). During her initial interrogation, her questioners enjoin Eva to comb her hair. Her refusal suggests that since she has been placed in the posture of Medusa, she is going to play the part with a vengeance and let her questioners deal with its effects. This detail is particularly relevant because Davis has refused to give Eva a comb while they were together in the hotel room; thus, Jones implies, Eva forces the authorities to live with the effects of what Davis, another representative of male domination, has begun. Medusa represents a fetishization of female difference, a mythological figure that simultaneously raises the specter of castration and alleviates the threat of it.[55] As Sarah Kofman points out, "the horror inspired by Medusa's head is always accompanied by a sudden stiffening, which signifies erection." Medusa, whose wild serpent-hair signifies the phallus, is also the representation of a lack or "hole" that is the female genital organs. Reading Freud, Kofman concludes that "if horror in the face of woman's genital organs always has as its apotropaic counterpart the erection of the male organ,...we can then understand how what was *supposed* to draw man away from woman is always at the same time what brings him closer to her" (85).

Kofman's reading of Freud evokes another version of the dialectic that Jones explores in her two novels, but that *Eva's Man* literalizes in terms of castration. When Eva says, "Men look at me and get hard-ons. I turn their dicks to stone" (130), she becomes the Medusa that Kofman argues represents the "inseparable blend of horror and pleasure" that characterizes constructions of woman (85).[56] This blend also characterizes what Bhabha refers to as the split between narcissism and aggressivity that marks the colonialist construction of the stereotype as fetish: "It is precisely these two forms of 'identification' that constitute the dominant strategy of colonial power exercised in relation to the stereotype which, as a form of multiple and contradictory belief, gives knowledge of difference and simultaneously disavows or masks it" ("The Other Question," 29). Bhabha is not interested in the stereotype as an always already received and receivable "image," but as a discursive strategy that produces and reproduces difference through an obsessive repetition.

Such an obsessive repetition is what characterizes the proliferation of the "overdetermined nominative properties" of the black woman, in Spillers's terms. It is a strategy geared to disempower actual black female subjects by containing those subjects within a metaphorical construction of Black Womanhood; the metaphors are threatening, but as metaphors, can be controlled. The castrating black woman who circulates in masculinist texts, both white and black, is a figure designed to provoke guilt on the part of actual black female subjects—a strategy that stems from a hegemonic desire to make the victim a criminal, and thus, to divide the black community and to ensure white innocence. Michele Wallace summarizes the paralyzing effects of this dynamic on black women: "Everytime she starts to wonder about her own misery, to think about reconstructing her life, to shake off her devotion and feeling of responsibility to everyone but herself, the ghosts pounce. She is stopped cold. The ghosts talk to her. '*You* crippled the black man. *You* worked against him. *You* betrayed him. *You* laughed at him. *You* scorned him. *You* and the white man'" (16). What Wallace describes here is a discursive strategy that functions to safeguard white male power and desire but, as Jones demonstrates, this strategy can be turned against itself; within the terms of the constructions of the black woman is implied the possibility of overturning that very construction. This is what Eva accomplishes by mimicking the strategy of obsessive repetition, and it is why she stands as a figure who cannot be assimilated into the system that endowed her with this potential power in the first place.

It is significant that the three mythological figures Eva identifies with come together when Eva recounts the scene of her castration of Davis. Even here, Eva refuses to *explain* herself, but the juxtaposition of Medusa, the Queen Bee, and Eve suggests that she is simply enacting the power assigned to her within these mythologies. When Eva literalizes the "vagina-dentata-myth,"[57] she thinks about Eve in a way that makes the apple of knowledge explicitly representative of the phallus: "I opened his trousers and played with his penis.... I got back on the bed and squeezed his dick hard in my teeth. I bit down hard. My teeth in an apple" (128). When she gets to the filling station, and reports her own crime, she looks at herself in the mirror, and says, "I'm Medusa, I was thinking. Men look at me and get hard-ons" (130). Eva completes the trio when she thinks "The queen bee. Men had to die for loving her" (131). The juxtaposition of these three images at the scene of castration produces an "explanation" of Eva's behavior more powerful than any "rational" explanation Eva could give. Her narrative *performs* a critique of masculinist and racist discourses and their positioning of woman, in much the same way as Luce

Irigaray's discourse performs a deconstruction of masculinist representations of the feminine.

Eva's narrative moves between the representation of gender as ideological construction, and "what that representation
leaves out or, more pointedly, makes unrepresentable" (de
Lauretis, *Technologies,* 26). What is unrepresentable in Eva's
case, according to the authorities who seek an explanation of
her behavior, is the fact that she has put into play the
metaphorical threat that woman poses to the dominant representational episteme. While the objectification of woman is,
arguably, the *basis* of masculine self-representation and the
culture's "master narratives," and functions through what
JanMohamed calls a "Manichean allegory";[58] when a textual
subject gendered female presumes to represent herself
across the contours of these master narratives, she participates in what de Lauretis calls a movement that characterizes
the subject of feminism: a movement between "inside" and
"outside" that provides for the constitution of other social and
discursive spaces, in "the margins (or 'between the lines,' or
'against the grain') of hegemonic discourses and in the interstices of institutions, in counter-practices and new forms of
community" (*Technologies,* 26). Implicit here is the possibility of a concurrent critique of the ways in which dominant
voices place their "Others" in positions of marginality, and
the affirmation that "marginal" subjectivities are not reducible
to Otherness, but in fact, can be empowered.

Critics of *Eva's Man* have failed to discern the power of
Eva's alternate construction of subjectivity, and have
reduced Jones's protagonist to a static figure who has no
discursive agency. Melvin Dixon, for example, chides Eva for
failing to acknowledge the "part she played in abusing men"
and, ironically, concludes with a statement that supports my
argument here: "Eva persists in acting out with Davis the
roles of women predators...which are really created by men
out of their own castration anxiety and fears about their
repressed femininity" (247). Because Dixon identifies so
fully with the men in the text, he misses the implications of
his own statement; he, like the male authorities in the text, is
so horrified at Eva's act that he shies away from considering

how Eva's behavior stands as a critique of the system those authorities represent: "Eva is inarticulate and brutally silent throughout most of the novel as if she were rebelling against language or had just lost her voice completely while filling up on cabbage and sausage and Davis' penis[!]" (246). Eva is indeed "rebelling" against a certain kind of language, but she certainly is not "silent"; she does, after all, maintain control over the place of enunciation even as she mimics others' discourses. As Jones points out, Eva "refuses to render her story *coherently*. By controlling what she will and will not tell, she maintains her autonomy" (Tate, *Black Women Writers*, 97; my emphasis). What Eva "brutalizes" by her silence, is the coherence of the official discourses which attempt to recuperate her; this is her "rebellion" and it is also her power.

It is not Eva's bizarre *behavior* that makes her subversive; rather, it is her excessive relation to official discourses that places her in a disruptive position.[59] In other words, Eva's is a *discursive* power despite what might appear to be her passive silence; if this power is negative it is because discourses of racism and sexism only allow black women negative positions. Indeed, *Eva's Man* deconstructs the opposition of activity/passivity by suggesting that Eva's seemingly passive resistance to systems of male domination is ultimately a more active refusal of these systems than Ursa was able to accomplish in *Corregidora*. Eva accomplishes her deconstruction of dominant discourses, and their construction of the black woman, both by taking those constructions to their exaggerated, but logical conclusion, and by refusing to *explain* her behavior as such. It is unlikely, in any case, that the representatives of official discourses, such as the "Dr. Frauds" in the prison, could make much sense of the narrative Eva offers to the reader. If Eva is indeed "crazy," she exhibits some surprisingly "sane" insights into the politics of male domination, even if uttered in an "irrational" or "incoherent" way. For example, Eva sees that the mythological power of the phallus has as its counterpart the vulnerability of the penis—an insight that the "Dr. Frauds" could not articulate any more forcefully than Eva does in her indirect way: "They kept his penis in the icebox, wrapped up like a ham, and then in the courtroom, wrapped up in a silk handkerchief, like a jewel" (49). The mythological power of the phallus, as emphasized in its being a "jewel" in the arena of law and order, is deconstructed by Eva's echoing the Alfonso's description of the penis as "meat."

The final scene of the novel works to further decenter the phallus/penis from its position of power, and to deconstruct the notion of sexuality as necessarily dependent on that power. The ending of *Eva's Man* mirrors the ending of *Corregidora* in its representation of oral sex—this time between two women. Whereas the ending of *Corregidora* foregrounds a heterosexual master/slave dialectic, and suggests the impossibility of overturning it, the ending of *Eva's Man* envisions another sexuality:

> Last night she got in the bed with me, Davis. I knocked her out, but I don't know how long I'm going to keep knocking her out...
>
> ...
>
> "Tell me when it feels sweet, Eva. Tell me when it feels sweet, honey."
>
> I leaned back, squeezing her face between my legs, and told her, "Now." (177; ellipses in the original)

The heterosexual bias of Dixon's reading of Jones leads him to argue that "when Eva allows herself to be seduced by her cellmate, Elvira Moody, she passively enjoys the act of cunnilingus..., whereas Ursa brings Mutt within the orbit of her control in the act of fellatio" (246). While Elvira has indeed seduced her, Eva is clearly taking the pleasure that Ursa gave to Mutt; to see the one as passive and the other as active amounts to discounting the possibility of a female pleasure that would not be dependent on the phallus. Dixon concludes that "Eva has failed to free herself or to speak anything more significant than the chilling 'Now' at the novel's close which announces her solo orgasm" (247).

For me, this ending and Eva's pleasure is *especially* "significant"—not because Jones presents lesbian sexuality as a particularly viable alternative to the heterosexual contract she has critiqued, but rather because the encounter between Eva and Elvira suggests yet another mode of female excess in relation to discourses and systems of male domination. It is also significant that this is the only place in Eva's narrative that she directly addresses Davis—which could be read as her need to invoke a male authority at this moment; but it can also be read as another slap in Davis's face, as it were, since he has refused to give Eva pleasure through oral sex earlier in the novel: "I'd only do that with a woman I'd lived with for years. I'd only do that with my wife" (142). Davis's comment here suggests that he is either repulsed by a non-phallic contact with a woman's genitals, or he is afraid of what that contact might signify in terms of a pleasure not wholly dependent on his penis. As we have seen in *Corregidora,* marriage means ownership of a woman's body; in this context, Davis's refusal suggests that it is only with the "pay-off" of this contract that he would be able to have oral sex with a woman without being, in some way, threatened by it.

Jones's critique of the representational paradigm whereby heterosexual relations are inscribed as a dangerous complementarity participates in a larger critique of binary representational politics based on race and gender differentiation. Insofar as heterosexual relations can be read as a microcosm of the power relations structuring patriarchal culture, a critique of these relations foregrounds the stakes involved in positing woman as male property, and in enforcing the objectification of female subjects. For the black female subject, the heterosexual contract has its roots in the *literal,* historical experience of gendered property relations, and brings into focus the intersections between racial and sexual definition within white patriarchal culture. The black female subject has been *spoken* by official discourses as a timeless essence that subtends a representational paradigm based on her cultural marginality; whether constructed in opposition to the white woman or the black man, the black woman has been systematically denied the privilege of *self*-representation. Obscured behind the mask of Jezebel, Sapphire, Mammy—or any of the other cultural constructions of her subjectivity—the black woman's cultural identity has always already been constituted as a non-identity, existing only in relation to other, similarly static, identities. Neither Ursa Corregidora nor Eva Medina Canada can simply "find" an identity that they can then occupy, for it is the logic of essential identity that has fostered their oppression and exploitation; rather, they must invent a subjectivity, based on the specificities of their experience, in order to speak against a history of *being spoken*. All subjectivities—whether "central" or marginal—are constituted across a field of contradictions.

One's interaction—or experience—with social practices, discourses, and institutions is discontinuous; that is, individual people take up diverse, sometimes contradictory, subject positions dependent, in large part, on how they are interpellated by different discursive formations. Both Ursa and Eva intervene in this interpellation by foregrounding the constitutive contradictions in the cultural production of black womanhood, and work to deconstruct the official discourses which enforce their marginality. As Caren Kaplan argues in an article on cultural marginality in relation to First- and Third-World feminists, "women have a history of reading and writing in the interstices of masculine culture, moving between use of the dominant language and a form of expression and specific versions of experience based on their marginality" (187). In Jones's two novels, that marginality is not only in relation to "masculine culture," but to a broader dominant or hegemonic culture, whose self-representation depends on hierarchical, "complementary" representations of its Others. Jones's reworking of the master/slave dialectic highlights that complementarity in representations of Self and Other, in that the existence of a master—whether literal or figurative—is structurally dependent on the existence of a slave. This dialectical conception of human relations ultimately serves to justify, or "naturalize," existing configurations of power relations; as in the discourse on American slavery, a static representation of the disempowered Other is necessary to the coherence of a certain discursive universe mobilized by a desire to rationalize the oppression of an entire social group by producing that group as Other to itself. I have argued here that it is possible to intervene into that universe and that desire by foregrounding the contradictions that threaten their coherence.

As Homi Bhabha suggests, the ambivalence in any colonial discourse can be seen in a constitutive contradiction: "colonial discourse produces the colonised as a fixed reality which is at once 'other' and yet entirely knowable and visible. It resembles a form of narrative whereby the productivity and circulation of subjects and signs are bound in a reformed and recognisable totality. It employs a system of representation, a regime of truth, that is structurally similar to Realism" ("The Other Question," 23). Bhabha's comment is particularly germane to my argument here, and to my overall project in this study. In my focus on the ways in which women's fiction strategically engages in official cultural narratives, I have argued that there are forces in traditional narrative structures that militate against female subjectivity and, in fact, depend on the objectification of Woman for their coherence and closure. Although I have not explicitly argued against realism as the place where a masculine desire is expressed by keeping "woman in her place," there is a sense in which the classic realist text best embodies that desire for closure and coherence. My reading of Derrida and Angela Carter foregrounded how Woman functions as the image of closure in masculinist narratives, particularly quest narratives, whether they be "traditional" or "radical." There, we saw that Carter intervenes into this mechanism of closure by making the feminine image speak as a woman and by showing her subversive appropriation of the gaze and her own narrative. In my chapter on Lessing, we saw that normalization is a form of closure that is predicated on bringing differentially determined subjects into line with an official version of "reality." My argument about the tension between humanist and posthumanist versions of subjectivity in Lessing was meant to suggest how, in spite of the "realist" spirit in which they were written, these novels seem structurally incapable of closure because of the disturbance of gender that I read into Martha's quest. And, here, I have argued that official versions of the "reality" of the black woman work toward a totalizing version of the Other that gives to official narratives their coherence and closure—a closure that demands a foreclosure of black female subjectivity.

While it is impossible for Jones's protagonists to "break free" from the historical construction of black womanhood, it is possible to tell another story in the margins of hegemonic discourses. To write in the margins means, for Jones, to push the hegemonic representations of black womanhood to their limits, and to empower black female subjects as agents capable of resisting those representations. The ambivalence that marks this textual strategy works to keep in suspension the contradictions that have structured Ursa's and Eva's experience, specifically the contradiction between their status as objects of discourse and their desire as subjects. Jones's protagonists cannot simply "forget" what Radhakrishnan calls "oppression, memory, and enforced identity" in favor of a "counter-memory" created whole from thin air, as it were; the "enforced identity" of Afro-American women must be deconstructed from the inside in order to forge a space for that "counter-memory." As Ursa puts it, "Shit, we're all consequences of something. Stained with another's past as well as our own" (45). It is the "consequences" of the historical production of black womanhood that both Ursa and Eva explore; and it is in the process of that exploration—the textual performance of critique and affirmation—that Ursa and Eva succeed in telling their own stories, and in empowering a self-representation of black female subjects. This self-representation exists in a dialogic relation to official representations and, as I have argued, both Ursa and Eva move between the "inside" of these representations and their outsides. It is in this movement that their subjectivities speak.

Epilogue
On Representation and Self-Representation

The process of representation, the sorting out of identity and difference, is the process of analysis: naming,
controlling, remembering, understanding. A process
so seemingly natural to us as to be beyond question.
Yet...it has been diagnosed as being at the very roots
of our Western drive to know all, and shown to be
inseparable from the imperial speaking subject...; it
has been denounced as complicitous with a violence
as old as Western history itself.

Alice Jardine, *Gynesis.*

On the one hand, *representation* serves as the operative term within a political process that seeks to
extend visibility and legitimacy to women as political
subjects; on the other hand, representation is the normative function of a language which is said either to
reveal or to distort what is assumed to be true about
the category of women.... The domains of political
and linguistic "representation" set out in advance the
criterion by which subjects themselves are formed,
with the result that representation is extended only to
what can be acknowledged as a subject. In other
words, the qualifications for being a subject must be
met first before representation can be extended.

Judith Butler, *Gender Trouble.*[1]

As my two epigraphs suggest, "representation" and "subjectivity" are two terms, or concepts, which cannot be separat-
ed. Jardine's comment implies that "representation" is an
act of violence, perpetrated by the self-present and knowing
subject against, one can only assume, the Others that that

subject desires to know and control. Thus, representation is a form of colonization, an imperial move on the part of the subject. Yet representation, as Butler suggests, has another, and contradictory, meaning: representation must also be made to signify the process by which ("invisible") subjects "legitimize" themselves by inscribing their experience, their desires, and their "reality" into discourse. The difference between these two meanings of representation, both political, is in the conceptualization of the subject of representation. For Jardine, that subject is akin to the humanist "self," who has been inscribed by Western discourse as white and male, the privileged subject of the human sciences. For Butler, the subject is "women," precisely that category that has been over-represented in Western discourses, and under-represented in political processes. "Linguistic" and "political" representation go hand in hand; for, normative discursive representations of Woman have de-legitimized women's participation in history. It is in order to analyze the complicities between the linguistic/discursive and the political that I have argued here that women become subjects by negotiating between normative representations of Woman—"what is assumed to be true of the category of women," in Butler's terms—and what those representations leave out: the possibility that women can be subjects of discourse and history. That possibility is realized through women's *self*-representation, my term for the processes by which subjects produce themselves as women and, thus, make "visible" the contradictions in hegemonic discursive and political systems. For every representation is also a production, not simply an imitation or re-presentation of an already constituted "reality."

Similarly, self-representation is a process of production, and what is produced through that process is subjectivity. Or, rather, self-representation engenders the subject of discourse, whether that subject be concerned with self-representation or not. All discursive practices engender a subject, and I have argued here that it is a key and explicit concern of feminist theory and practice to foreground, rather than transcend, that engendering. For, while some narrative and theoretical practices might seek to obscure the subject that they engender—or, seek to inscribe that subject as sexually and racially in-different—feminist discursive practices have a stake in bringing that subject to light. The subject that Jardine invokes—in order to deconstruct—is not the only subject that can be theorized. On the contrary, I have suggested here that the singular and unified (white male) subject of humanist discourses can be *disturbed* by theorizing how all subjects are marked by gender and race. For the white male subject—the standard against which all differences are measured—(self)representation has not historically been a problem. But, as Butler forcefully suggests, the "qualifications for being a subject must be met first before representation can be extended." For women, those qualifications cannot be simply met by usurping the (masculine) place of enunciation, without changing the politics of enunciation. Rather, what is needed is a radical rethinking of what it means to be a subject and, specifically, what it means to become a woman-subject in patriarchal cultures.

Homogeneous representations of Woman and women's heterogeneous self-representations exist in a complex and often contradictory relationship. I have charted this relationship here by arguing that contemporary women's texts strategically engage with official narratives of sexual difference, of subjectivity and of history; that this engagement proceeds by a movement "inside" and "outside" gender as ideological representation; and that it is in the interstices between these two types of cultural and narrative positioning that female subjectivity is engendered in discourse. I have also offered what I hope are a number of convincing arguments about how official narratives conspire to close off the possibility of a female subjectivity, both in discourse and in social relations. In my readings of the fictional texts, I have wedged open the contradictions that disrupt the fit between Woman and women, suggesting that the humanist ideal of unitary and singular selfhood cannot accomodate the contradictory positions subjects occupy in relation to discourses of gender and racial difference. It occurs to me, as I attempt to draw some conclusions to this study that I have actively worked to avoid the very contradictions that I began by identifying as productive. In other words, I have attempted to present a *seamless representation* of women's fiction and the problematics of gendered subjectivity by forcing on these very diverse texts my own desire to make a coherent argument about them. I have, in short and unwittingly, been working toward the type of closure I have identified as a strategy of containment in the theoretical discourses I have critiqued.

I have not, however, meant to offer such a closed representation of contemporary women's fiction. The field of late twentieth-century women's fiction is wide and heterogeneous. The texts I have chosen to discuss here captured my attention because they all seemed to respond, in one way or another, to theoretical issues that currently preoccupy feminist critics and theorists, particularly the questions that have emerged through a re-thinking of identity politics. My choice to focus on a limited number of texts, and to perform detailed readings of them, was a result of my desire to trace the complicated processes by which female subjectivity is engendered in narrative discourse. There are many other texts that I might have discussed here, and I hope that my arguments will lead other feminist critics to think in new ways about the specificity of women's writing.[2] Readings of other women's novels, by different critics and theorists with different perspectives and investments, will necessarily (and productively) extend and revise the arguments I have made here. Indeed, my work here has been enabled by recent theoretically informed readings of women's texts. The identity politics within feminism—the attempts to refigure the women as subjects—are paralled by the identity politics of feminism. Rather than consolidate the identity of feminism, it is important to keep that identity as an open question, to embrace diverse, and perhaps even contradictory, feminist practices. Claiming a singular identity for woman and for feminism —making them speak as *the* difference from man and from sexually in-different critical practices—can lead to containment and recuperation, both colonialist strategies that function to short-circuit radical change.

The theoretical materials from which I have drawn in this study are as widely various as the fictional texts, but there are plentiful connections, resonances, and most importantly, similarities in political agendas. Deconstruction, French feminist theory, critiques of colonial discourses, feminist film theory, and revisionist Afro-American histories—all these theoretical endeavors share, to one extent or another, a desire to disrupt an old and well established order of things and to envision, if not a new order, at least the possibility of transformation in discursive and social relations. The most important connection between these diverse projects, for my purposes here, is a destabilization of the unitary subject of humanist discourses and, correspondingly, a deconstruction of that subject's Others. The different strategic forms of that deconstruction that I have identified here—mimicry, masquerade, radical indeterminacy—all participate in the important project of theorizing the relationship between central and marginal subjectivities and discourses. These strategies, that I have read into both fiction and theory, do not proffer an Utopian leap beyond hegemonic discursive systems; rather, they proceed by staging dialogues between homogeneous representations of "identity" and heterogeneous representations of identities and differences. In my focus on the slippages between official representations of gender and racial difference and heterogeneous self-representations, I have also staged such a dialogue. My aim has been to engender the subject of (self)representation and, specifically, feminist (self)representation.

Notes

Introduction

1. Judith Butler advances the radical claim that "gender must...designate the very appartus of the production whereby the sexes themselves are established. As a result, gender is not to culture as sex is to nature; gender is also the discursive/cultural means by which 'sexed nature' or a 'natural sex' is produced and established as 'prediscursive,' prior to culture, a politically neutral surface *on which* culture acts" (7).

2 . Elizabeth Meese also addresses this crisis of feminist theory in the first chapter of her *(Ex)Tensions,* arguing against the consolidation of the Identity of feminism she sees as an impulse toward territorialism.

3. See, particularly, the essays collected in Elizabeth Weed, ed., *Coming to Terms,* and Linda Nicholson, ed. *Feminism/Postmodernism.* Meese also provides an intelligent accounting of the positivities and negativities in the alliances between feminism and poststructuralism, particularly Derridean deconstruction.

4. The most devastating of these criticisms can be found in Toril Moi, *Sexual/Textual Politics,* where Anglo-American feminist critics become the spokespieces for the masculinist tradition.

5. Linda Alcoff suggests that if we take theorists like Foucault and Derrida to their logical conclusions, we must content ourselves with the idea that "an effective feminism could only be a wholly negative feminism, deconstructing everything and refusing to construct anything" (418).

6. Radhakrishnan, "Negotiating Subject Positions in an Uneven World," 277. Radhakrishnan's comment appears in the context of his consideration of Rosa Burger's multiple subjective positioning in Nadine Gordimer's *Burger's Daughter.* He writes: "On the one hand, those in dominant subject positions, like whites who are against apartheid in South Africa, are in the process of de-authorizing themselves and seeking affiliation with emerging revolutionary subjects. On the other hand, those in emerging revolutionary positions, like

blacks in South Africa, are striving to affirm and legitimate themselves by creating their own 'insider space'" (277).

7. See de Lauretis, *Technologies of Gender* for a detailed discussion of this "twofold pull in contradictory directions" of feminist
theory (26).

8. I use the capitalized Woman to denote an essentialized and
essentializing figure, distinct from *a* woman and women—except
when use of the capital "W" would be inconsistent with the usage of
a writer under consideration, for example, Derrida.

9. De Lauretis addresses this "liability of feminist thought" in
some detail in *Technologies of Gender.*

10. See, particularly, bell hooks, *Ain't I a Woman?;* Elly Bulkin,
Minnie Bruce Pratt, and Barbara Smith, *Yours in Struggle;* Cherrie
Moraga and Gloria Anzaldua, eds., *This Bridge Called My Back;*
and, Gloria Hull, Patricia Bell Scott, and Barbara Smith, eds., *All
the Women are White.*

11. Chandra Talpade Mohanty gives a particularly convincing
account of how Western feminist work on "Third world women" falls
prey to these exclusionary strategies. See her "Under Western
Eyes: Feminist Scholarship and Colonial Discourses."

12. Bordo suggests that "while in theory, all 'totalizing' narratives may be equal, in the context of Western history and the actual
relations of power characteristic of that history, key differences dis-
tinguish the universalizations of gender theory from the metanarratives arising out of the propertied, white, male, Western intellectual
tradition" (141). In this, Bordo echoes Nancy Hartsock's claims
that women and other minority subjects have a significantly different relation to the "center" and culture's master narratives than do
white, Western men.

13. Meese, 10; and Weed, xxiv.

14. The idea that it might be possible and productive to "risk"
essence comes from Gayatri Spivak's "Subaltern Studies: Deconstructing Historiography." She sees the group as formulating a
notion of consciousness that goes against the poststructuralist critiques of humanism that they, otherwise, draw from. She reads their
project as an attempt "to retrieve the subaltern consciousness" in
order to "undo a massive historiographic metalepsis and 'situate'
the effect of the subject as subaltern." For Spivak this project is "a

strategic use of positivist essentialism in a scrupulously visible political interest" (*In Other Worlds,* 205). This claim has quickly become notorious in critical circles, and since making it, Spivak has warned against taking a "strategy" for a "theory." See Spivak with Ellen Rooney, "In a Word: Interview," especially 126–30.

15. Alcoff would reject Fuss's use of the term "nominal essence" because, for Alcoff, this is precisely what poststructuralist theory would reduce "women" to. She claims that nominalism is "the idea that the category 'woman' is a fiction and that feminist efforts must be directed toward dismantling that fiction" (417). Yet, I do not think that this is what Fuss means by her terms "nominal essence"; her term represents an effort to think the category of "women" beyond its "essence" as an "idea."

16. Elaine Showalter's separation of "feminist critique" from "gynocritique" is the classic example of this, and has shaped most discussions of the specificity of women's writing. See her "Feminist Criticism in the Wilderness."

17. My conceptualization of subjectivity has been gleaned from recent theoretical texts, most especially Henriques et. al., de Lauretis's *Alice Doesn't,* and Paul Smith.

18. I refer here to psychoanalytic conceptualizations of the origin of subjectivity.

19. For an exchange on the question of gendered authorship, see Nancy K. Miller, "Changing the Subject" in *Subject to Change* and Peggy Kamuf, "Replacing Feminist Criticism." See, also, Elizabeth Weed, xxi–xxii, for a discussion of identity and authorship.

20. Diana Fuss notes that the problem with humanist conceptualizations of "experience" as a guarantee of authentic knowledge has led poststructuralists not to discount experience per se, but rather, to question it as "the ground (and the most stable ground) of knowledge production. The problem with categories like 'the female experience' or 'the male experience' is that, given their generality and seamlessness, they are of limited epistemological usefulness" (27). Fuss, however, sees de Lauretis's reconceptualization of "experience" as much more useful, as does Linda Alcoff.

21. See, particularly, "The Subject and Power." For a valuable commentary on Foucault and subjectivity, see Henriques et. al., *Changing the Subject.*

22. Meese proposes a theory of the "use value" of literature in her *(Ex)Tensions,* arguing that the reading lessons particular texts provide their readers indicate most forcefully their strategic value in different contexts. In this argument, Meese is going against the assumption that we must have a canon that establishes value across all contexts. I find her theory very promising for intervening into debates about canon formation.

23. There have been some attempts to devise a feminist narrative theory and feminist theories of reading, although none have taken quite the tact I will take here. Robyn Warhol, in *Gendered Interventions,* distinguishes between "masculine" and "feminine" modes of narrative address, but does not touch on how the texts she studies *construct* readers in gender-specific ways. Susan Lanser works "Toward a Feminist Narratology" by offering gender as a salient factor for categorizations of narrative point of view. Perhaps because, like Warhol, Lanser is invested in a structuralist account of narrative, she does not ask the questions about narrative's construction of gender that I am asking here. Finally, Patrocinio Schweickart offers a feminist theory of reading that accounts for how already gendered readers react to texts in different ways. My difference from Schweickart, and from Judith Fetterley's theory of the "resisting reader" from which Schweickart draws, is that I am concerned with how gender is produced *through* narrative processes, not prior to them.

24. See, especially, Chapter Five of *Alice Doesn't.*

25. Mulvey, "Visual Pleasure and Narrative Cinema" and, "Afterthoughts on 'Visual Pleasure and Narrative Cinema.'"

26. R. Radhakrishnan makes this point in his reading of Gordimer's *Burger's Daughter:* "While poststructuralism teaches us that 'common reality' can only be understood trhough multiple and contradictory narratives, the politically aware reader has to choose positions that are either 'inside' or 'outside', despite her awareness that the very terms 'inside' and 'outside' can be deconstructed. Otherwise, Gordimer's/Rosa's narratives end up resembling Botha's" ("Negotiating Subject Positions in an Uneven World," 287). While I agree with Radhakrishnan's general point here, I am not so sure that one can so easily, consciously "choose" to occupy these positions.

27. See Hutcheon, *A Poetics of Postmodernism* and *The Politics of Postmodernism.*

28. I will discuss Spillers's article, "Mama's Baby, Papa's Maybe" in detail in relation to Jones.

Chapter One

1. Lessing's implicit definition of "humanism," however, is not my own; it seems to me that she is addressing a "humanitarianism" when she argues for the political responsibility of the writer in the modern world. This humanitarianism is indeed evident in *Children of Violence,* a series of texts that actually problematize "humanism" and its founding illusion of a rational, coherent self.

2. I will use the following abbreviations to cite these novels in my text: *MQ, APM, ARS,* and *LL.*

3. Despite this very interesting suggestion, however, Brooks goes on to generalize about "narrative," "the novel," and "human desire" throughout his study. His book, thus, engenders the reader and writer—and, indeed, the "human"—as male.

4. Few critics have considered the centrality of racial issues in Children of Violence, and those who have tend to applaud Lessing's "humanist" vision of universal equality. Lars Hartveit, for example, places Martha's consciousness of the "colour bar" at the center of her development, and concludes that "the focus on Martha's changing moods and her progress from phase to phase singles her out as a suffering human being fully 'tuned in' to the human condition" (35). For other, mainly biographical, studies of Lessing and Africa, see: Michael Thorpe, *Doris Lessing's Africa,* and Linda Susan Beard, "Doris Lessing, African Writer."

5. Claire Sprague suggests that, alongside or even *within* the linear progression of the series, we can discern another kind of progression, one she describes as a kind of "ebb and flow." While Sprague sees this second type of movement as a rhythm between the "dominant and recessive forces" always already in "embryo" *inside* both the individual and society, and accessible to the reader on the level of plot or theme; I see it more as a rhythm of repetition and resistance, certainty and contradiction, located in the interstices between subjectivity and sociality. Where Sprague gages the dominant and recessive forces in reference to Martha's "true self," I will suggest that this process-oriented movement ultimately deconstructs the idea that such a product rests at the end of Martha's

quest. (Sprague, *Rereading Doris Lessing,* 86; "Dialectic and Counter-Dialectic," 40 and 45.) The article, written before the book, seems to me much more interesting, in its attempt to look at the dialectical movement in the *Children of Violence* texts. Basically, Sprague argues that the pattern of Martha's development approximates the Marxist rhythm of "dying and becoming," where the new is always already inherent in the old. The problem with this account is, I think, that it cannot address the *production* of these "dominant and recessive forces," and thus reifies both the "individual" and the "society." Nevertheless, this reading does recognize a certain political analogue to Martha's development. Sprague's book, however, seems much more interested in imposing a formal pattern on the texts and, indeed, on Lessing's entire work. This pattern has to do with the use of names and numbers and, in my view, is not only too formulaic, but also adds little by way of a "rereading" of Lessing.

6. For readings of *Children of Violence* as *Bildungsroman,* see: Ellen Cronan Rose, *The Tree Outside the Window;* Sydney Kaplan, "The Limits of Consciousness in the Novels of Doris Lessing"; and Catharine Stimpson, "Doris Lessing and the Parables of Growth."

7. See Barthes, *S/Z.*

8. Robert Scholes and Peter Brooks both essentialize narrative desire as male by implying that narrative follows a model of male sexuality. See de Lauretis, *Alice Doesn't,* Chapter Five, and Susan Winnett, "Coming Unstrung: Women, Men, Narrative, and the Principles of Pleasure," for critiques of these models. Both Hélène Cixous and Luce Irigaray have argued that certain modes of writing are essentially masculine, modeled on male sexuality, and speculate on a "feminine" mode of writing which would be rooted in female sexuality. In my view, this reading of the sex of the text does not go far enough in theorizing the specificity of men's or women's writing.

9. In this sense, Lessing's precursor is George Eliot who, in *Middlemarch,* as D.A. Miller so convincingly argues in *Narrative and Its Discontents,* represents her characters (especially Rosamond Vincy) as being "stuck" in middles.

10. The language describing the hero of the *Bildungsroman* is Dagmar Barnouw's, (82), but the *gendering* of this paradigm is my own, via de Lauretis.

11. When I began to formulate this argument I was unaware that Rachel Blau DuPlessis had suggested a similar reading in her

Writing Beyond the Ending. However, DuPlessis's claim that "Women, as Lessing makes Martha richly aware, are the point of production of this replica building" (190)—what I am referring to by the phrase "ideological reproduction"—suggests that women, in fact, *are* responsible for this conservatism. This seems a particularly problematic claim in a feminist text. I am arguing, on the other hand, that the text encodes this conservative force as feminine—a rather different story.

12. Denise Riley, "Does Sex Have a History? 'Women' and Feminism." I learned of this essay through Elizabeth Weed's introduction to *Coming to Terms,* where she makes an interesting argument about the vicissitudes of the feminist slogan "the personal is the political" (Weed, xiv–xv).

13. In this sense, Martha is akin to the "great heroes" of American literature—and those who have canonized them—whom Nina Baym analyzes in "Melodramas of Beset Manhood."

14. The focus of Sukenick's article is a reading of Lessing in relation to the "female" tradition of novels of sensibility, and she basically argues that Lessing eschews this tradition *because* it is female and thus not concerned enough with "larger" political issues. Here, Sukenick points out that Lessing's reluctance to endorse feminism—as seen in her introduction to *The Golden Notebook*—stems from this same dichotomy between primary and secondary issues. This is, as Marxist feminists have pointed out, the traditional male leftist line on the "woman question."

15. Catharine Stimpson points out that Martha must learn "the value of negation. Saying no, saying I will not, is halfway between submission to the life she despises and one she might actively build for herself; halfway between conformity and authenticity" (196).

16. Rachel Blau DuPlessis, in *Writing Beyond the Ending,* suggests that this passage describes a specifically *female desire,* and thus, naturalizes a feminine position that Peter Brooks also identifies as an integral part of the "female plot." See Brooks, *Reading for Plot,* chapter on "Narrative Desire."

17. In extreme form, this encounter results in a complete negation of "native" subjectivity that works hand in hand with the enforced subjugation of the indigenous population. JanMohamed writes that "the native, who is considered too degraded and inhuman to be credited with any specific subjectivity, is cast as no more

than a recipient of the negative elements of the self that the European projects onto him" (66–67). I discuss JanMohamed's thesis in more detail in my chapter on Gayl Jones.

18. Hollway, in *Changing the Subject,* (252 and 258–59). She makes this point in the context of a discussion of defense mechanisms in heterosexual relations. She writes: "What is projected onto another person represents the material which is unacceptable because of contradictions in the one who is doing the projecting" (258). The focus of Hollway's article is on the ways in which men and women take up gender-differentiated positions that are made available through historically specific networks of discourses on sexuality.

19. Homi Bhabha discusses this contradictory desire in the colonial project in his work on colonial discourses. I will discuss this work in Chapter Three.

20. See Gayatri Spivak, "Subaltern Studies: Deconstructing Historiography" in *In Other Worlds,* for a discussion of "metalepsis, or the substitution of a cause for an effect" in the positivist humanist conceptualization of the subject of consciousness (especially, 202–07).

21. As convincing—and, indeed, seductive—as Smith's *negative* points are throughout this study, a nagging question persists, and in fact, becomes more insistent as the study progresses. In the final chapter, called "Responsibilities," Smith raises this question himself, through the voice of a "colleague" who, after reading a draft of the text, asked: "'So where *is* the subject?'"—to which Smith replies: "For the most part I've wanted to not answer this question; rather I've intended to displace it" (153). Here, I cannot help but recall Smith's convincing critique of Derridean displacement, which is perhaps the most severe this book has to offer. To what end has Smith "displaced" this question? In a book that focuses on how the human sciences have *abstracted* the subject, it seems odd indeed that Smith fails to specify "his" human agent and, perhaps more importantly, to specify *what* it is that these human agents might be resisting. Apart from a few vague references to "the new right" and "multinational economic exploitation," Smith's discussion of the "target" of resistance reduces to an unspecified notion of Ideology—the very problem for which he criticizes Marx and Althusser. Finally, what these vague human agents might be said to "resist" appears to be simply their "cernment" in/by the disciplines that Smith critiques.

22. Smith's text practices its own kind of ideological interpellation, as, of course, do all texts. *Discerning the Subject* constructs a
subject who already "knows" why it is that the unitary, rational subject is "bad."

23. It has been pointed out to me, by Carolyn Allen, that the
difference between these two texts on the subject can be described
as a difference between a social science perspective that makes
use of current critical theory, and a wholly literary theoretical perspective, *Changing the Subject* and *Discerning the Subject,* respec-
tively. While this seems a valid distinction for the most part, I would
add that Smith's book attempts to bring a social science perspective to literary theory.

24. See de Lauretis, *Alice Doesn't,* (132–34), for an analysis of
how Freud's narrative of "Femininity" is governed by this kind of
seduction logic.

25. de Lauretis deploys this theoretical construct in the title
essay of her collection, *Technologies of Gender.* The phrase comes,
I think, from Henriques et. al.'s reading of Foucault, to which de
Lauretis refers.

26. Judith Williamson analyses this phenomena in advertising,
perhaps the most forceful arena of contemporary ideological interpellation. See her *Decoding Advertisements.*

27. See Hollway, (230–38), in *Changing the Subject.*

28. It is not until Martha becomes politically active that the
derogatory term, *kaffir,* is qualified by quotation marks. The fact
that the narrator also uses the term, unqualified, up until this point
suggests that the narrating consciousness parallels Martha's—or,
that, in the years between the first two texts and the second two,
Lessing has developed an awareness of the ways in which racism is
produced through language use.

29. See, for example, Jean Pickering. Ellen Cronan Rose, on the
other hand, argues that Lessing dissociates herself from Martha's
adolescent vision by maintaining an ironic distance on it (142), an
interpretation with which I agree. But Rose does not elaborate on
what, exactly, constitutes Martha's "evasion of reality" in this vision.

30. See Henriques, "Social psychology and the politics of
racism," where he argues that "the rotten apple theory of racism,"
as exemplified in key psychological texts on prejudice, serves to

displace the causes of racism, first, onto the individual—thus exon-
erating institutions of racism—and, second, onto the victim of that
racism. Within this framework, "we cannot ask about the social and
economic causes of differences between blacks and whites in racist
societies such as Britain" (*Changing the Subject,* 73). And, by constructing the subject of racism as simply ignorant, the "net effect [of
such theories] is to leave power relations intact" (63).

31. While I would agree with this as an accurate assessment of
Martha's position, I would argue that the irony that marks Lessing's
presentation of Martha's politics undermines a simple identification
between the two. The irony is most likely directed against left politics in general, however, rather than against the narrow humanist
doctrine of "liberal individualism."

32. See, particularly, Jean Pickering's "Marxism and Madness:
The Two Faces of Doris Lessing."

33. As many critics of Lessing have noted, she is influenced by
Jung and R.D. Laing, as well as Sufi mysticism; such influence
leads her to posit some kind of universal consciousness. See, particularly, Marion Vlastos, "Doris Lessing and R.D. Laing: Psychopolitics and Prophecy"; and Nancy Shields Hardin, "Doris Lessing and
the Sufi Way"; and Rotraut Spiegel, *Doris Lessing: The Problem of
Alienation.*

34. Henriques et. al. describe the ways in which the theoretical
construct of "intersubjectivity" supports an individual-society dual-
ism, in that it militates against any theorization of the relation
between the subject and the social. Instead, social psychology's
theories of interaction between individual and society, or individual
"internalization" of social norms, etc., posit an unproblematic *content* of the social and an equally unproblematic concept of the
coherent individual. Such theories fail "to address the social in any
form other than the personal" (*Changing the Subject,* 17).

35. Ironically, the meeting place for the group is called "Black
Ally's Café"—a place that is definitely off limits to the "natives."

36. Martin and Mohanty derive the idea of "home" from Minnie
Bruce Pratt's essay from *Yours in Struggle.* They extrapolate from
Pratt the idea that location "is constructed on the tension between
two specific modalities: being home and not being home. 'Being
home' refers to the place where one lives within familiar, safe, protected boundaries; 'not being home' is a matter of realizing that

home was an illusion of coherence and safety based on the exclusion of specific histories of oppression and resistance, the repression of differences even within oneself" (196). Martha and Jasmine, thus, are securely "at home."

37. One of the reasons that I have chosen not to discuss *The Four-Gated City* in any detail is because, in that text, it seems to me that the "watcher" takes over to such a degree that the double movement I have been tracing in the earlier novels is not operative in it. Another way to look at this is that the narrator and Martha effectively merge in *The Four-Gated City,* perhaps because, as Lynn Sukenick argues, *history* takes over Martha's place as protagonist in this text (see Sukenick, 102).

38. This pronouncement comes in the midst of Lessing's infamous, and incredulous, response to the fact that *The Golden Notebook* has been appropriated by feminists. "Introduction" (viii–ix).

Chapter Two

1. The new explorations of the place of woman in theory have taken a number of different forms. Alice Jardine's *Gynesis* is an excellent introduction to, and critique of, the place of woman in "high" French theory. See, also, Jonathan Culler's remarks on "reading as a woman" in his *On Deconstruction* and Terry Eagleton's comments on feminist strategies of reading in *Literary Theory*. Jean-François Lyotard's "One of the Things at Stake in Women's Struggles" also links feminism up with the larger "postmodern condition" and the essays collected in *Men in Feminism* provide a vigorous and interesting sampling of the debates around these theoretical issues and what is at stake in them. Tania Modleski's "Feminism and the Power of Interpretation" comments on the (male) desire to read as a woman, and Diana Fuss's *Essentially Speaking,* in turn, comments on Modleski's readings.

2. "Veiled Lips" is a translated excerpt from Irigaray's book on Nietzsche, *Amante marine: de Friedrich Nietzsche,* (Paris: Editions de Minuit, 1980).

3. Jardine cites an unpublished paper written by Danielle Haase-Dubuosc and Nancy Huston, "L'un s'autorise et l'autre pas," which addresses this "coincidence," as well as Rosi Braidotti's doctoral dissertation, "Feminisme et philosophie" (University of Paris I,

1981). She also cites Joan Kelly's work on a similar coincidence during the Renaissance, "Early Feminist Theory and the Querelle des Femmes, 1400–1789." *Signs* 8, no. 1 (1982). See also Teresa de Lauretis, *Technologies of Gender,* and the collection *Men in Feminism,* especially Rosi Braidotti's essay, "Envy: Or, With Your Brains and My Looks." In the context of art criticism and theory, see Rosa Lee, "Resisting Amnesia: Feminism, Painting and Postmodernism."

4. In Wiegman's doctoral dissertation, "Negotiating the Masculine: Configurations of Race and Gender in American Culture" (University of Washington, 1988), she focuses on how various constructs of difference (especially gender and race) are used in patriarchal culture to "negotiate" the very terms of that culture. As she writes, "Through the manipulation of gender, race, and class differences, the white male structure negotiates the terms of its own existence, establishing itself as a universal, all encompassing perspective while elaborating a complex system of empowerment based on exclusions." The white male position is therefore neither homogenous nor stable; its representations change in order to contain within itself questioning or radical discourses that threaten its hegemony. These changes are historically specific, and are prompted by crises in dominant ideologies.

5. I find it odd that a writer so concerned with the openness of texts could levy the charge of "misreading," as Derrida does in "Choreographies." Here, Derrida addresses the question of feminist reaction to *Spurs,* and chides certain (unnamed) feminists for basically "missing the point," of simplifying his text: "Some have reacted at times even more perfunctorily, unable to see beyond the end of phallic forms projecting into the text; beginning with style, the spur or the umbrella, they take no account of what I have said about the difference between style and writing or the bisexual complication of those and other forms. Generally speaking, this cannot be considered reading" (69). If certain readers cannot "see past" certain elements of his text, it is because readers are differently invested in different discourses; and because different subjects are interpellated differently by those discourses. *Any* reading will be selective, although not in the same way. Derrida "takes no account" of differential discursive investments which might influence any reading of his text.

6. In quite another context, a reading of popular Vietnam narratives, Susan Jeffords addresses a similar "occupation" of the fem-

inine by the masculine. She observes that "Men do not *become* women in these narratives, they occupy them" (105). She continues to argue that the apparent gender fluidity in these narratives is only that, apparent: "such boundary crossings are not transgressions but confirmations: the masculine can move into the 'female position' by occupying that position, not altering its own....There is not an exchange of gender roles, but an elimination of them, so that all that exists, all that speaks,...is the voice of the masculine point of view" (*The Remasculinization of America: Gender and the Representation of the Vietnam War,* 107). The parallel between narratives of "popular culture" and those of "high theory" suggests that the crisis in masculinity is far-reaching, and doesn't respect such categories. I wish to thank Robyn Wiegman for bringing this work to my attention.

7. For discussions of the implications of theories of subjectivity for feminist theory, see de Lauretis, *Alice Doesn't* and Kaja Silverman, *The Subject of Semiotics.*

8. Both Cixous and Irigaray have been working to this end by positing the possibility of a "feminine language" and exploring the question of a female desire. In my view, however, the most promising work on female subjectivity can be found in feminist film theory, especially in those texts interested in theorizing a female spectator. See de Lauretis *Alice Doesn't* and *Technologies of Gender* and Mary Ann Doane, *The Desire to Desire* for overviews of, and contributions to, this work.

9. See, especially, Irigaray, "Any Theory of the 'Subject' Has Always Been Appropriated by the 'Masculine'" in *Speculum of the other Woman;* and "Women's Exile."

10. Like Irigaray, Cixous identifies the desire to know as a masculine strategy for containing an always disruptive feminine. See, especially, "Castration or Decapitation?" Derrida, of course, would be in full agreement with this assessment of the desire to know; that does not mean that he escapes from this desire, although he might say that he does.

11. Heather Findlay, in "Is There a Lesbian in this Text?", reads the second woman as a lesbian separatist feminist, who is "scapegoated" by Derrida as well as Elizabeth Berg (in "The Third Woman"). Findlay argues "that various moments in the rhetoric of deconstruction require heterosexuality as a characteristic of its affirmative heroine, and erase the possibility of a specifically female

homosexual practice" (59). Findlay further makes a clever analogy between Derrida's desire for heterogeneity and the heterosexual desire of the text. While her reading of *Spurs* is focused differently than mine, I am in complete sympathy with her reading.

12. See, especially, *Positions* (39–42), where Derrida speaks of the "double gesture" of deconstruction.

13. Following upon the heels of a dismissal of Lacan, Derrida describes the reactive feminist in what I read as an oblique reference to Irigaray; this woman is "castration's confederate, who has now become the inverted image of his pupil, the rowdy student, the master's disciple" (61).

14. de Lauretis takes Derrida's warning to feminists to heart—or rather, pretends to. If she were to argue that "Derrida's discourse denies the fact of gender" she would become a "castrating woman": "I shall not do so, therefore. Decency and shame prevent me, though nothing more." In order to avoid earning Derrida's contempt, she decides to "approach Derrida's text obliquely" through Spivak's reading of it in "Displacement and the Discourse of the Woman." (*Technologies of Gender,* 47). She is, of course, playing on the notion of decency and modesty as articulated in *Spurs.*

15. Irigaray never openly refers to *Spurs,* but it seems clear enough that she is responding to Derrida's reading of Nietzsche with her own reading. Interestingly, the translator of Irigaray's piece, Sara Speidel, keeps referring to *Spurs* in her copious translator's notes. She prefaces each of these references by the phrase, "Cf. Derrida, *Spurs.*" She quotes extensively from *Spurs* without comment, except this one rather suggestive observation: "Irigaray's response to Nietzsche responds to Derrida's text as well. In a sense (a traditional one), Derrida seems to become-'woman' in Veiled Lips—his expression veiled, silenced and effaced, mediating between Irigaray and Nietzsche" (Trans. note 8, 123).

16. See, especially the two *Cultural Critique* special issues on the "Nature and Context of Minority Discourse" and particularly Abdul R. JanMohamed and David Lloyd's introductions to the two issues.

17. Speidel refers to *Ecce Homo* as a Nietzschean text which discusses Athena.

18. Speidel interprets Athena's "burial" of the Furies quite nicely: "Athena assuages the anger of the Furies, promising them a

'cult, rites, sacrifices...' if they will retire to underground caverns, 'bury' themselves beneath the town, subordinating their power to the good of Athens and remaining 'loyal and propitious to the land.'" She also suggests that this play has often been read "in terms of the psychological and political conflict between matriarchal and patriarchal orders," and cites Cixous's *La jeune née* as one such reading. (Trans. n3, 121–22).

19. If, as Domna Stanton argues, Irigaray "declares the murder of the mother to be the foundation of Western culture and society" in her *Amante marine: de Frederich Nietzsche* (Stanton, 160), it is in order to question the logic at work in this masculine displacement of the feminine. She writes: "Even God needs femininity in order to present himself as the only creator" ("Veiled Lips," 98).

20. Interestingly, Irigaray's exploration of a feminine space seem most insistent when she leaves the masters behind. See, especially "When Our Lips Speak Together" in *This Sex*. The critiques of French feminist theories of the feminine by American critics are well known. While I would agree that Irigaray sometimes posits a monolithic femininity in opposition to a monolithic masculinity, I think it is reductive to reject her work as "essentialist." What I find productive in Irigaray is her method or style of reading; that is, the textual operation by which she mimes or parodies master discourses in order to dis-cover the desire which mobilizes these discourses. Still, I think it would be productive to critique the ways in which Irigaray tends to recontain women within Woman, especially in texts where she attempts to "speak female." Despite some disagreement with Stanton, I find her article one of the most productive critiques of these theories that I've seen. See also, Diana Fuss's chapter on Irigaray in *Essentially Speaking;* and Naomi Schor, "This Essentialism Which Is Not One: Coming to Grips with Irigaray."

21. In both of Hutcheon's books, *A Poetics of Postmodernism* and *The Politics of Postmodernism,* she insists, repetitively that postmodernism's "complicitous critique" can only question; it paradoxically "both legitimizes and subverts that which it parodies" (*Politics,* 101). I will question Hutcheon's certainty about the political ambidexterity of postmodernism later in this chapter.

22. Brian McHale, in *Postmodernist Fiction,* points to the text's Manichean opposition between the Apollonian Minister of Justice and the Dionysian Hoffman. But, in describing Hoffman as the "agent of fantasy and pleasure" (143), he banishes gender from this

scene, and elides the question that is central to the text: *Whose* fantasy, and *whose* pleasure?

23. See Brooks, *Reading for the Plot* for an analysis of desire as the (phallic) "piston" of narrative, its "motor force."

24. Mulvey, "Visual Pleasure" (15–17). de Lauretis, in *Alice Doesn't,* explores the reversal of Mulvey's claim. See, particularly, 103 and 109.

25. For other, interesting, feminist discussions of *The Story of O,* see Kaja Silverman, "*Histoire d'O:* The Construction of a Female Subject," and Nancy K. Miller, "The Text's Heroine."

26. I wish to thank the students in my seminar on "Gender, Desire and Contemporary Fiction" at Case Western Reserve University for prompting me to consider these difficult questions.

27. Interestingly, when Hutcheon focuses explicitly on feminist postmodernist practice, her certainty about postmodernism's operations breaks down, particularly in her reading of Hannah Wilke's nude self-portrait. Wilke offers her image to the spectator between the two slogans—"Marxism and Art" and "Beware of Fascist Feminism"—and Hutcheon is troubled by what she senses as the text's legitimation of masculinist images of female desire, as well as its seemingly anti-feminist ideology. Hutcheon's response to this photograph deserves quotation in its entirety: "If 'fascist feminism' meant prudish feminism, then the commodification of the female body in male art...might be what such feminism underwrites by refusing woman the use of her own body and its pleasures. But what about the position of the addressed viewer: is it voyeuristic, narcissistic, critical? Can we even tell? Does the work problematize or confirm the maleness of the gaze? I really cannot tell. In the face of the manifest contradictions of this work, it is tempting to say that, while Wilke is clearly playing with the conventions of pornographic address (her eyes meet and engage the viewer's), she is also juxtaposing this with the discourse of feminist protest—but turned against itself in some way. She does not make her own position clear and thus risks reinforcing what she might well be intending to contest, that is, patriarchal notions of female sexuality and male desire" (*Politics,* 159). This reading of the photograph, if we took out the questions and uncertainties, would qualify Wilke's work as postmodernist in the terms Hutcheon has set up and developed throughout both her books. That is, postmodernist art both "problematizes and confirms"—or legitimizes and subverts—the politics

of representation. But the questions she asks here, it is worth noting, do not inform her readings of the texts of postmodernism produced by men. Nowhere else in her study does Hutcheon ask about the position of the viewer or reader, nor does she seem to think it problematic that postmodernist art does not "make its own position clear." There are two possible conclusions we could reach here: one, that feminist art doesn't really "qualify" as postmodernist; and, two, that feminist artists might have a slightly different stake in their articulations of "complicitous critique."

28. See Mulvey, "Afterthoughts" and Doane, "Film and the Masquerade."

29. According to Carter, pornography is "art with work to do"—its chief function being the arousal of sexual desire (*The Sadeian Woman,* 12). Carter disdains the opposition between pornography and erotica on the grounds of a class analysis, noting that erotica is "the pornography of the elite" (17).

30. Jardine never explicitly makes this point, but implies it in her discussions of fictional fantasies of (female) dismemberments and the like.

31. See my "Misappropriations of the Feminine" for a much more detailed analysis of fetishism in Derrida/Freud.

32. See Mary Ann Doane, "Veiling Over Desire: Close-ups of the Woman," for a fascinating and theoretically broad reading of the trope of the veil in Nietzsche, Derrida, Lacan, Irigaray, and various films which feature veiled women.

33. Roof's notion of the decoy is elaborated in her discussion of Diane Kurys' film *Entre Nous,* in her forthcoming book *A Lure of Knowledge.* At one point, in reference to Lacan, Roof makes a suggestive connection between the fetish and the decoy: "the decoy, like the fetish, represents something which is essentially absent and its reassuring presence hides the threat of castration that lurks behind its production." Briefly, Roof argues that the film creates a series of decoys through its subversive use of conventional cinematic narrative techniques, such as a narrative economy which raises in the spectator both the expectation of and desire for what Roof calls "a traditional male narrative climax"—that is, a desire for the visual "revelation and representation of female *jouissance* in a lesbian confrontation between the two protagonists." What is subversive in the film is that the spectator is, in effect, "seduced" by

this series of decoys—which chart the illusory trajectory of male desire—only to find that the decoys stand in for what is not there. Because the sexual encounters between the two women all take place off screen, Roof suggests that the film not only subverts the spectator's identification with a controlling male gaze—in the camera—but also, in effect, decenters the conventional cinematic apparatus and the scopophilic and fetishistic economies supported by that apparatus. Although I don't do it here, it would be possible to read the woman and the fetish as decoys in Roof's particular sense of the term to argue that Derrida attempts to seduce a (possibly feminist) reader. In this case, however, the "subversion" would fall to the reader.

34. Page references to *Glas* cite page number and column. The "i" indicates an insert in the column.

35. This comment can be found in "Femininity," 116, and relates to woman's "inferior" genital apparatus.

36. Linda Hutcheon notes that this episode "reveals the extreme of...ex-centric ethnicity" and that Carter "uses this society to ironic and satiric ends" (*Poetics*, 71).

37. Carter here is mimicking a scene from Sade, in which a woman sports her "flexible clitoris-cum-prick" (*The Sadeian Woman*, 112).

38. Robert Clark comes to an opposite conclusion in his reading of "Angela Carter's Desire Machine." For Clark, Carter's work, in general, fails to include "within its own critical representation an understanding of the complicity of that representation with the social forces it appears to reject" (154). Further, according to Clark, "Carter's insight into the patriarchal construction of femininity has a way of being her blindness: her writing is often a feminism in a male chauvinist drag, a transvestite style, and this may be because her primary allegiance is to a postmodern aesthetics that emphasizes the non-referential emptiness of definitions. Such a commitment precludes an affirmative feminism founded in referential commitment to women's historical and organic being. Only in patriarchal eyes is femininity an empty category, the negation of masculinity" (158). Apart from the fact that the second statement seems to contradict the first, underlying these comments is an assumption of an essential femininity—an "organic being"—that Carter's "transvestite" style, in fact, works to deconstruct. Clark would have Carter leave behind what I am reading as her radical

critique and focus, instead, on some affirmation that would place women *outside* patriarchal eyes.

39. In *The Sadeian Woman,* Carter discusses the myths surrounding maternity in especially great detail (105–121), but also devotes a significant amount of attention to other "feminine" figures. Her exposé of the ideology behind mothering, in particular reference to Sade's subversion of it, is perhaps the most telling I've ever encountered—especially because she refers to psychoanalytic theory without remaining within its closed ideological system for her analysis.

40. Hutcheon, who coins the term "ex-centricity" in *A Poetics of Postmodernism,* seems a little too quick to assume that postmodernist practice disrupts gender, race, and class hierarchies by displacing the "central" in favor of the "ex-centric."

41. Irigaray, however, distinguishes between mimicry as a subversive strategy, and masquerade as a conservative one. The first escapes masculine control, while the second captures woman within the terms of masculine desire. See *This Sex,* 220, for the distinction between the two strategies.

42. See Mulvey, "Visual Pleasure," E. Ann Kaplan, "Is the Gaze Male," and Kaja Silverman, "Lost Objects and Mistaken Subjects," for discussions of the gaze in cinema.

43. Doane derives the terms of her analysis from Joan Riviere's "Womanliness as a Masquerade" in Henrik M. Ruitenbeek, ed., *Psychoanalysis and Female Sexuality* (New Haven: College and University Press, 1966).

44. Butler's comments appear in the context of a reading of Lacan's theory of feminine masquerade and the essentially "comedic" nature of heterosexual relations. The reference is to Jacques Lacan, "The Meaning of the Phallus" in Juliet Mitchell and Jacqueline Rose, eds.

45. See Laura Mulvey's discussion of Hitchcock in her "Visual Pleasure and Narrative Cinema."

46. Judith Mayne, in a reading of "Marlene Dietrich, *The Blue Angel,* and Female Performance," warns against assuming that a simple reversal of the terms of the duality structuring the filmic gaze along gender lines will necessarily displace this duality. In my view, thinking of female performance and masquerade as an operation

whereby the woman turns the gaze on herself is one step toward disrupting the duality.

47. Carter argues that West could "get away" with such a threatening "castratory wit" because she entered the Hollywood scene when she was safely past the age of menopause. She writes: "The middle-aged woman...may say what she pleases, wink at and nudge whomever she desires but we know it is all a joke upon her, for she is licenced to be free because she is so old and ugly that nobody will have her. Mae West relied on this freedom, even if she turned it on its head" (*The Sadeian Woman,* 61).

48. Carter charges Mailer with mythologizing Monroe without having any sense of the fact that it is *his* desire that places her in the position he claims she occupied. She points out, for example, his "approving" quotation of Diana Trilling's description of Monroe as "a young woman trapped in some never-never land of unawareness" (*The Sadeian Woman,* 64). The reference is to Mailer's *Marilyn* (London: Hodder and Stoughton, 1973). Carter gives no reference for Trilling's comments.

49. Mayne's comment appears in the context of a reading of the carnivalesque in *The Blue Angel,* and is meant as a corrective to those who see in Bakhtin's work, especially his *Rabelais and His World,* an asocial privileging of the carnival. She notes that "in feminist terms, flirtation with the carnivalesque is equally risky. Equating the carnivalesque with female resistance to the patriarchal order may be a celebration of precisely those qualities that define women as irrelevant in patriarchal terms" (40). Mary Russo also warns against this risk, noting that women are often put in danger in actual, historical, carnival scenes. Yet, both Russo and Mayne imply that the risk is worth taking for, in Russo's terms, "the hyperboles of masquerade and carnival suggest, at least, some preliminary 'acting out' of the dilemmas of femininity" (225).

50. This "museum of woman monsters" is an idea that Carter takes from Sade. See *The Sadeian Woman,* (25–26).

51. Carter uses this phrase to refer to the naive, but empiricist, Walser at the beginning of Nights at the Circus (10), and in her discussion of Justine in *The Sadeian Woman:* "[Justine] is not in control of her life; her poverty and her femininity conspire to rob her of autonomy. She is always the dupe of an experience that she never experiences *as* experience; her innocence invalidates experience and turns it into events, things that happen to her but do not change

her. This is the common experience of most women's lives, conduct-
ed always in the invisible presence of others who extract the meaning of her experience for themselves and thereby diminish all meaning, so that a seduction, or a birth, or a marriage, the central events
in the lives of most women, the stages of a life, are marginal occur-
rences in the life of the seducer, the father or the husband" (51).

52. Carter argues, in *The Sadeian Woman,* that all mythologies—particularly those that universalize sexual difference—work
by a "savage denial of the complexity of human relations" and are
thus, "consolatory nonsense" (6).

53. Radhakrishnan invokes Derrida's "double session" as a
strategy that, "when politicized is not all that different from the
"Manichean" *episteme* as invoked by Abdul JanMohamed" in his
"The Economy of Manichean Allegory: The Function of Racial Difference in Colonialist Literature." The "political" difference, of
course, is key here. The reference to Derrida is to his *Dissemination.* Radhakrishnan is primarily interested in theory "proper," but I
am, in sense, arguing here, following Barbara Christian, that "theorizing" goes on in fiction, as well. See her "The Race for Theory."

Chapter Three

1. One example of the omission of Jones in feminist criticism
of black women's writing can be found in Hazel V. Carby's *Recon-
structing Womanhood: The Emergence of the Afro-American
Woman Novelist.* In an extensive list of "Texts by Black Women
Authors" at the end of Carby's book, which includes texts by
anonymous authors and which certainly is not limited to the writers
Carby discusses in her book, Gayl Jones is not even mentioned.
Similarly, Barbara Christian's influential *Black Women Novelists:
The Development of a Tradition,* omits any mention of Jones.

2. In an interview with Claudia Tate, Jones responds to her critics' tendency to "castigate" her, in Tate's terms, for writing "about
characters who do not conform to positive images of women or
black women." Jones replies: "'Positive race images' are fine as
long as they're complex and interesting personalities. Right now I'm
not sure how to reconcile the various things that interest me with
'positive race images'" (Tate, ed. *Black Women Writers at Work,*
97). In a piece entitled "About My Work," Jones argues that "Eva
Canada stands for no one but Eva Canada," and suggests that criti-

cal response to Eva's "negative image" "raises the questions of possibility. Should a Black writer ignore such characters, refuse to enter 'such territory' because of 'negative image' and because such characters can be misused politically by others, or should one try to reclaim such complex, multidimensional, contradictory characters as well as try to reclaim the idea of the 'heroic image'?" (233). As I will argue here, it *is* possible to do both, and Jones's novels do indeed practice such a double strategy.

3. Claudia Tate discusses *Corregidora*'s exploration of "racial and mythic histories," but oddly tries to situate the text within a humanist frame by arguing that the novel's strength lies in its portrayal of "the universality of the protagonist's plight" (139). Gloria Wade-Gayles criticizes Jones for breaking out of a pattern of Afro-American fiction, as she writes: "The verdict on *Eva's Man* is that its author's neglect of particulars about the black man's victimization results in his appearing to be innately a victimizer rather than a victim turned victimizer unwittingly" (176).

4. Janice Harris's "Gayl Jones' *Corregidora*" is, in some senses, an exception to this. Harris does focus on ambivalence as Ursa's defining characteristic, but does so in her reading of *Corregidora* as a "portrait of the artist" novel, akin to Joyce's *A Portrait of the Artist as a Young Man* and Lawrence's *Sons and Lovers*. Harris makes it clear that she is not attempting to obscure the race and gender specificity of Jones's text, nor is she attempting to validate *Corregidora* by comparing it to "male masters" of the genre. Still, Harris's interpretive frame leads her to focus too much on Ursa's intensely personal struggle to free herself from the "twin nets" of past and present, and ignores the larger historical and ideological implications of that struggle. Harris also fails to consider the ways in which *Corregidora* might comment on and critique the more male-centered, white portraits of artists that she compares it to. She concludes with a call to appreciate the text for its (implicitly) timeless and universal qualities: "My point is that what Paul [Morel], Stephen [Dedalus], and Ursa go through includes but also transcends race, class, and sex" (5). Harris claims that there are so few artist novels with women at "their center"—and implies that there are no portraits of black artists—and thus misses the chance to compare *Corregidora* to works such as Jean *Toomer's Cane*, Christina Stead's *The Man Who Loved Children*, and May Sinclair's *Mary Olivier: A Life*—just to name three modern novels which do deal with the artist in the context of race, gender, and/or class.

5. See, also, JanMohamed, "Humanism and Minority Literature: Toward a Definition of Counter-hegemonic Discourse": "If minority literature repeatedly explores the political, collective, and marginal aspects of human experience, then minority criticism must also systematically avoid the temptation of a seductively inclusive, apolitical humanism; it must articulate and help to bring to consciousness those elements of minority literature that oppose, subvert, or negate the power of hegemonic culture, and it must learn to celebrate marginality in its specific manifestations without fetishizing or reifying it" (297–98). The only quarrel I have with Jan-Mohamed's argument in this article is his persistent use of the term "emasculate" to describe what humanist theories have done to minority literature; in this word, I read an implicit assessment of integrity as "masculine."

6. See discussion of R. Radhakrishnan at the end of Chapter Two.

7. The phrase is Houston Baker's. See his *Blues, Ideology, and Afro-American Literature: A Vernacular Theory,* Chapter One.

8. See White, Giddings, and Jacqueline Jones for more on the divergences between black women's lived experiences and what has been conceived as their "essence."

9. Again, this process is similar in many ways to Martha Quest's projection of difference onto the body of her "invisible black sister" in *A Proper Marriage.*

10. For examples of proslavery documents as they construct the black woman, see Elliott, ed. *Proslavery Arguments,* especially Simms, "The Morals of Slavery"; Harper, "Harper on Slavery"; Hammond, "Hammond's Letters on Slavery."

11. See, particularly, Hélène Cixous, "Sorties," in Cixous and Catherine Clément, *The Newly Born Woman.*

12. In recent work on black women's history there is little or no critique of the notion that female bodies should be "owned" by anybody; that is, while historians critique the white ownership of female slaves' bodies, they tend to unproblematically reinscribe both the black woman and the black man within the property nexus by referring to heterosexual relations as obtaining between a black man and "his" woman, and vice versa. Even the radical stance of Michele Wallace's book does not prevent her from following this strategy.

13. There is a significant amount of disagreement among historians of slavery as to the relative strengths and weaknesses of the slave family, and whether or not men and women followed traditional—i.e., patriarchal—patterns of interaction. See Jacqueline Jones for a discussion of the sexual division of labor in the slave community, and for a discussion of the bonds between men and women. The literature on the black family in slavery has been, in part, an attempt to demonstrate the ways in which slaves were able to create communities despite white efforts to prevent this. For studies of the slave family, from a male perspective, see: John Blassingame, *The Slave Community, Plantation Life in the Antebellum South;* Robert Fogel and Stanley Engerman, *Time on the Cross, The Economics of American Negro Slavery;* Eugene Genovese, *Roll, Jordan Roll, The World the Slave Made;* and Herbert Gutman, *The Black Family in Slavery and Freedom, 1715–1925.* As White points out, these books were all concerned with placing the black man firmly at the head of the slave family and, thus, had little to say about the family from the female slave's perspective. See White, Giddings, Sterling, and Jacqueline Jones for discussions of the black woman in the slave family.

14. Stanley Elkins, *Slavery, A Problem in American Institutional and Intellectual Life.*

15. See White for a detailed consideration of this imaginary construct.

16. Wallace's book presents the most detailed critique of "black macho." See, also, Giddings (314–324; and 337–340 [on sexism in the Shirley Chisolm campaign]); Wade-Gayles (36–40); and bell hooks, *Ain't I a Woman?* (106–117 and 182–185).

17. Daniel Moynihan, *The Negro Family: The Case for National Action,* United States Department of Labor, 1965. Rpt. as "The Moynihan Report" in Lee Rainwater and William L. Yancey, *The Moynihan Report and the Politics of Controversy.* Moynihan's report, albeit unwittingly, spurred a productive debate within the community of black scholars.

18. Bond and Peery cite films and radio shows of the 1930's and 1940's as texts which "invariably peddled the Sapphire image of the Black woman" (116).

19. Charles Johnson, *Being and Race: Black Writing Since 1970* (109).

20. George Breitman, *Malcolm X Speaks* (New York: Merit Publishers, 1965) (cited in Staples, p. 8, n. 1). See, also, Angela Davis, *Women, Race, and Class* for an analysis of this strategy, especially Chapter 11, "Rape, Racism and the Myth of the Black Rapist."

21. While Staples's argument against the "Myth of the Black Matriarchy" is useful and important within this debate, his conclusions about the "true" place of the black woman are rather more troubling, and in fact, give convincing evidence of what Michele Wallace calls "Black Macho" in the struggle for racial liberation. Staples writes: "The role of the black woman in the black liberation struggle is an important one and cannot be forgotten. From her womb have come the revolutionary warriors of our time" (16). Staples's reduction of the black woman's productivity to her reproductivity serves to naturalize the dominant (and sexist) position of black men in the civil rights movement, as can be seen in his note to the above statement: "It is interesting to note that, despite unfounded rumors about the emasculation of the black male, the thrust of the black liberation struggle has been provided almost exclusively by a black male leadership. In selecting leaders of black organizations, black females inevitably defer to some competent black male, an act which shows how much they really prefer the dominating position they supposedly have in black society" (16, note 29). See also, Deborah E. McDowell, "Reading Family Matters," for a critique of Staples in the context of recent debates over gender and Afro-American literary reception.

22. Moynihan (75); quoted in Spillers (66, her ellipses).

23. Henderson's article, "Speaking in Tongues," makes an argument similar to the one I am offering here, in specific reference to black women's fiction. She focuses on black women writers' complex relationship to hegemonic and "ambiguously (non)hegemonic" discourses, placing the black woman in a position of negotiating between "testimonial discourse," which signify affinity and community, and "competetive discourses," which signify challenge and difference. She argues that "if black women speak a discourse of racial and gendered difference in the dominant or hegemonic discursive order, they speak a discourse of racial and gender identity and difference in the subdominant discursive order" (20–21). In this astute formulation, Henderson points to the "multiple voices that enunciate [the black woman's] complex subjectivity" (20). The phrase "ambiguously (non)hegemonic" comes from Rachel Blau DuPlessis's "For the Etruscans," Hester Eisenstein and Alice Jar-

dine, eds., *The Future of Difference* (Boston: G.K. Hall, 1980). For DuPlessis, this term refers to white women who are privileged by race but not by gender; Henderson uses it to refer, as well, to black men who are privileged by gender and not by race.

24. Degler cites a nineteenth century Brazilian aphorism which makes clear that a woman's function was determined by her color:

> White women are for marrying
> Mulatto women are for fornicating
> Black women are for service (188).

The middle term here suggests that the mulatto woman was not used for reproduction; her sexuality was not defined by her ability to produce children, for that was the duty of the white wife. Degler argues that Brazilian slavery was essentially harsher than American, partially because the Portuguese had no interest in reproducing the slave labor force. Masters could treat their slaves as harshly as they wanted because they did not need to nurture the proper conditions for reproduction. Unlike in the United States, the international slave trade was allowed in Brazil almost to the time of slavery's legal abolition (69–70). See, also, A.J.R. Russell-Wood, *The Black Man in Slavery and Freedom in Colonial Brazil*.

25. Bastide's article is sympathetic to the plight of the black woman in Brazilian slavery, but suffers from an acceptance of certain codes of gendered behavior and assumptions about marriage. For example, he suggests that "if miscegenation were to take place in the form of marriage, and *thus in mutual respect and equality between the sexes,* it would indeed show an absence of racial prejudice" (11, my emphasis).

26. Davis makes an interesting comparison between the practice of rape during slavery and during the American involvement in Vietnam, arguing that rape in both cases amounted to a "weapon of mass political terrorism" against an entire race, executed on the women (23–24).

27. Critiquing Eugene Genovese's romanticization of the relationship between slave concubines and their white masters, Angela Davis writes: "It was as oppressors—or, in the case of non-slaveowners, as agents of domination—that white men approached Black women's bodies. Genovese would do well to read Gayl Jones' *Corregidora*...which chronicles the attempts of several generations of women to 'preserve the evidence' of the sexual crimes committed during slavery" (26). The reference is to Genovese, *Roll, Jordan, Roll.*

28. A. da Costa Pinto, *O negro no Rio de Janeiro. Relaçoes de raça numa sociedade em mudança* (Sao Paulo, 1953, 214; quoted in Degler, 189). See Russell-Wood (30 ff.), for a discussion of white women and convents.

29. While my quotations from Wallace might suggest that she focuses on sexism within the black community, at the expense of an analysis of racism within American culture, this is not so. Her analysis of black sexism is firmly based in an historical reading of the ways in which ideologies of race have "seduced" the black man into buying into certain patriarchal notions of power. See, also, bell hooks, Chapter Three, "The Imperialism of Patriarchy." Deborah McDowell, in "Reading Family Matters," analyzes the literary debates which took up the question of black women's negative portrayals of black men, mostly in mainstream journals. What was at stake in this mid-1980's debate, according to McDowell, was a desire on the part of black male critics to keep black women writers from enjoying center-stage in the literary marketplace. These male critics were engaged in chiding black women writers for aligning themselves with (white) feminists, instead of with the black community. McDowell reads the debate as a "family romance" that had as its impetus the (male) desire to keep the black woman "in her place." As McDowell points out, these critics focused "their gaze" on one "tiny aspect of [black women writers'] immensely complex and diverse project—the image of black men—despite the fact that, if we can claim a center for these texts, it is located in the complexities of black female subjectivity and experience. In other words, though black women writers have made black women the subject of their own family stories, these male readers/critics are attempting to usurp that place for themselves and place it at the center of inquiry" (84).

30. Kaplan reads contemporary Western feminist discourse within the context of poststructuralist thought, particularly Deleuze and Guattari's essay, "What is a Minor Literature" (in *Kafka: Towards a Minor Literature,* trans Dana Polan [Minneapolis: University of Minnesota Press, 1986]). She applauds their inscription of a "paradoxical movement between minor and major—a refusal to admit either position as final or static. The issue is positionality" (189). She critiques Deleuze and Guattari, however, by writing: "What gets lost in Deleuze and Guattari's formulation is the acknowledgement that oppositional consciousness (with its benefits and costs) stems from the daily, lived experience of oppression"; she admits she is "con-

fused by the universalizing of the term 'us'" in their text, and asks: "Who is the 'us' that is circulating in the essay 'What is a Minor Literature?'" (191–92). What Kaplan is questioning is the politics of enunciation, the position from which a First-World critic speaks about "minority texts," and what is implicit in the desire to occupy the margins of discourse, or the "minor" perspective.

31. Dixon, Tate, and Byerman all discuss the importance of the blues motif in Jones's novels.

32. See Spillers for an indepth analysis of this problematic.

33. JanMohamed's article focuses on texts by white writers such as Joyce Cary, Joseph Conrad, Nadine Gordimer, and E.M. Forster, and argues that there are two types of colonialist texts: "imaginary" and "symbolic." The former are those that participate in the fetishization of the native Other, as I've described it in the body of my text; the latter attempt to get beyond this dialectical relation by either avoiding the "Othering" of the native, or by explicitly critiquing it. This "Othering" is part of the larger "Economy of Manichean Allegory" that JanMohamed reads in colonialist literature, and is the subject of his book, *Manichean Aesthetics: The Politics of Literature in Colonial Africa.*

34. Claudia Tate reads the ending as a "catharsis, dramatized in sexual terms" (141). Melvin Dixon sees the ending as a "healing communication between reconciled opposites" (245). Both of these comments suggest that the asymmetry of power relations has been "healed"—an idealistic reading that I don't think can be supported by the text.

35. See "Gayl Jones," in Tate, *Black Women Writers at Work* (95 ff).

36. See Byerman, Dixon, and Wade-Gayles.

37. See Byerman (184), for a discussion of Eva's narrative as blues performance.

38. See "About My Work" (235).

39. Henderson sees this as the objective of black women writers, in general.

40. Keith Byerman takes this tact when he argues that Eva's act is precipitated when "the epitome of sexual domination is reached; the actions and attitudes of her father, her husband, her

cousin, and all other men she and other women encounter culminate in Davis's reification of her" (183).

41. Gloria Wade-Gayles ignores Eva's response, and quotes the psychiatrist's words, attributing them to Eva, as a valid explanation of her act; she writes "Eva understands that she castrated Davis and poisoned him because 'he came to represent all the men she had known'" (182).

42. I am indebted to Keith Byerman's reading of *Eva's Man* for his articulation of Eva's strategy of "literalization." He points out that Eva "chooses to literalize the metaphor of the queen bee's power to destroy the drones" (183)

43. Giddings cites Calvin Hernton as a black intellectual who promoted the notion that black mothers "castrate" their sons; and William Grier and Price Cobbs as psychiatrists who "accused Black mothers of inflicting 'senseless pain on their sons'" (Giddings, 319–320). The references are to: Hernton, "The Negro Male," in Doris Y. Wilkinson and Ronald Taylor, ed., *The Black Male in America: Perspectives on His Status in Contemporary Society* (Chicago: Nelson-Hall, 1977); and, Grier and Cobbs, *Black Rage* (New York: Bantam, 1968, 51). Both Giddings and Michele Wallace suggest that if the black mother has taught her son not to be aggressive, it is in order to shield him from the consequences of practicing that aggression against the dominant group in American society—not least of which is the threat of lynching.

44. As I argued in the first part of this chapter, notions of the "feminine" are complicated by race and the specificity of the Afro-American woman's historical experience of racial and sexual definition. Irigaray's formulation, at times, approaches an essentialism that risks positing *the* feminine in opposition to the masculine.

45. See Tania Modleski, "Feminism and the Power of Interpretation" (128–29) for a discussion of Irigaray's "elsewhere" as the space of "women's desire for power."

46. Although Bhabha undertakes, in "The Other Question," to talk about both racial and sexual difference, his reading of the stereotype as fetish tends to conflate the two—which is problematic considering that he begins the article by chiding Stephen Heath for "read[ing] too singularly, too exclusively under the sign of sexuality" in Heath's analysis of Welles's *A Touch of Evil* in "Film and System, Terms of Analysis," *Screen* 6, no. 2 (Summer 1975), (Bhabha, 21).

Gender does not really interest Bhabha, except to the extent that he is interested in theorising how a gendered construct—i.e., fetishism—might be translated into terms of race. He writes: "For fetishism is always a 'play' or vacillation between the archaic affirmation of wholeness/similarity—in Freud's terms: 'All men have penises'; in ours 'All men have the same skin/race/culture'—and the anxiety associated with lack and difference—again, for Freud 'Women do not have penises'; for us 'Some do not have the same skin/race/culture'" (27). And, some, I would add, have neither.

47. See Bhabha, "The Other Question," for a detailed discussion of the stereotype as fetish in colonial discourses.

48. I have borrowed this summary of Bhabha from Benita Parry's "Problems in Current Theories of Colonial Discourse" (40). Bhabha's arguments are extremely difficult to represent—á la Derrida—and, as Parry puts it, his "flagrantly ambivalent presentation...leaves it vulnerable to innocent misconstruction" (42).

49. It is in "Signs Taken for Wonders" that Bhabha begins to articulate how this might work, but only at the end of the article.

50. Bhabha's work owes much to Frantz Fanon, especially *Black Skin White Masks*.

51. Again, critics of the novel have posited interpretations of this identification that the novel itself undermines. Melvin Dixon argues that Eva fails to come to terms with her past and to forge an identity because she "chooses to embrace received images of *femmes fatales*" (245). Gloria Wade-Gayles similarly misses the subversive implications of Eva's excessive mimicry when she argues that *Eva's Man* falls within the tradition of "female erotic novels" and that it "reads at times like the script of an X-rated movie" (175). For Wade-Gayles, this is problematic; but I would argue that Jones's text reads more like a *male* erotic novel and that its quasi-pornographic scenes carry a critique of the male desire that mobilizes "X-rated" movies. Dixon is right when he argues that received images of *femmes fatales* are masculine constructions, but he fails to see how Eva's excessive identification with these images carries with it an implicit critique of their construction.

52. See Paula Giddings, especially Chapter One on "Ida B. Wells and the First Antilynching Campaign"; and Angela Davis, Chapter Eleven, on "Rape, Racism and the Myth of the Black

Rapist." Both Giddings and Davis critique white feminist anti-rape movements for buying into the myth of the black rapist.

53. Gerda Lerner, ed. *Black Women in White America: A Documentary History* (New York: Pantheon Books, 1972, 193; quoted in Davis, 174). Davis insists on the historical connection between rape and racism, and argues that the rape of black women has received little attention from white feminists, whose silence on this question implicates them in the structures of American racism. She writes: "One of racism's salient historical features has always been the assumption that white men—especially those who wield economic power—possess an incontestable right of access to Black women's bodies" (175); and this right has justified the institutionalized pattern of rape as a weapon of racist domination.

54. Wallace argues that after a while, black men began to see that having sex with white women would get back at white men. So, the black man "decided he would do exactly what he thought the white man wanted him to do least. He would debase and defile white women. He would also show the white man that black women had no influence over him and that they would have to pay for fucking white men for all those years. He too would make his woman submissive, but he would not be the chump the white man had been. He'd give his woman nothing for her submissiveness" (72–72). I would suggest that Wallace is speaking more of the psychic legacies of slavery than she is about the material practices of contemporary life.

55. This fetishization is similar to that identified by JanMohamed in his reading of the dynamics of the colonialist imaginary, and is similarly marked by a static sense of essentialized difference between Self and Other—in Freud's case, male Self and female Other.

56. Deborah Gray White suggests that the mythological images of the black female slave as, alternately, Jezebel and Mammy, participates in the broader cultural construction of Woman, regardless of race. She writes: "They are black images, but, being almost as old as the images of Eve and the Virgin Mary, they are also universal female archetypes" (60–61). In *Eva's Man,* Jones considers all of these "archetypes," not in order to demonstrate their "universality," but to consider the specific effects that they have on black women.

57. Sabine Brock and Anne Koenen argue that "Jones sug-

gests...by her intensive and frequent exploration of the vagina-den-tata-myth that women are not only (and not the only) victims of sexual violence and that they can turn sexuality into a weapon by exploiting male fears" (171). This line of argument is fine as far as it goes; as I argued in my reading of *Corregidora*, Ursa does realize a certain kind of power in Mutt's vulnerability. But what Brock and Koenen neglect to take into account is that when women "turn sex-uality into a weapon," they are only taking to its logical conclusion the representation of female sexuality as constructed from a "male-centered frame of reference" (de Lauretis, *Technologies*, 26).

58. See de Lauretis, *Alice Doesn't,* Chapter One, for a discus-sion of Woman as the ground of masculine (self)representation.

59. Byerman argues that, in turning herself in to the police, Eva "reenters the world of male domination" that she had tem-porarily disrupted, "but she enters now not as a victim but as an alternative power, a queen bee" (184). While Byerman's descrip-tion seems accurate as far as it goes, I find this reading problematic in its suggestion that the only possible form of female power is to forcefully remind the "oppressor of his vulnerability" by attacking male control at its "point of greatest weakness"—by literally cas-trating man (Byerman, 184).

Epilogue

1. Jardine, 118–19; Butler, 1–2. See, also, Gayatri Spivak, "Can the Subaltern Speak?," for a consideration of the dual mean-ing of "representation."

2. A few writers and texts come immediately to mind: Toni Morrison's novels, especially *Beloved;* Sherley Anne Williams's *Dessa Rose;* Audrey Thomas's *Mrs. Blood;* Margaret Atwood's *The Handmaid's Tale;* Joanna Russ's *The Female Man;* Maxine Hong Kingston's novels; and, Lois Gould's *La Presidenta* and *A Sea-Change.*

Bibliography of Works Cited

Aeschylus. *Oresteia*. Trans. Richmond Lattimore. Chicago: University of Chicago Press, 1953.

Alcoff, Linda. "Cultural Feminism versus Poststructuralism: The Identity Crisis in Feminist Theory." *Signs* 13, No. 3 (1988): 405–36.

Althusser, Louis. "Ideology and Ideological State Apparatuses." *Lenin and Philosophy and Other Essays*. Trans. Ben Brewster. London: New Left Books, 1971.

Baker, Houston A. *Blues, Ideology, and Afro-American Literature: A Vernacular Theory*. Chicago: University of Chicago Press, 1984.

Bakhtin, Mikhail. *Rabelais and His World*. Trans. Helen Iswolsky. Bloomington: Indiana University Press, 1984.

Barnouw, Dagmar. "Disorderly Company: From *The Golden Notebook* to *The Four-Gated City*." Pratt and Dembo, eds., 74–97.

Barthes, Roland. *S/Z*. 1970. Trans. Richard Miller. New York: Hill and Wang, 1974.

Bastide, Roger. "Dusky Venus, Black Apollo." Trans. Michael Wood. *Race* 3, No. 1 (Nov 1961): 10–18.

Baym, Nina. "Melodramas of Beset Manhood: How Theories of American Literature Exclude Women Authors." *American Quarterly* (Summer 1981): 123–39.

Beard, Linda Susan. "Doris Lessing, African Writer." Carolyn A. Parker and Stephen H. Arnold, eds. *When the Drumbeat Changes*. Washington, D.C.: African Literature Association and Three Continents Press, Inc., 1981.

Beck, Antony. "Doris Lessing and the Colonial Experience." *Journal of Commonwealth Literature* 19, No. 1 (1984): 64–73.

Belsey, Catherine. *Critical Practice*. London and New York: Methuen, 1980.

Berg, Elizabeth. "The Third Woman." *Diacritics* 12 (1982): 11–20.

Bhabha, Homi. "Of Mimicry and Man: The Ambivalence of Colonial Discourse." *October* 28 (Spring 1984): 125–33.

227

————. "The Other Question." *Screen* 24, No. 6 (1983): 18–36.

————. "Signs Taken For Wonders: Question of Ambivalence and Authority under a Tree Outside Delhi, May 1817." *Critical Inquiry* 12, No. 1 (Fall 1985): 144–65.

Blassingame, John. *The Slave Community, Plantation Life in the Antebellum South.* New York: Oxford Univ. Press, 1972.

Bond, Jean Carey and Patricia Peery. "Is the Black Male Castrated?" *Liberator* 9, No. 5 (May 1969). Rpt. Toni Cade, ed. *The Black Woman: An Anthology.* New York: New American Library, 1970.

Bordo, Susan. "Feminism, Postmodernism, and Gender-Scepticism." Linda J. Nicholson, ed., 133–56.

Braidotti, Rosi. "Envy: or With My Brains and Your Looks." Jardine and Smith, eds., 233–41.

————. "Féminisme et philosophe," Diss. University of Paris I, 1981.

Brock, Sabine and Anne Koenen. "Alice Walker in Search of Zora Neale Hurston: Rediscovering a Black Female Literary Tradition." Gunter H. Lenz, ed. *History and Tradition in Afro-American Culture.* Frankfurt and New York: Campus Verlag, 1984.

Brooks, Peter. *Reading for the Plot: Design and Intention in Narrative.* New York: Alfred A. Knopf, 1984.

Bulkin, Elly, Minnie Bruce Pratt and Barbara Smith. *Yours in Struggle: Three Perspectives on Anti-Semitism and Racism.* Brooklyn, NY: Long Haul Press, 1984.

Butler, Judith. *Gender Trouble: Feminism and the Subversion of Identity.* New York and London: Routledge, 1990.

Byerman, Keith. *Fingering the Jagged Grain: Tradition and Form in Recent Black Fiction.* Athens and London: University of Georgia Press, 1985.

Carby, Hazel V. *Reconstructing Womanhood: The Emergence of the Afro-American Woman Novelist.* New York: Oxford University Press, 1987.

Carter, Angela. *The Infernal Desire Machines of Doctor Hoffman.* 1972. Rpt. New York: Penguin Books, 1985.

————. *Nights at the Circus.* 1984. New York: Viking Books, 1985.

————. *The Sadeian Woman and the Ideology of Pornography.* 1978. Rpt. New York: Pantheon Books, 1988.

Christian, Barbara. *Black Women Novelists: The Development of a Tradition, 1892–1976.* Westport, CN: Greenwood Press, 1980.

————. "The Race for Theory." *Cultural Critique* No. 6 (1987): 51–63.

Cixous, Helene. "Castration or Decapitation?" *"Le sexe ou la tête?"* 1976. Trans. Annette Kuhn. *Signs* 7, No. 1 (1981): 41–55.

Cixous, Hélène and Catherine Clément. *The Newly Born Woman.* 1975. Trans. Betsy Wing. Minneapolis: University of Minnesota Press, 1986.

Clark, Robert. "Angela Carter's Desire Machine." *Women's Studies* 14, No. 2 (1987): 147–61.

Culler, Jonathan. *On Deconstruction: Theory and Criticism after Structuralism.* Ithaca: Cornell University Press, 1982.

Davis, Angela. *Women, Race and Class.* New York: Vintage Books, 1981.

Degler, Carl. *Neither Black nor White: Slavery and Race Relations in Brazil and the United States.* New York: MacMillan, 1971.

de Lauretis, Teresa. *Alice Doesn't: Feminism, Semiotics, Cinema.* Bloomington: Indiana University Press, 1984.

————., ed. *Feminist Studies/ Critical Studies.* Bloomington: Indiana University Press, 1987.

————. *Technologies of Gender: Essays on Theory, Film, and Fiction.* Bloomington: Indiana University Press, 1987.

Derrida, Jacques. *Dissemination.* Trans. Barbara Johnson. Chicago: University of Chicago Press, 1981.

————. *Glas.* 1974. Trans. John P. Leavey, Jr. Lincoln: University of Nebraska Press, 1986.

————. "Otobiographies: The Teaching of Nietzsche and the Politics of the Proper Name." 1970. Trans. Avital Ronell. Christie V. MacDonald, ed. *The Ear of the Other: Otobiography, Transference, Translation.* New York: Schocken Books, 1985.

————. *Positions.* Trans. Alan Bass. Chicago: University of Chicago Press, 1981.

————. *Spurs/Eperons.* 1976. Trans. Barbara Harlow. Chicago: University of Chicago Press, 1979.

Derrida, Jacques and Christie V. McDonald. "Choreographies." *Diacritics* 12 (Summer 1982): 66–76.

Di Stefano, Christine. "Dilemmas of Difference: Feminism, Modernity, and Postmodernism." Linda J. Nicholson, ed., 63–82.

Didion, Joan. *The White Album.* New York: Pocket Books, 1979.

Dixon, Melvin. "Singing a Deep Song: Language as Evidence in the Novels of Gayl Jones." Mari Evans, ed. *Black Women Writers (1950–1980).* Garden City, NY: Anchor Press/ Doubleday, 1984, 236–48.

Doane, Mary Ann. *The Desire to Desire: The Woman's Film of the 1940's.* Bloomington: Indiana University Press, 1987.

————. "Film and the Masquerade: Theorising the Female Spectator." *Screen* 23 (Sept./ Oct. 1982): 74–87.

————. "Veiling Over Desire: Close-ups of the Woman." Richard Feldstein and Judith Roof, eds. *Feminism and Psychoanalysis.* Ithaca: Cornell University Press, 1989, 105–41.

DuPlessis, Rachel Blau. *Writing Beyond the Ending: Narrative Strategies of Twentieth-Century Women Writers.* Bloomington: Indiana University Press, 1985.

Eagleton, Terry. *Literary Theory: An Introduction.* Minneapolis: University of Minnesota Press, 1983.

Elkins, Stanley. *Slavery, A Problem in American Institutional and Intellectual Life,* 2nd Ed. Chicago: University of Chicago Press, 1968.

Elliot, E. N. *Cotton is King and Proslavery Arguments.* 1860. Rpt. The Basic Afro-American Reprint Library. New York: Johnson Reprint Corporation, 1968.

Fanon, Frantz. *Black Skin White Masks.* London: Paladin, 1970.

Felman, Shoshana. "Rereading Femininity." *Yale French Studies* No. 62 (1981): 19–44.

Fetterley, Judith. *The Resisting Reader: A Feminist Approach to American Fiction.* Bloomington: Indiana Univ. Press, 1978.

Findlay, Heather. "Is There a Lesbian in this Text? Derrida, Wittig, and the Politics of the Three Women." In Elizabeth Weed, ed., 59–69.

Finke, Laurie. "The Rhetoric of Marginality: Why I Do Feminist Theory." *Tulsa Studies in Women's Literature* 5, No. 2 (Fall 1986): 251–72.

Fogel, Robert and Stanley Engerman. *Time on the Cross, The Economics of American Negro Slavery.* Boston: Little, Brown, 1974.

Foucault, Michel. "The Subject and Power." *Critical Inquiry* 8 No. 4 (1982): 777–89.

Fraser, Nancy and Linda J. Nicholson. "Social Criticism with Philosophy: An Encounter between Feminism and Postmodernism." Linda J. Nicholson, ed., 19–38.

Freud, Sigmund. "Femininity." In *New Introductory Lectures on Psychoanalysis.* 1933. Trans. James Strachey. New York: W.W. Norton, 1965, 99–119.

———. "Fetishism." 1927. *The Standard Edition of the Complete Psychological Works.* 24 Vols. Trans. James Strachey. London: Hogarth, 1955. 21: 152–57.

Fuss, Diana. *Essentially Speaking: Feminism, Nature and Difference.* New York and London: Routledge, 1989.

Gates, Henry Louis Jr. "Authority, (White) Power and the (Black) Critic." *Cultural Critique* No. 7 (Fall 1987): 19–46.

Genovese, Eugene. *Roll, Jordan Roll, The World the Slaves Made.* New York: Vintage Books, 1974.

Giddings, Paula. *When and Where I Enter: The Impact of Black Women on Race and Sex in America.* New York: William Morrow and Co., Inc., 1984.

Gutman, Herbert. *The Black Family in Slavery and Freedom, 1715–1925.* New York: Pantheon, 1976.

Hardin, Nancy Shields. "Doris Lessing and the Sufi Way." Pratt and Dembo, eds., 148–64.

Harris, Janice. "Gayl Jones' *Corregidora.*" Frontiers 5, No. 3 (1980): 1–5.

Hartsock, Nancy. "Rethinking Modernism: Minority vs. Majority Theories." *Cultural Critique* No. 7 (Fall 1987): 187–206.

Hartveit, Lars. "Commitment and the Novelist's Craft: The Racial Issue in the African Volumes of Doris Lessing's *Children of Violence*." Daniel Massa, ed. *Individual and Community in Commonwealth Literature*. Malta: Old University Press, 1979, 28–35.

Henderson, Mae Gwendolyn. "Speaking in Tongues: Dialogics, Dialectics, and the Black Woman Writer's Literary Tradition." Cheryl A. Wall, ed., 16–37.

Henriques, Julian, Wendy Hollway, Cathy Urwin, Couze Venn, and Valerie Walkerdine. *Changing the Subject: Psychology, social regulation and subjectivity*. London and New York: Methuen, 1984.

hooks, bell. *Ain't I a Woman? Black Women and Feminism*. Boston: South End Press, 1981.

Howe, Florence. "A Conversation with Doris Lessing (1966)." Pratt and Dembo, eds., 1–19.

Hull, Gloria, Patricia Bell Scott, and Barbara Smith, eds. *All the Women Are White, All the Blacks Are Men, but Some of Us Are Brave*. Old Westbury, NY: The Feminist Press, 1982.

Hutcheon, Linda. *A Poetics of Postmodernism: History, Theory, Fiction*. New York and London: Routledge, 1988.

———. *The Politics of Postmodernism*. New York and London: Routledge, 1989.

Irigaray, Luce. *Speculum of the Other Woman*. 1974. Trans. Gillian Gill. Ithaca: Cornell University Press, 1985.

———. *This Sex Which is Not One*. 1977. Trans. Catherine Porter with Carolyn Burke. Ithaca: Cornell University Press, 1985.

———. "Veiled Lips." *Amante marine: de Frederich Nietzsche*. 1980. Trans. Sara Speidel. Mississippi Review (Winter/Spring 1983): 93–131.

———. "Women's Exile: An Interview." Trans. Couze Venn. *Ideology and Consciousness* 1, No. 1 (1977): 62–76.

JanMohamed, Abdul. "The Economy of Manichean Allegory: The Function of Racial Difference in Colonialist Literature." *Critical Inquiry* 12, No. 1 (Autumn 1985): 59–87.

———. "Humanism and Minority Literature: Toward a Definition of

Counter-hegemonic Discourse." *Boundary 2* 12–3, Nos. 3–1 (Spring/Fall 1984): 281–99.

——. *Manichean Aesthetics: The Politics of Literature in Colonial Africa*. Amherst, Mass: University of Massachusetts Press, 1983.

——. "Negating the Negation as a Form of Affirmation: The Construction of Richard Wright as Subject." *Cultural Critique* No.7 (1987): 245–66.

JanMohamed, Abdul R. and David Lloyd, eds. "The Nature and Context of Minority Discourse." *Cultural Critique* Nos. 6 and 7 (Spring and Fall 1987).

Jardine, Alice. *Gynesis: Configurations of Woman and Modernity*. Ithaca: Cornell University Press, 1985.

Jardine, Alice and Paul Smith, eds. *Men in Feminism*. New York: Methuen, 1987.

Jeffords, Susan E. *The Remasculinization of America: Gender and the Representation of the Vietnam War*. Bloomington: Indiana University Press, 1989.

Johnson, Charles. *Being and Race: Black Writing Since 1970*. Bloomington: Indiana University Press, 1988.

Jones, Gayl. "About My Work." Mari Evans, ed. *Black Women Writers (1950–1980)*. Garden City, NY: Anchor Press/ Doubleday, 1984, 233–35.

——. *Corregidora*. 1975. Rpt. Boston: Beacon Press, 1986.

——. *Eva's Man*. 1976. Rpt. Boston: Beacon Press, 1987.

Jones, Jacqueline. *Labor of Love, Labor of Sorrow: Black Women, Work and the Family from Slavery to the Present*. New York: Vintage Books, 1985.

Kamuf, Peggy. "Replacing Feminist Criticism." *Diacritics* 12 (1982): 42–47.

Kaplan, Caren. "Deterritorializations: The Rewriting of Home and Exile in Western Feminist Discourse." *Cultural Critique* No. 6 (1987): 187–98.

Kaplan, Sydney Janet. "The Limits of Consciousness in the Novels of Doris Lessing." Pratt and Dembo, eds., 119–32.

Kermode, Frank. *The Sense of an Ending*. London: Oxford University Press, 1966.

Kofman, Sarah. *The Enigma of Woman*. Trans. Catherine Porter. Ithaca: Cornell University Press, 1985.

Kojève, Alexander. *Introduction to the Reading of Hegel*. Ed. Allan Bloom. Trans. James H. Nichols, Jr. Ithaca, NY: Cornell University Press, 1969.

Kuhn, Annette. "Women's Genres." *Screen* (January/February, 1984): 18–28.

———. *Women's Pictures*. London: Routledge & Kegan Paul, 1982.

Lanser, Susan. "Toward a Feminist Narratology." *Style* 20, No. 3 (Fall 1986): 341–63.

Lee, Rosa. "Resisting Amnesia: Feminism, Painting and Postmodernism." *Feminist Review* No. 26 (Summer 1987): 5–28.

Lessing, Doris. *The Four-Gated City*. 1969. Rpt. New York: Plume Books, 1976.

———. *The Golden Notebook*. 1962. Rpt. New York: Bantam Books, 1979.

———. *Landlocked*. 1958. Rpt. New York: Plume Books, 1970.

———. *Martha Quest.* 1952. Rpt. New York: Plume Books, 1970.

———. *A Proper Marriage*. 1952. Rpt. New York: Plume Books, 1970.

———. *A Ripple From the Storm*. 1958. Rpt. New York: Plume Books, 1970.

———. *A Small Personal Voice*. 1956. Rpt. New York: Vintage Books, 1975.

Lyotard, Jean-François. "One of the Things at Stake in Women's Struggles." *SubStance* 20 (1978): 9–17.

Martin, Biddy and Chandra Talpade Mohanty. "Feminist Politics: What's Home Got to Do with It?" de Lauretis, ed., 191–212.

Mayne, Judith. "Marlene Dietrich, *The Blue Angel,* and Female Performance." Dianne Hunter, ed. *Seduction and Theory: Readings of Gender, Representation, and Rhetoric*. Urbana and Chicago: University of Illinois Press, 1989, 28–46.

McDowell, Deborah E. "Reading Family Matters." Cheryl A. Wall, ed., 75–97.

McHale, Brian. *Postmodernist Fiction.* New York and London: Methuen, 1987.

Meese, Elizabeth. *(Ex)Tensions: Re-Figuring Feminist Criticism.* Urbana and Chicago: University of Illinois Press, 1990.

Michel, Frann. "Displacing Castration: *Nightwood, Ladies Almanack,* and Feminine Writing." *Contemporary Literature* 30, No. 1 (Spring 1989): 33–58.

Miller, D.A. *Narrative and Its Discontents: Problems of Closure in the Traditional Novel.* Princeton, NJ: Princeton University Press, 1981.

Miller, Nancy K. *Subject to Change: Reading Feminist Writing.* New York: Columbia University Press, 1988.

————. "The Text's Heroine: A Feminist Critic and Her Fictions." *Diacritics* 12 (1982): 48–53.

Mitchell, Juliet and Jacqueline Rose, eds. *Feminine Sexuality: Jacques Lacan and the* école freudienne. 1982. Rpt. New York: W.W. Norton & Company, 1985.

Modleski, Tania. "Feminism and the Power of Interpretation: Some Critical Readings." de Lauretis, ed., 121–38.

————. "The Search for Tomorrow in Today's Soap Operas." *Film Quarterly* 32, No. 1 (Fall 1979). Rpt. Donald Lazere, ed. *American Media and Mass Culture.* University of Californa Press, 1987, 266–78.

Mohanty, Chandra Talpade. "Under Western Eyes: Feminist Scholarship and Colonial Discourses." *Boundary 2* 12–13, Nos. 3–1 (Spring/Fall 1984): 333–58.

Moi, Toril. *Sexual/Textual Politics: Feminist Literary Theory.* 1985. London and New York: Routledge, 1988.

Moraga, Cherrie and Gloria Anzaldua, eds. *This Bridge Called My Back.* 1981. New York: Kitchen Table/ Women of Color Press, 1983.

Mulvey, Laura. "Afterthoughts on 'Visual Pleasure and Narrative Cinema' Inspired by 'Duel in the Sun' (King Vidor, 1946)." *Framework* Nos. 15, 16, 17 (1981): 12–15.

————. "Visual Pleasure and Narrative Cinema." *Screen* 16, No. 3 (1975): 6–18.

Nicholson, Linda J., ed. *Feminism/Postmodernism.* New York and London: Routledge, 1990.

Nietzsche, Frederich. *The Gay Science.* 1887. Trans. Walter Kaufmann. New York: Random House, 1974.

Parry, Benita. "Problems in Current Theories of Colonial Discourse." *Oxford Literary Review* 9 (1988): 27–58.

Pickering, Jean. "Marxism and Madness: The Two Faces of Doris Lessing's Myth." *Modern Fiction Studies* 26, No. 1 (Spring 1980): 17–30.

Pratt, Annis, and Dembo, L.S., eds. *Doris Lessing: Critical Studies.* Madison, WI: University of Wisconsin Press, 1974.

Pryse, Marjorie and Hortense Spillers, eds. *Conjuring: Black Women, Fiction, and Literary Tradition.* Bloomington: Indiana University Press, 1985.

Radhakrishnan, R. "Ethnic Identity and Post-Structuralist Differance." *Cultural Critique* No. 6 (1987): 199–220.

————. "Negotiating Subject Positions in an Uneven World." In Linda Kauffman, ed. *Feminism and Institutions: Dialogues on Feminist Theory.* Cambridge, MA: Basil Blackwell, 1989, 276–90.

Rainwater, Lee and William L. Yancey, ed. *The Moynihan Report and the Politics of Controversy: A Transaction Social Science and Public Policy Report.* Cambridge, MA: MIT Press, 1967.

Riley, Denise. "Does Sex Have a History? 'Women' and Feminism." *New Formations* 1 (Spring 1987).

Robinson, Sally. "The 'Anti-Logos Weapon': Multiplicity in Women's Texts." *Contemporary Literature* 29, No. 1 (Fall 1988): 105–24.

————. "Misappropriations of the Feminine." *SubStance* 59 (Fall 1989): 48–70.

Roof, Judith. *A Lure of Knowledge: Lesbian Sexuality and Theory.* New York: Columbia Univ. Press, forthcoming, 1991.

Rose, Ellen Cronan. *The Tree Outside the Window: Doris Lessing's Children of Violence.* Hanover, NH: University Press of New England, 1976.

Rubin, Gayle. "The Traffic in Women: Notes on the 'Political Economy' of Sex." Reiter Raynor, ed. *Toward an Anthropology of Women*. New York: Monthly Review Press, 1978, 157–210.

Russell-Wood, A.J.R. *The Black Man in Slavery and Freedom in Colonial Brazil*. London and Basingstoke: The MacMillan Press, LTD., 1982.

Russo, Mary. "Female Grotesques: Carnival and Theory." de Lauretis, ed., 213–29.

Scholes, Robert. *Fabulation and Metafiction*. Urbana: University of Illinois Press, 1979.

Schor, Naomi. *Reading in Detail: Aesthetics and the Feminine*. New York and London: Methuen, 1987.

———. "This Essentialism Which Is Not One: Coming to Grips with Irigaray." *differences* 1, No. 2 (Summer 1989): 38–58.

Schweickart, Patrocinio. "Reading Ourselves: Toward a Feminist Theory of Reading." In Eliazabeth Flynn and Patrocinio Schweickart, eds. *Gender and Reading: Essays on Readers, Texts and Contexts*. Baltimore: The Johns Hopkins University Press, 1986, 31–62.

Showalter, Elaine. "Feminist Criticism in the Wilderness." *Critical Inquiry* 8 (Winter 1981). Rpt. Showalter, ed., 243–70.

———. ed. *The New Feminist Criticism: Essays on Women, Literature, Theory*. New York: Pantheon Books, 1985.

Silverman, Kaja. "*Histoire de'O:* The Construction of a Female Subject." Carole Vance, ed. *Pleasure and Danger: Exploring Female Sexuality*. Boston: Routledge & Kegan Paul, 1984, 320–49.

———. "Lost Objects and Mistaken Subjects: Film Theory's Structuring Lack." *Wide Angle* 7 (1985): 14–29.

———. *The Subject of Semiotics*. New York: Oxford University Press, 1983.

Smith, Paul. *Discerning the Subject*. Minneapolis: University of Minnesota Press, 1988.

Spiegel, Rotraut. *Doris Lessing: The Problem of Alienation and the Form of the Novel*. Frankfurt A.M., Bern, Cirencester/U.K.: Peter D. Lang, 1980.

Spilka, Mark. "Lessing and Lawrence: The Battle of the Sexes." *Contemporary Literature* 16 (1975). Rpt. Sprague and Tiger, eds., 69–86.

Spillers, Hortense. "Mama's Baby, Papa's Maybe: An American Grammar Book." *Diacritics* 17, No. 2 (Summer 1987): 65–81.

Spivak, Gayatri Chakravorty. "Can the Subaltern Speak?" Cary Nelson and Lawrence Grossberg, eds. *Marxism and the Interpretation of Culture.* Urbana and Chicago: University of Illinois Press, 1988, 271–313.

———. "Displacement and the Discourse of the Woman." Mark Krupnick, ed. *Displacement: Derrida and After.* Bloomington: Indiana University Press, 1983, 169–95.

———. *In Other Worlds: Essays in Cultural Politics.* New York: Methuen, 1987.

———. "Love Me, Love My Ombre, Elle." *Diacritics* 14, No. 4 (1989): 19–36.

Spivak, Gayatri Chakrarorty with Ellen Rooney. "In a Word: Interview." *differences* 1, No. 2 (Summer 1989): 124–56.

Sprague, Claire. "Dialectic and Counter-Dialectic in the Martha Quest Novels." *Journal of Commonwealth Literature* 14, No. 1 (1979): 39–52.

———. *Rereading Doris Lessing: Narrative Patterns of Doubling and Repetition.* Chapel Hill and London: University of North Carolina Press, 1987.

Sprague, Claire and Virginia Tiger, eds. *Critical Essays on Doris Lessing.* Boston: G.K. Hall, 1986.

Stanton, Domna. "Difference on Trial: A Critique of the Maternal Metaphor in Cixous, Irigaray, and Kristeva." Nancy K. Miller, ed. *The Poetics of Gender.* New York: Columbia University Press, 1986, 157–82.

Staples, Robert. "The Myth of the Black Matriarchy." *The Black Scholar* 1, Nos. 3–4 (Jan–Feb 1970): 8–16.

Sterling, Dorothy, ed. *We Are Your Sisters: Black Women in the Nineteenth Century.* New York: W.W. Norton, 1984.

Stimpson, Catharine, R. "Doris Lessing and the Parables of Growth." Elizabeth Abel, Marianne Hirsch, and Elizabeth Langland, eds.

The Voyage In: Fictions of Female Development. Hanover, NH and London: University Press of New England, 1983.

Sukenick, Lynn. "Feeling and Reason in Doris Lessing's Fiction." Pratt and Dembo, eds., 98–118.

Tate, Claudia, ed. *Black Women Writers at Work*. New York: Continuum, 1983.

———. "Corregidora: Ursa's Blues Medley." *Black American Literature Forum* 13 (1979): 139–41.

Thorpe, Michael. *Doris Lessing's Africa*. London and Ibadan, Nigeria: Evans Brothers Limited, 1978.

Todd, Janet. *Feminist Literary History*. New York: Routledge, 1988.

Vlastos, Marion. "Doris Lessing and R.D. Laing: Psychopolitics and Prophecy." *PMLA* 91 (March 1976). Rpt. Sprague and Tiger, eds., 126–41.

Wade-Gayles, Gloria. *No Crystal Stair: Visions of Race and Sex in Black Women's Fiction*. New York: The Pilgrim Press, 1984.

Wall, Cheryl A., ed. *Changing Our Own Words: Essays on Criticism, Theory, and Writing by Black Women*. New Brunswick and London: Rutgers University Press, 1989.

Wallace, Michele. *Black Macho and the Myth of the Superwoman*. New York: The Dial Press, 1978.

Warhol, Robyn. *Gendered Interventions: Narrative Discourse in the Victorian Novel*. New Brunswick and London: Rutgers University Press, 1989.

Weed, Elizabeth, ed. *Coming to Terms: Feminism, Theory, Politics*. New York and London: Routledge, 1989.

———. "Introduction: Terms of Reference." Elizabeth Weed, ed., ix–xxxi.

White, Deborah Gray. *Ar'n't I a Woman? Female Slaves in the Plantation South*. New York: W.W. Norton & Co., 1985.

Wiegman, Robyn. "Negotiating the Masculine: Configurations of Race and Gender in American Culture." Doctoral Dissertation, University of Washington, 1988.

Williamson, Judith. *Decoding Advertisements: Ideology and Meaning in Advertising*. New York: Boyars, 1978.

Winnett, Susan. "Coming Unstrung: Women, Men, Narrative, and Principles of Pleasure." *PMLA* 105, No. 3 (May 1990): 505–18.

Woolf, Virginia. *A Room of One's Own.* 1929. New York: Harcourt, Brace & World, Inc., 1957.

Index